WEBER'S REAL GRILLING

 BY JAMIE PURVIANCE

PHOTOGRAPHY BY TIM TURNER

Sunset

 weber

AUTHOR: Jamie Purviance

MANAGING EDITOR: Marsha Capen

PHOTOGRAPHER AND PHOTO ART DIRECTION: Tim Turner

FOOD STYLIST: Lynn Gagné

ASSISTANT FOOD STYLIST: Nina Albazi

PHOTO ASSISTANTS: Takamasa Ota, Josh Sears, Christy Clow, Patrick Kenney

INDEXER: Becky LaBrum

COLOR IMAGING: Vicki LaVigne, Paul Christon

IN-HOUSE PREPRESS: Amy Dorsch, Sara Sweeney

CONTRIBUTORS: Christina Schroeder, Marsha Capen, Russell Cronkhite, Lynn Gagné,
Andrew Hunter, Fran Purviance, Amelia Saltsman, David Shalleck, Bob and
Coleen Simmons, Marie Simmons, Amy Vogler, Jan Weimer,
Weber Grill Restaurant Executive Chefs: Randy Waidner, Tony Fraske, Eric Crouse

RECIPE TESTERS: Bob and Coleen Simmons, Edna Schlosser

WEBER-STEPHEN PRODUCTS CO.: Mike Kempster Sr., Executive Vice President

SUNSET BOOKS: Richard A. Smeby, Vice President, General Manager; Bob Doyle, Vice President,
Editorial Director; Linda Barker, Retail Sales Development Manager

EXECUTIVE PRODUCERS: rabble+rouser, inc.: Christina Schroeder, President and CEO;
Marsha Capen, Head of Client Services

DESIGN AND PRODUCTION: Michael Mabry Design: Michael Mabry, Peter Soe Jr., Margie Chu

ISBN 0-376-02046-6
Library of Congress Control Number: 2004097601

For additional copies of
Weber's Real Grilling,™
visit our web site at www.sunset.com
or call 1-800-526-5111

Printed in the United States
by RR Donnelley

www.weber.com®
www.sunset.com

Acknowledgements

The fact that Mike Kempster and Christina Schroeder at Weber asked me to write this book makes me the luckiest food writer I know. They created an exciting vision for an unprecedented cookbook and trusted me to fulfill it. I will always be grateful for that.

I owe enormous appreciation to my editor, Marsha Capen. Her tireless work ethic and creative ideas are on every page of this book. She led the editorial team with a blend of kindness and determination that made each of us better at what we do.

Photographer Tim Turner and food stylist Lynn Gagné excelled in the face of an awesome assignment: photograph every single recipe, plus dozens of instructive scenes. Thankfully, each of them possess a rare gift for finding a compelling way to see each plate of food. Certainly it helped that the meat came courtesy of my friends at Lobel's of New York [www.lobels.com]. The Lobel family's expertise as butchers and purveyors of the finest and freshest meats goes back to the 1840s, and it really shows.

For the imaginative, accessible design of this book, my thanks go to Michael Mabry and his team, Margie Chu and Peter Soe Jr. They adapted to a horrendous schedule and designed the book as if they had all the time in the world.

I was fortunate to rely on some very talented recipe developers and testers. In particular, I want to acknowledge the work of David Shalleck, Bob and Coleen Simmons, and Amy Vogler.

Thanks are certainly due to Susan Maruyama of Round Mountain Media for introducing me to Rich Smeby and Bob Doyle at Sunset Books. It is an honor to work with all three of these leaders in the publishing industry. I hope that this is just the beginning of our collaborations.

Several books were helpful to me during the research of this book. The ones I found particularly good are: *The Complete Meat Cookbook*, by Bruce Aidells and Denis Kelly; *The Best Recipe Grilling and Barbecue*, by the editors of *Cook's Illustrated* magazine; *How to Cook Meat*, by Chris Schlesinger and John Willoughby; and *How to Grill*, by Steven Raichlen.

Finally, some personal acknowledgements. My wife, Fran, and our three children, Julia, James, and Peter, give me the most important kind of support every day. I also want to thank my parents, Ginny and Jim Purviance. They have instilled in me an enduring love of food and family. I owe them more than I can ever imagine.

This icon identifies step-by-step fundamentals. For more, go to www.realgrilling.com

Introduction

This book's purpose is to tell the story of how we Americans grill today. It reflects the many hours I spent talking and grilling with outdoor cooks from coast to coast. I asked them why they grill, how they grill, and what they grill. In the following pages, I have tried to cover the diversity of what I have learned, although the focus is on what is most real. I wanted to capture a true sense of grilling today. That means simple and fun. The recipes here are designed to be easy enough to shop for and easy enough to prepare so that grilling never feels like a chore. Of all the things I heard while writing this book, one was the most consistent: "We cook because we have to, but we grill because we want to."

It's not surprising that some of what we grill today is the same as what Americans have been grilling for decades. The classics remain popular regardless of time or trends. I am talking about recipes like Filet Mignon with Lemon-Parsley Butter [a perennial favorite on steakhouse menus] and Smoked Baby Back Ribs with Cola Barbecue Sauce [a must-have at my house for the Fourth of July]. This book features these recipes and several other classics as tributes to American grilling traditions, including traditional recipes that we have borrowed from other parts of the world, like Carne Asada Fajitas and West Indies Pork Chops with Black Bean-Mango Salsa.

But what about the recipes that have changed? Aren't they an important part of real grilling, too? What about my version of Ginger Chicken Satay with Peanut Sauce, for instance? It's not exactly the one I learned from an Indonesian chef while I was traveling in Southeast Asia. Back in the United States I couldn't find the same tiny red chile that she used in the sauce, but a green serrano chile works just as well. To me, this version is as real as the original. Actually it's hard to say what the original recipe was. I am sure it didn't call for peanut butter, which is what the Indonesian chef used. The point is, recipes

We cook because we have to, but we grill because we want to.

can change for very good reasons. As we adapt them to our own circumstances, they don't necessarily lose their integrity. Some keep their essential qualities while they change to meet the needs of people who cook them.

I have three young children, a wife who

Photograph by Henry Diltz

works full time, and a writing career that requires all the attention I can give it, so at the end of some days I am completely whooped. I am also the cook in my house, so I need some recipes I can use to make quick, respectable dinners without messing up a bunch of pots and pans. For ridiculously busy days, I rely on recipes like Hurry Up I'm Hungry Chicken Breasts, Grill-Roasted New Potatoes, and Basic Grilled Asparagus. These dishes, and many easy ones like them, are an important part of this book not only because they take less than thirty minutes to prepare but also because a lot of beginning grillers get started with these. One day you are making Chicago-Style Hot Dogs and before you know it you are ready for something a little more daring, like T-Bone Steaks with Eggplant Caponata.

Even when we have more time for grilling, who wants to spend it driving from store to store for ingredients? Not me and not anyone else I asked. That's why you can cook any recipe in this book with the ingredients sold at a well-stocked supermarket. Also, I have streamlined the prep work in these recipes so you don't have to bother with unnecessary steps. I don't expect you to make chicken stock from scratch or grind your own hamburger meat when you can buy perfectly good

versions of these. Let's be real.

I have learned from people all over America that grilling is about much more than food and fire. It is also about us and our lifestyles. It is about how we personalize recipes with our own choices, like arranging the coals in a certain way or adding a little more hot sauce to a marinade because that's how you like it. Outdoor cooks have always developed their own touch and they enjoy sharing it with their families and friends. Ultimately, that is the story of grilling today. Flavors and tastes change from one part of the country to the next, but we all want to be part of this relaxed, communal way of cooking. It is the nature of real grilling.

Jamie Purviance

THE GRILL

How to Choose it. How to Use it.

If you ask ten people what makes you a success at the grill, most would tell you it's a combination of the ingredients, the recipe, and the chef. I go a step further and say a lot has to do with the grill itself. In my own totally unscientific grill-side research, I've found that most people think all grills work pretty much the same. But they don't. A grill is an appliance and just like you would take care to get a good and reliable stove, you should approach your grill choice the same way.

Choosing a Gas Grill

1. How is the heat distributed across the cooking grate? It used to be that all gas grills used lava rocks, but that is old technology today. They've been replaced by inverted v-shaped metal bars that do a much better job of channeling away grease and preventing flare-ups. Look for ones that are solid, with no holes or cutouts. Otherwise grease could get to the burners. If you don't want to replace the bars every year, look for thick stainless steel or porcelain-enamel coated bars. They'll hold up a lot better.

Also look at the burners. Because propane contains trace levels of H_2O, they should also be made of stainless steel. Otherwise they could rust.

2. Where does the grease go? This seems like a no-brainer question, but many people don't even think about it until they get the grill home. Grease build up in your grill can cause flare-ups [which is why you should keep your grill clean, but we'll talk about that later]. Your best bet is a grill with a system that channels grease into a deep catch pan with a removable liner. This will make it much easier to clean up. Watch out for grills that have shallow pans that look like baking sheets. Once they are filled with grease, they are almost impossible to remove without spilling on the patio or deck. Not good.

I think it's easier to get to the catch pan if it is accessible from the front of the grill. Otherwise, you have to move the grill to get access from the back. Call me lazy, but I prefer not to have to bother with that. Whatever you decide, front or back, try taking the catch pan out a couple of times to make sure it is easy to remove.

3. What about safety? It's hard to find a store that actually lets you test drive a grill, so sometimes it's hard to judge how safe it's going to be to use. I tell people just to imagine that the grill is hot. Lift the lid. Is there plenty of clearance for your hand on the handle? Is it designed so that your arm stays clear of the hood when lifting the lid? Look underneath the grill. Are the electrical wires and gas-line plumbing set away from hot surfaces and from the grease catch pan? Give the grill a good shake. How sturdy is it? If a strong gust of wind came up while the lid was open, would it stand firm? These things aren't as sexy as a shiny lid or a powerful side burner, but it's the stuff underneath the exterior that really matters.

4. BTUs. The common logic is that more is better, but honestly, that's not true. A good grill will get up to searing temperatures of 500° to 550°F using the least amount of gas possible. Think of it like the fuel efficiency of a car. If you can use less gas to get the performance you want, wouldn't that be nice?

Choosing a Charcoal Grill

1. Look for good thick grates: One for the charcoal and one to cook the food on.

2. Good solid construction and materials. A porcelain-enamel finish on the bowl and lid will make it practically indestructible.

3. Make sure the grill has top and bottom vents. These provide good airflow and can be closed to put out the fire and save unused charcoal for next time.

You can get a basic charcoal grill that will serve you just fine, but since I am a charcoal fanatic, I like my grill to be tricked out. Here's how mine's equipped:

Ash removal system. I don't like to hassle with clean up, so I use a grill that has a damper that sweeps ashes into an ash catcher. Then I can easily dispose of them.

Hinged cooking grate. If you like to grill using the indirect method, a hinged cooking grate is a must. It lets you add more coals to the fire without having to take off the entire cooking grate. You just lift up the sides and add the coals.

Gas assist. In my household, using charcoal lighter fluid is a sin. It imparts a chemical taste that fights with the food. A better alternative is to use a chimney starter to light the coals. Even better, get a charcoal grill with a gas assist. It's the ultimate. You just add the coals and turn on the gas. In a few minutes, the coals are lit. Then you turn off the gas and wait until the coals are ashed over.

Grill Upkeep and Maintenance

Many people I meet tell me that they never clean their grills. Usually that's followed by stories of how everything they cook burns. Hmmm. If you don't keep your grill clean, your probability of flare-ups and burnt food rises exponentially. So even though it's not much fun, I advise people to spend a few minutes every time they grill, and a few minutes every month, to keep things in good working order. It's not hard. If you are diligent, it will put the kibosh on flare-ups and extend your investment in your grill.

Every time you grill: Do the burn-off. Turn all the burners on high, close the lid, let it go for 10 to 15 minutes, then brush the cooking grates thoroughly with a long-handled grill brush.

Now, there is some debate about when to do the burn-off. Some say to do it before grilling, and there are those who say to do it after grilling. There is no one right way. Personally, I just do it while preheating the grill. It saves time and it saves a lot of propane, because I've been known to forget to turn the grill off, particularly when I am entertaining friends and pouring a really nice bottle of wine. But that's just me. If the thought of leaving the crispies on your grill gives you the creeps, do it afterwards; but set a timer so that you don't leave the grill running more than 15 minutes. On a charcoal grill, unless you have a very hot fire going when you are finished grilling, do it beforehand.

Once a month: I recommend that you roll up your sleeves once a month (more often if you are grilling daily) and do a more thorough cleaning.

The instructions below are for a gas grill. I also recommend you read the care instructions in your owner's manual before getting started. Every grill is different, so the steps below may not exactly apply to you, but the objective is the same: get the grease and debris out of the grill. These suggestions apply to grills with angled bars over the burners.

1. Turn off the gas supply and let the grill cool down completely.
2. While the lid is warm—but not hot to the touch—wipe down the inside of the lid using a sponge and some warm, soapy water. This will help stop the build up of carbon.
3. Brush the grates. Remove them and place them to the side.
4. Brush the angled metal bars covering the burners. Remove them and place them to the side.
5. Carefully brush the burner tubes with a stainless steel brush, being careful to brush up and down, not across the ports [openings].
6. Clean the bottom of the grill. If you have a removable collection tray, scrape the debris into the collection tray. A small plastic putty knife is a handy tool to help get into tight places.
7. Remove all the debris and dispose of the grease.
8. Using warm, soapy water, wash the inside of the grill [avoid getting water inside the burner tubes]. Rinse.
9. Put the angled bars and grates back into place and you are good to go.

Note: There are a few degreasers and grill cleaners [similar to oven cleaners] on the market. Read your owner's manual before using any of these products or any abrasive cleansers. Some of them can harm your grill and may void your warranty, so beware. The same goes for putting parts in the dishwasher or taking your grill through the car wash [yes, it has been done].

The regular maintenance on a charcoal grill is a little more straightforward. Here the objective is to make sure you are regularly cleaning out the ashes from the bottom of the grill and the catch pan. Ash has a slight amount of water in it naturally, so if you leave it sitting, it can rust your grill.
1. Brush the grate when the grill is hot. When cool, remove the ashes and dispose of them in a fireproof container.
2. Brush the inside of the grill, the charcoal grate, and any other parts inside the grill.
3. Just like you would on a gas grill, wipe down the inside of the lid and the bowl with warm, soapy water. Rinse.

It's NOT Paint!
If it looks like paint is peeling off the inside of your lid, don't worry. It's not paint. The flakes you see are just accumulated cooking vapors that have turned into carbon. They are not harmful, but you can get rid of them by brushing the lid with a brass-bristle brush or a crumpled piece of aluminum foil.

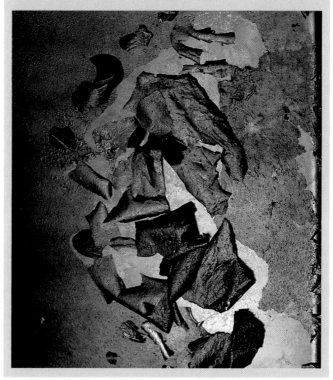

THE FIRE

Whether you are talking about the glowing embers of a charcoal grill or the flickering flames of a gas grill, the fire provides you with several options for developing flavors, textures, and aromas. As you get better and better at mastering the fire to suit your needs, your ability will show in the food, and the ancient art of grilling will be more fun than ever before.

Direct or Indirect?

Direct heat means the fire is directly below the food. This arrangement works well for grilling thin, tender foods such as hamburgers, boneless chicken breasts, fish fillets, and sliced vegetables. These foods develop golden brown and delicious surfaces in the same amount of time that it takes to cook their centers just right. Generally speaking, it is best to use direct heat for foods that need less than 20 minutes of grilling time.

Indirect heat means the fire is off to one side of the grill, or better yet, on opposite sides of the grill, and the food is cooked over the unlit part. Large foods such as turkeys, prime rib, and pork shoulders do well in this arrangement, because the indirect heat cooks them evenly from all sides, allowing their centers to cook just right before their surfaces are overdone. Generally speaking, it is best to use indirect heat for foods that need more than 20 minutes of grilling time.

Sometimes a combination of direct and indirect heat will give you the best results. For example, bone-in chicken pieces will develop rich, smoky flavors and crispy skins when you grill them over direct heat for about 10 minutes. Then, if you move them over indirect heat, the meat at the center and near the bone will cook to a juicy, tender doneness before the skins get too dark. I call this second step "grill-roasting," because the grill works like an oven, with indirect heat penetrating from all sides rather than primarily from below.

How Hot is High?

Choosing direct heat vs. indirect heat is one thing. Another important decision is whether to use high, medium, or low heat [or any other heat level in between]. The recipes in this book recommend which temperature[s] to use, but if you are working with a charcoal grill with no knobs to turn, how can you tell the differences between the levels of heat?

Ideally your grill has a thermometer mounted in the center of the lid. High, medium, and low correspond to these temperature ranges on the thermometer:

High	450° to 550°F
Medium	350° to 450°F
Low	250° to 350°F

Charcoal

Charcoal is what's left when wood logs are burned with very little oxygen. This controlled burning removes water and resins from the logs, but it doesn't consume the wood. As a result, you have black lumps of combustible carbon. This "lump charcoal" burns more slowly and evenly than logs, though it still delivers a truly live-fire experience as it sparks and pops and casts woodsy aromas on the food. Don't walk away from lump charcoal; you need to watch it carefully. It burns very hot at the start and then looses heat quickly, so be ready to replenish the fire.

Today briquets are more popular than lump charcoal, probably because they are inexpensive and widely available. These compressed black bundles are made from sawdust, coal, starch binders, and other fillers like glue and clay. Some of them include lighter fluid, which I don't recommend. Most briquets contribute very little woodsy aroma, however they do produce good, even heat. When fat and juices drip into the glowing embers, the drippings turn to smoke, flavoring the food in wonderful ways.

Best of Both Worlds: If you want the woodsy aromas of lump charcoal and the slow burning of briquets, use both. Start the fire with briquets. When they are all covered in gray ash, bury the lump charcoal among the briquets. The fire will be ready for grilling 15 to 20 minutes later. The lump charcoal will provide the flavor while the briquets prolong the heat.

Ways To Build A Fire

A simple way to light any type of charcoal is to use a chimney starter—an aluminum cylinder with a handle outside and wire rack inside. Remove the top grate from your grill and set the chimney starter on the charcoal grate below. Fill the space under the wire rack with a few sheets of wadded-up newspaper or a few paraffin cubes. Fill the space above the rack with charcoal. Light the newspaper or paraffin cubes through the holes on the side. The coals will be glowing bright orange in 20 to 25 minutes. Wearing barbecue mitts, pour the coals carefully over the charcoal grate.

Note: Never place a hot chimney starter on the grass or deck. Set it on a heatproof surface, such as concrete, and keep children and pets away.

Alternatively, light a few paraffin cubes in the middle of the charcoal grate. Build a pyramid of coals over the paraffin cubes. When the coals in the middle are lit, use long tongs to pile the unlit coals on top. When all the coals are glowing bright orange, arrange them on the grate.

How Many Coals?

The number of coals you need to start depends on the size of your grill. In most cases, you should start with enough to create a single layer of coals across the charcoal grate.

Diameter of Grill	Briquets Needed
14½"	30
18½"	40
22½"	50
37½"	150

Use a long spatula or tongs to move the coals in whatever configuration you need. The most basic configuration is a 1-zone fire, where you have even heat all the way across the grill. Notice that the coals have a light coating of grey ash. Wait until they reach this point before grilling. It looks like this:

Basic Direct Fire

If you want the option of grilling over both direct and indirect heat, push the coals to the opposite sides of the grill and put a disposable drip pan in the middle [for long-cooking recipes, add water to the drip pan to keep drippings from burning]. The middle area is for indirect grilling. You will need about one-third fewer coals for this configuration. It looks like this:

Basic Indirect Fire

For even more flexibility, arrange a fire with 3 zones of heat. On one side of the grill, pile the coals 2 or 3 briquets deep. Then slope the coals down to a single layer of coals across the center of the grill, and have no coals on the opposite side. When the coals are completely ashed over and they have burned for about 10 minutes more, you should have high heat on one side, medium heat in the center, and indirect heat on the opposite side. It looks like this:

3-Zone Fire

Controlling the Heat

For high heat [450° to 550°F] with a 1-zone fire, let the coals burn until they have a light coating of ash. Then put the lid on and preheat the cooking grate for about 10 minutes. For medium heat [350° to 450°F], once the coals have a light coating of ash, let them burn for about 15 minutes more with the lid off. Then put the lid on and preheat the cooking grate for about 10 minutes. With the lid on, the temperature will drop about 100 degrees over the course of the hour.

Maintaining the Heat

If the temperature is dropping below the range you want, add more coals [see amounts below], scattering them among the lit coals. To light the new coals, be sure to sweep the old ashes into the ash catcher, bury the new coals among the lit ones, and leave the lid off for 10 to 15 minutes.

To skip this waiting period, light the new coals in a chimney starter and add them whenever you need them.

Diameter of Grill	Briquets to add after each hour
14½"	12
18½"	14
22½"	16
37½"	44

Controlling Flare-Ups

Occasionally a charcoal fire will flare-up. A little bit of this is fine. In fact, it creates desirable carmelization. A lot of this is not. It could scorch the food. Flare-ups are the result of fats or oils dripping into the flame of the grill and igniting. To limit the amount of dripping, trim your meats of excess fat, and brush or spray only a light coating of oil on your food. If your food has been soaking in an oil-based marinade, drain it well and pat the marinade off the surface with paper towels.

It also helps to limit the amount of air getting to the flame. Keep the lid on the grill as much as possible. The vents on the lid should be open almost always [to keep the fire lit], but if flare-ups are a problem, close the vents on the lid until the flare-ups die down.

Some grillers will tell you to use a water gun or spray bottle to extinguish flare-ups, yet this tends to knock ashes onto your food. A better solution is to move the food over indirect heat temporarily. With no flame directly below the food, the flare-ups should die down in less than 10 seconds. Then move the food back over direct heat.

Gas

Recent improvements in the quality of gas grills have revolutionized grilling. You can now control the heat of a good gas grill with the kind of precision that previously you would only get from an indoor gas stove. With options like side burners, infrared burners for rotisserie cooking, and smoker boxes, outdoor cooks now have tremendous flexibility, not to mention a gas grill's long-standing advantage over charcoal—push-button convenience. Some of my charcoal buddies claim that gas grills don't get hot enough to sear properly, and I have heard people say that food doesn't pick up the same kind of smokiness with a gas grill. I disagree on both counts. Turn all the burners of a gas grill on high and watch the temperature climb to 500°F and beyond. That's hotter than any food requires for searing. As for the smokiness, gas grills generate a lot of smoke when juices and fat drip into the grill. For more aroma of woodsy smoke [the same kind a charcoal grill provides], I use wood chips with excellent results [more on that on pages 22-23].

Lighting a Gas Grill

Lighting a gas grill, in most cases, is as simple as lifting the lid, opening the valve at the top of the tank, turning a knob or two on the burner controls, and pushing a button. The spark of the igniter lights the gas vapors and presto, you have flickering flames.

Before grilling, preheat the grill with the lid closed and all burners on high for about 10 minutes [the temperature should rise to at least 500°F]. This makes the grate much easier to clean and it improves the grill's ability to sear. Then adjust the burners, if necessary, to the desired temperature.

To grill over direct heat, place the food directly over a lit burner and close the lid. It looks like this:

Direct Heat

To grill over indirect heat, place the food over an unlit burner and leave the other burner[s] on. It looks like this:

Indirect Heat

Tools Every Griller Should Own

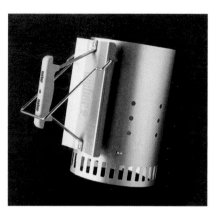

Barbecue Mitts Fire is hot. Protect yourself at all times when cooking. This is especially important when you are dumping coals out of a chimney starter or moving them around the charcoal grate.

Chimney Starter This handy invention provides a simple way to light charcoal. The cylindrical shape promotes a fast, even burn. Buy one big enough to light as many coals as will fit in a single layer across your charcoal grate [see page 15].

Grill Brush The best tool for keeping your grill grate clean. Get one with stiff brass bristles. My new favorite is shaped like a triangle and gets in between the grates better than other brushes I've used. If you have cast-iron cooking grates, you'll need a brush with steel bristles.

Basting Brush Good for basting but even more useful for brushing oil on food before grilling. Get one with soft, flexible bristles and wash by hand after every use. Don't put it in the dishwasher; it is very hard on the bristles.

Disposable Pans These are essential for catching grease and drippings. Also handy for carrying food to and from the grill. In a pinch, they make half-decent smoker boxes [see page 23].

Pans for Cooking A skillet with an ovenproof handle lets you use your grill to roast, braise, or bake anything you would cook in your oven. Cast-iron is the most traditional, though nonstick sauté pans perform really well, too. Heavy-duty aluminum pie plates are ideal for baking pies, cakes, and cobblers in the grill.

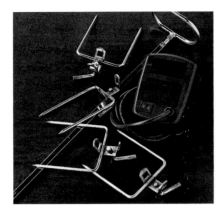

Rotisserie Look for a really strong rod, good forks to keep the meat firmly in place, wood or heat-resistant plastic handles, and a good motor. If you have a side burner, make sure the design won't obstruct its use while the rotisserie is operating.

Spatula Required for turning burgers, delicate fish fillets, and wide items like pizzas. Don't bother with an extra-long spatula with a flimsy blade—the blade should be long, wide, and sturdy.

Timer If timing is everything, then a timer can make all the difference. It's like a sous chef who always has you covered. Why not have two of them?

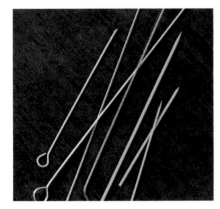

Skewers Wood skewers are fine for occasional use, but metal is much better if you like to make kabobs or satays a lot. Look for a flat design rather than round, or get double-prong metal skewers; this will keep food from spinning on the skewers as you turn them over.

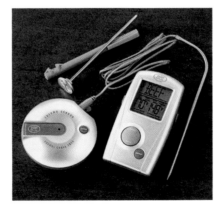

Thermometer An instant-read thermometer is the surest way to know about the doneness of your food before you cut into it. Some digital thermometers allow you to leave the probe in the food and walk away with a wireless beeper that will tell you when the food reaches the internal temperature you selected. Very cool.

Tongs They get the most use of all. Have at least three pairs: one for picking up raw food, one for handling cooked food, and one for arranging coals. The best are stainless steel and spring loaded.

1. With the breast side facing up, slide a 3-foot piece of twine under the back and drumsticks.

2. Cross the twine just above the drumsticks.

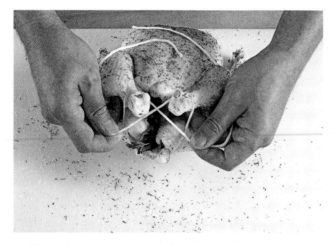

3. Wrap the twine around the drumsticks and pull toward the outside to bring the drumsticks together.

4. Pull the twine tightly along each side of the chicken between the joints of the drumsticks and the thighs.

5. Tie the two ends of twine together between the neck bone and the top of the breast. Pull tightly to bring the legs up against the breast.

6. After you cut off any dangling twine, the chicken is ready for grill-roasting or cooking on a rotisserie.

1. The screws that tighten each fork should be on the bottom of the spit.

2. The second chicken should face the same direction as the first.

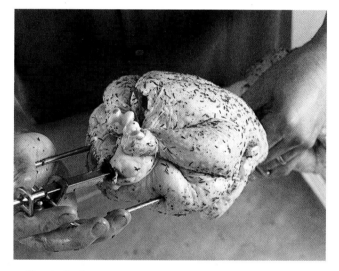

3. Each fork should be deep inside the meat.

4. The chickens should be centered on the spit.

Adapting Recipes to the Rotisserie

Almost any recipe that calls for indirect heat does really well on the rotisserie. As long as the meat can be evenly balanced on the spit, it's a prime candidate for the rotisserie. For example, try one of these:

By the same token, if your grill doesn't have a rotisserie, you can still cook any recipe that calls for one. Just put the meat right on the grate over indirect heat, with the fire on opposite sides of the food. The cooking time and temperature will be almost exactly the same. Here are a couple rotisserie recipes in this book that can also be grilled over indirect heat:

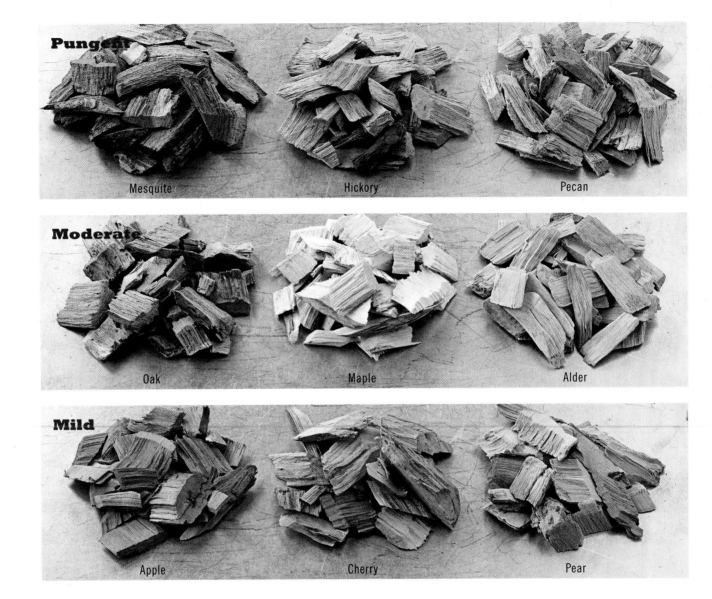

Pungent
Mesquite Hickory Pecan

Moderate
Oak Maple Alder

Mild
Apple Cherry Pear

Smoking

I hope that at some point in your life, even just once, you experience the tremendous satisfaction of succulent baby back ribs cooked for hours and hours over the wafting aromas of wood smoke. I hope you cook those ribs yourself and share them with people you love. This is authentic barbecue, a proud American tradition. I also hope that you add a touch of smoke to foods that cook much more quickly. Believe me, steaks, chops, and even vegetables are transformed by smoke into something inexpressible.

Start by soaking wood chunks in water for at least 1 hour; chips need only 30 minutes of soaking. Shake all the excess water off the woods before adding them to your fire or smoker box. You can use any of the hardwoods [see above]. Mesquite and hickory are the most popular, but start with just a few handfuls and see how you like it. You might want to blend a pungent wood with something more moderate like oak or maple. Don't use softwoods like pine and fir, because they have an unsavory, resinous character. Also avoid any woods that have been treated with chemicals.

Pungent

Best for beef, lamb, or pork

Mesquite

Hickory

Pecan

Moderate

Best for fish, pork, or poultry

Oak

Maple

Alder

Mild

Best for fish, poultry, or vegetables

Apple

Cherry

Pear

Preparing Your Charcoal Grill, Gas Grill, or Vertical Water Smoker

Charcoal Grill: Use the indirect method by arranging charcoal briquets on each side of the charcoal grate. Place a heavy aluminum foil pan between the piles of briquets; add 2 cups water and any flavorings, such as barbecue sauce, wine, beer, or juice. Allow 30 minutes for the coals to heat up [they should have a light coating of grey ash]. Place the soaked wood chunks or chips directly on the prepared coals and allow them to smoke fully before you begin cooking. Place the food on top of the cooking grate over the water pan. Cover the grill. Add 5 to 7 briquets to each side every hour and replenish the water and flavorings as needed.

Gas Grill: A smoker attachment makes it easy to turn your gas grill into a hot smoker. Before preheating your grill, simply fill the water pan on the smoker attachment with hot tap water. Place the presoaked wood chunks or chips in the other compartment. Begin cooking after preheating and when the grill is fully smoking.

You can also improvise with a foil pan. Place presoaked wood chips in a foil pan, cover with aluminum foil (poke holes in the aluminum foil to allow the smoke to escape), and place directly on the bars over the lit burner. Place the cooking grates on top, make sure the burners are on high, and close the lid. Begin cooking when the grill is fully smoking, adjusting the temperature as desired.

Water Smoker: A vertical water smoker is shaped like an upright bullet with 3 sections. Light the coals in a chimney starter. When they have a light coating of grey ash, spread them evenly across the inside of the charcoal chamber. If you are using the water pan, place it in the middle section and fill it with hot water. Add flavorings to the water, if desired.

Place the soaked woods on the coals through the door on the front of the smoker. Keep all the vents partially closed for smoke cooking. Place the food on the top and/or middle cooking grate. Arrange the food in a single layer on each grate, leaving space for smoke to circulate around each piece. Add 12 to 14 briquets and as many wood chunks as needed to the fire, and replenish the water and flavorings as needed. With the lid closed, the low heat and aromatic smoke will rise with the steam and barbecue whatever you like: ribs, turkey, chicken, pork shoulder, brisket, etc.

RUBS, MARINADES, AND SAUCES

Most grillers I know are looking for an edge, a certain something that will take their food to the next level. In the pages ahead, you will find many tips for working the fire and applying insider techniques, but perhaps nothing is easier and more effective than a judicious use of good rubs. A rub is a mixture of spices, herbs, and other seasonings [often including sugar]. The term comes from the practice of massaging meat with the mixture. Quite simply, a rub is the fastest way to add flavor to food.

Marinades work more slowly than rubs, but they seep in a little deeper. Typically, a marinade is made with some acidic liquid, some oil, and a combination of herbs and spices. These ingredients can "fill in the gaps" when a particular meat, fish, or vegetable [yes, vegetable] lacks enough taste or richness. They can also give food characteristics that reflect regional/ethnic cooking styles. The acidity in a marinade is often helpful in tenderizing food, but if it works too long, the surface of meat turns mushy and fish actually gets tougher, so timing is crucial.

And then there are the sauces, especially the barbecue sauces. Most barbecue sauces in America today are tomato based, though we have a fair share of brisk vinegar-based sauces, even some based on strange things like milk, espresso, or jelly. In the end, a good barbecue sauce is unexplainable magic. When the right ingredients simmer over time and coalesce into a rich concoction, you can't really describe the fabulous taste. You just slather it on the meat and thank your lucky stars!

Let's take a closer look at the fundamentals of rubs, marinades, and sauces. I believe that if you know something about the individual components of each, you will be better at making your own and doctoring the ones you buy at the store. That's when grillers find their edge. That's when they develop a certain something.

Hot
prepared chili powder
pure chile powder
black pepper
cayenne pepper
crushed red chile pepper

Sweet
granulated sugar
brown sugar
cinnamon
allspice
Chinese five-spice
cloves
nutmeg

Earthy
cumin
paprika
coriander
celery seed

Herbaceous
(dried herbs)

thyme	fennel
oregano	bay
parsley	sage
rosemary	dill
marjoram	basil

Sharp
granulated garlic
granulated onion
dry mustard
mustard seed
turmeric

Salty
kosher salt
sea salt
smoked sea salt

The Yin and Yang of Rubs

Each ingredient in a rub belongs to one of the six categories pictured above. Some rubs have ingredients from only three or four categories. That's fine. As you add a little of this and a little of that to your rubs, consider each category and keep a sense of balance in mind. Hot spices such as pure chile powder and cayenne pepper have a real affinity for sweet elements like brown sugar and cinnamon. Similarly, earthy spices and dried herbs complement each other. The herbs tend to brighten and lighten the deep flavors of spices like cumin and paprika. And if you are using sharp spices like granulated garlic and onion, try adding a bit more salt to mellow their bite.

How Long?

If you leave a rub on for a long time, the seasonings intermix with the juices in the meat and produce more pronounced flavors, as well as a crust. This is good to a point, but a rub with a lot of salt and sugar will draw moisture out of the meat over time, making the meat tastier, yes, but also drier. So how long should you use a rub? Here are some guidelines.

1 to 15 minutes	15 to 30 minutes
Small foods, such as shellfish, cubed meat for kabobs, and vegetables	Thin cuts of boneless meat, such as chicken breasts, fish fillets, pork tenderloin, chops, and steaks
30 to 90 minutes	**2 to 8 hours**
Thicker cuts of boneless or bone-in meat, such as leg of lamb, whole chickens, and beef roasts	Big or tough cuts of meat, such as racks of ribs, whole hams, pork shoulders, and turkeys

A Word about Freshness

Ground spices loose their aromas in a matter of months [eight to ten months maximum]. If you have been holding onto a little jar of coriander for years, waiting to blend the world's finest version of curry powder, forget about it. Dump the old, tired coriander and buy some freshly ground. Better yet, buy whole coriander and grind the seeds yourself. Some people who are far more exacting than I am actually date each jar when they buy it. Whatever you do, store your spices and spice rubs in air-tight containers away from light and heat, to give them a long, aromatic life. The spice rack by your stove may look absolutely darling, but it is murder on your spices.

Rub Recipes

Rubs are often ethnic, meat-specific, or just down-right personal. I have included some of my favorites on this page, but don't be restricted by the titles. For example, I happen to love the beef rub for the way that pure chile powder, onion, garlic, and a touch of cumin work with the juices and fat of a well-marbled steak, but if you want to have the same rub on chicken, be my guest. Better still, use these rubs as a starting point for making your own.

Classic Barbecue Rub

- 2 teaspoons kosher salt
- 1 teaspoon freshly ground black pepper
- 1 teaspoon dried thyme
- 1 teaspoon paprika
- 1 teaspoon pure chile powder
- 1 teaspoon granulated sugar
- 1 teaspoon celery seed
- 1/2 teaspoon mustard seed
- 1/2 teaspoon ground mustard
- 1/2 teaspoon ground cumin
- 1/2 teaspoon ground fennel

Makes about 1/4 cup

Chicken and Seafood Rub

- 4 teaspoons granulated onion
- 4 teaspoons granulated garlic
- 1 tablespoon kosher salt
- 2 teaspoons prepared chili powder
- 2 teaspoons freshly ground black pepper

Makes about 1/4 cup

Pork Rub

- 2 teaspoons pure chile powder
- 2 teaspoons freshly ground black pepper
- 2 teaspoons kosher salt
- 2 teaspoons ground cumin
- 2 teaspoons dried oregano
- 1 teaspoon granulated garlic

Makes about 1/4 cup

Beef Rub

- 4 teaspoons kosher salt
- 1 tablespoon pure chile powder
- 1 tablespoon granulated onion
- 1 1/2 teaspoons granulated garlic
- 1 teaspoon paprika
- 1 teaspoon dried marjoram
- 1/2 teaspoon ground cumin
- 1/2 teaspoon freshly ground black pepper
- 1/4 teaspoon ground cinnamon

Makes about 1/4 cup

Southwest Rub

- 2 teaspoons pure chile powder
- 2 teaspoons granulated garlic
- 2 teaspoons paprika
- 2 teaspoons kosher salt
- 1 teaspoon ground coriander
- 1 teaspoon ground cumin
- 1 teaspoon freshly ground black pepper

Makes about 1/4 cup

Caribbean Rub

- 1 tablespoon light brown sugar
- 1 tablespoon granulated garlic
- 1 tablespoon dried thyme
- 2 1/4 teaspoons kosher salt
- 3/4 teaspoon freshly ground black pepper
- 3/4 teaspoon ground allspice

Makes about 1/4 cup

Acids

vinegar
citric juices
tomatoes
wine
yogurt

Oils

olive oil
sesame oil
canola oil

Good Flavors

fresh or dried herbs
spices
condiments
finely chopped vegetables
the zest of citrus fruits

Building a Better Marinade

The rules to building a marinade are: there aren't any rules, and you can add whatever you want. But before you start dumping ingredients into a bowl with all the restraint of a sailor on leave, let me give you some advice. Start with the basics. That means a little acid, a little oil, and a whole bunch of good flavors.

I usually start with a ratio of 1:3 [acidity: oil], just like in salad dressings. The acidity in the marinade tenderizes the food [especially the surface] and contributes some tanginess. The oil provides moisture and richness. It also mellows the sharp taste of the acid. The good flavors...well, they just taste good.

Actually, there is one rule about marinades. When they include an acid, be sure to use non-reactive containers. These are dishes and bowls made of glass, plastic, or ceramic. Containers made of aluminum or other metals react with acids and add a metallic flavor to food.

My favorite container is a resealable plastic bag. I set the bag in a bowl so the liquid comes up the sides of the food and covers it evenly. If there is not enough liquid, I turn the bag over every hour or so.

How Long?

The right times vary depending on the strength of the marinade and the food you are marinating. If your marinade includes intense ingredients such as soy sauce, liquor, or hot chiles and spices, don't overdo it. A fish fillet should still taste like fish, not a burning-hot, salt-soaked piece of protein. Also, if an acidic marinade is left too long on meat or fish, it can make the surface mushy or dry. Here are some general guidelines to get you going.

15 to 30 minutes	1 to 3 hours
Small foods, such as shellfish, fish fillets, cubed meat for kabobs, and tender vegetables	Thin cuts of boneless meat, such as chicken breasts, pork tenderloin, chops, and steaks, as well as sturdy vegetables
2 to 6 hours	**6 to 12 hours**
Thicker cuts of boneless or bone-in meat, such as leg of lamb, whole chickens, and beef roasts	Big or tough cuts of meat, such as racks of ribs, whole hams, pork shoulders, and turkeys

Note: Marinades work faster at room temperature, but if the food requires more than 1 hour of marinating time, put it in the refrigerator. For most meats, remove them from the refrigerator (with or without the marinade) 20 to 30 minutes before grilling.

After a marinade has been in contact with raw fish or meat, either discard it or boil it for at least 1 minute. The boiling will destroy any harmful bacteria that might have been left by the fish or meat. A boiled marinade often works well as a basting sauce.

Lots of People Do It But Never Admit to It
Go ahead. Use that bottled Italian dressing as a marinade. It is actually pretty good, and when you are pressed for time and need to make dinner fast after a busy day, it will work just fine. I won't tell.

Marinade Recipes

Beer Marinade
- 1 cup dark Mexican beer, such as Negra Modelo
- 2 tablespoons dark sesame oil
- 1 tablespoon finely chopped garlic
- 1 teaspoon dried oregano
- 1 teaspoon kosher salt
- 1/2 teaspoon freshly ground black pepper
- 1/4 teaspoon ground cayenne pepper

In a small bowl, whisk the ingredients.

Makes about 1 1/4 cups

Jerk Marinade
- 1/2 cup roughly chopped yellow onion
- 1 jalapeño chile pepper, roughly chopped
- 3 tablespoons white wine vinegar
- 2 tablespoons soy sauce
- 2 tablespoons canola oil
- 1/2 teaspoon ground allspice
- 1/4 teaspoon granulated garlic
- 1/4 teaspoon ground cinnamon
- 1/4 teaspoon kosher salt
- 1/4 teaspoon freshly ground black pepper
- 1/8 teaspoon ground nutmeg

In a food processor, combine the ingredients. Process until smooth.

Makes about 3/4 cup

Pacific Rim Marinade
- 1 small yellow onion, roughly chopped [about 1 cup]
- 1/3 cup soy sauce
- 1/4 cup fresh lemon juice
- 1/4 cup vegetable oil
- 2 tablespoons dark brown sugar
- 2 tablespoons minced garlic
- 1/2 teaspoon ground allspice

In a medium bowl, whisk the ingredients until the sugar is dissolved.

Makes about 2 cups

More Marinade Recipes

Mediterranean Marinade

2 tablespoons extra virgin olive oil
2 teaspoons paprika
1 teaspoon ground coriander
1 teaspoon ground cumin
1 teaspoon granulated garlic
1 teaspoon kosher salt
1/4 teaspoon freshly ground black pepper

In a small bowl, mix the ingredients.

Makes about 1/4 cup

Southwest Marinade

1/2 cup fresh orange juice
3 tablespoons extra virgin olive oil
2 tablespoons red wine vinegar
1 tablespoon minced garlic
2 teaspoons pure chili powder
1 1/2 teaspoons dried oregano
1 teaspoon kosher salt
1/2 teaspoon freshly ground black pepper
1/2 teaspoon ground cinnamon

In a medium bowl, whisk the ingredients.

Makes about 1 cup

Spicy Cayenne Marinade

1/4 cup extra virgin olive oil
2 tablespoons fresh lemon juice
1 tablespoon minced garlic
2 teaspoons dried oregano
2 teaspoons paprika
1 1/2 teaspoons kosher salt
1 teaspoon celery seed
1 teaspoon ground cayenne pepper

In a small bowl, whisk the ingredients.

Makes about 1 cup

Bourbon Marinade

1/2 cup bourbon
1/4 cup ketchup
2 tablespoons extra virgin olive oil
2 tablespoons soy sauce
1 tablespoon white wine vinegar
2 teaspoons minced garlic
1/2 teaspoon Tabasco® sauce
1/2 teaspoon freshly ground black pepper

In a medium bowl, whisk the ingredients.

Makes about 1 cup

Honey-Mustard Marinade

1/2 cup Dijon mustard
1/4 cup honey
2 tablespoons extra virgin olive oil
2 teaspoons curry powder
1 teaspoon freshly grated lemon zest
1/2 teaspoon granulated garlic
1/2 teaspoon kosher salt
1/4 teaspoon ground cayenne pepper
1/4 teaspoon freshly ground black pepper

In a medium bowl, whisk the ingredients.

Makes about 1 cup

Tarragon-Citrus Marinade

1/4 cup extra virgin olive oil
1/4 cup roughly chopped fresh tarragon
Zest and juice of 1 orange
Zest and juice of 1 lemon
2 tablespoons sherry vinegar
2 teaspoons kosher salt
1 teaspoon minced garlic
1 teaspoon grated ginger
1/2 teaspoon prepared chili powder
1/2 teaspoon freshly ground black pepper

In a medium bowl, whisk the ingredients.

Makes about 1 cup

Mongolian Marinade

1/2 cup hoisin sauce
2 tablespoons oyster sauce
2 tablespoons soy sauce
2 tablespoons dry sherry
2 tablespoons rice vinegar
2 tablespoons canola oil
1 tablespoon honey
1 tablespoon minced ginger
1 tablespoon minced garlic
1/2 teaspoon crushed red pepper flakes [optional]

In a medium bowl, whisk the ingredients.

Makes about 1 1/4 cups

Tequila Marinade

- 1 cup fresh orange juice
- 1/2 cup tequila
- 2 tablespoons fresh lime juice
- 2 tablespoons light brown sugar
- 2 teaspoons ground cumin
- 1 jalapeño chile pepper, cut into 1/8-inch slices

In a small bowl, whisk the ingredients until the sugar is dissolved.

Makes about 1 3/4 cups

Cuban Marinade

- 1/2 cup fresh orange juice
- 1/2 cup fresh lemonade
- 1/2 cup finely chopped yellow onion
- 1/4 cup extra virgin olive oil
- 2 tablespoons minced garlic
- 2 tablespoons dried oregano
- 2 tablespoons fresh lime juice

In a medium bowl, whisk the ingredients.

Makes about 2 cups

Tandoori Marinade

- 1 cup plain yogurt
- 1 tablespoon grated fresh ginger
- 1 tablespoon paprika
- 1 tablespoon vegetable oil
- 2 teaspoons minced garlic
- 2 teaspoons kosher salt
- 1 1/2 teaspoons ground cumin
- 1 teaspoon ground turmeric
- 1/2 teaspoon ground cayenne pepper

In a blender or food processor, process the ingredients until smooth.

Makes about 1 1/4 cups

Chinese Hoisin Marinade

- 1/2 cup hoisin sauce
- 2 tablespoons red wine vinegar
- 1 tablespoon canola oil
- 2 teaspoons minced garlic
- 1 teaspoon grated ginger
- 1 teaspoon Tabasco® sauce
- 1 teaspoon dark sesame oil

In a medium bowl, whisk the ingredients.

Makes about 3/4 cup

Mojo Marinade

- 1/2 cup fresh orange juice
- 2 tablespoons fresh lime juice
- 2 tablespoons soy sauce
- 2 tablespoons extra virgin olive oil
- 1 tablespoon minced garlic
- 1/2 teaspoon Tabasco® sauce
- 1/2 teaspoon ground cumin
- 1/4 teaspoon kosher salt
- 1/4 teaspoon freshly ground black pepper

In a medium bowl, whisk the ingredients.

Makes about 1 cup

Barcelona Marinade

- 5 scallions, cut into 1-inch pieces
- 1 cup lightly packed fresh basil leaves
- 3 large garlic cloves
- 2 serrano chile peppers, roughly chopped
- 1/4 cup extra virgin olive oil
- 2 tablespoons sherry vinegar
- 1 teaspoon kosher salt
- 1/2 teaspoon freshly ground black pepper

In a food processor or blender, process the ingredients to a smooth paste, 1 to 2 minutes.

Makes about 3/4 cup

Cilantro Pesto Marinade

- 2 tablespoons coarsely chopped walnuts
- 2 medium garlic cloves
- 1 1/2 cups loosely packed fresh cilantro leaves and tender stems
- 1/2 cup loosely packed fresh Italian parsley leaves and tender stems
- 1/2 teaspoon kosher salt
- 1/4 teaspoon freshly ground black pepper
- 1/4 cup extra virgin olive oil

In a food processor, finely chop the walnuts and garlic. Scrape down the sides of the bowl. Add the cilantro, parsley, salt, and pepper and process until finely chopped. With the motor running, slowly add the oil to create a smooth purée.

Makes about 1 cup

Sweet

granulated sugar

light or dark
brown sugar

honey

molasses

corn syrup

maple syrup

hoisin sauce

soda pop

Sour

distilled vinegar

cider vinegar

red or white
wine vinegar

balsamic vinegar

rice wine vinegar

lemon or lime juice

mustard

the juice from a
pickle or relish jar

capers

Spicy

hot sauces

fresh or
dried chiles

black pepper

cayenne pepper

crushed red
pepper flakes

horseradish

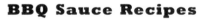

Salty

kosher or sea salt

soy sauce

fish sauce

Worcestershire
sauce

olives

anchovies

Anatomy of a Barbecue Sauce

Most respectable sauces made at home and some
of the better bottled sauces achieve a balance of
sweet, sour, spicy, and salty. For your own sauces,
choose from the categories above, but don't forget
to add what really sets a great sauce apart. I call it
the "x" factor. It could be almost anything. Here
are just some of the options to consider.

The "x" factor:

any spice imaginable	pork fat
fruit preserves	butter or olive oil
liquid smoke	chicken or beef stock
liquor	coffee or espresso
wine	you name it...
tomato sauce	

BBQ Sauce Recipes

Cola Barbecue Sauce

  1 tablespoon extra virgin olive oil
  ½ teaspoon granulated garlic
  ½ teaspoon pure chile powder
  ½ teaspoon ground cumin
  ⅔ cup ketchup
  ⅓ cup cola
  2 tablespoons soy sauce
  2 tablespoons cider vinegar
  ¼ teaspoon freshly ground black pepper
  ⅛ teaspoon mesquite liquid smoke

In a medium saucepan over medium heat, warm
the oil. Add the garlic, chile powder, and cumin.
Cook for 30 seconds, stirring occasionally. Add the
remaining ingredients, whisk them, and allow the
sauce to simmer for about 5 minutes.

Makes about 1 cup

Ancho Barbecue Sauce

- ⅓ cup slivered almonds
- 2 medium dried ancho chile peppers, about ½ ounce total
- 6 tablespoons fresh orange juice
- ⅓ cup roughly chopped roasted red bell peppers from a jar
- 3 tablespoons ketchup
- 2 tablespoons extra virgin olive oil
- 1 tablespoon red wine vinegar
- ½ teaspoon granulated garlic
- ¼ teaspoon kosher salt
- ¼ teaspoon freshly ground black pepper

In a medium skillet over medium heat, toast the almonds until golden brown, 3 to 5 minutes, stirring occasionally. Transfer the almonds to a food processor. Remove the stems from the chiles, make a slit down the side of each one with scissors, and remove the veins and seeds. Flatten the chiles and place them in the skillet over medium heat. With a spatula hold the chiles flat for 5 seconds, turn over and repeat for another 5 seconds. Transfer the chiles to a medium bowl and soak in hot water for 15 minutes. Remove the chiles, squeeze out the excess water, and then roughly chop [you should have about ¼ cup]. Place the chiles and the remaining ingredients in the food processor with the almonds. Process to create a coarse purée.

Makes about 1 cup

Sassy Barbecue Sauce

- ½ cup ketchup
- 2 tablespoons molasses
- 1 tablespoon white wine vinegar
- 1 tablespoon Dijon mustard
- 1 tablespoon light brown sugar
- 2 teaspoons Worcestershire sauce
- ½ teaspoon kosher salt
- ¼ teaspoon Tabasco® sauce
- ¼ teaspoon granulated garlic
- ¼ teaspoon freshly ground black pepper

In a small, heavy saucepan, whisk the ingredients with ½ cup water. Bring to boil over medium heat, then reduce the heat and simmer for 10 minutes, stirring occasionally.

Makes about 1 cup

Red Chile Barbecue Sauce

- 4 dried pasilla chile peppers, about ¾ ounce total
- 2 tablespoons canola oil
- ½ cup ketchup
- 3 tablespoons soy sauce
- 2 tablespoons balsamic vinegar
- 3 medium garlic cloves, crushed
- 1 teaspoon ground cumin
- ½ teaspoon dried oregano
- ¼ teaspoon kosher salt
- ¼ teaspoon freshly ground black pepper

Remove the stems and cut the chiles crosswise into sections about 2 inches long. Remove most of the seeds. In a medium skillet over high heat, warm the oil. Add the chiles and toast them until they puff up and begin to turn color, 2 to 3 minutes, turning once. Transfer the chiles and oil to a small bowl. Cover with 1 cup of hot water and soak the chiles for 30 minutes. Pour the chiles, along with the oil and water, into a blender or food processor.

Add the remaining ingredients and process until very smooth.

Makes about 2 cups

Pasilla Barbecue Sauce

- 2 tablespoons extra virgin olive oil
- 6 medium garlic cloves, peeled
- ⅓ cup finely chopped red onion
- 2 dried pasilla chile peppers, stemmed, seeded, and cut into strips
- 1 cup diced canned tomatoes with juice
- 1 cup amber Mexican beer
- 1 tablespoon cider vinegar
- 1 teaspoon kosher salt
- ½ teaspoon dried oregano
- ¼ teaspoon freshly ground black pepper

In a small, heavy saucepan over medium heat, warm the oil and cook the garlic until lightly browned, 4 to 5 minutes, turning occasionally. Add the onion and chiles. Cook for about 3 minutes, stirring occasionally. Add the remaining ingredients, bring to a boil, then simmer for 15 minutes. Remove the saucepan from the heat and let the mixture stand for 15 minutes to soften the chiles and blend the flavors. Purée in a blender.

Makes about 2 cups

Sauce Recipes

Chimichurri Sauce

- 4 large garlic cloves
- 1 cup loosely packed fresh Italian parsley leaves
- 1 cup loosely packed fresh cilantro leaves
- 1/2 cup loosely packed fresh basil leaves
- 3/4 cup extra virgin olive oil
- 1/4 cup rice vinegar
- 1 teaspoon kosher salt
- 1/2 teaspoon freshly ground black pepper
- 1/2 teaspoon Tabasco® sauce

In a food processor with the motor running, mince the garlic. Add the parsley, cilantro, and basil. Pulse to finely chop the herbs. With the processor running, slowly add the oil in a thin stream, and then add the remaining ingredients.

Makes about 1 1/2 cups

Garlic and Red Pepper Sauce

- 1 large red bell pepper
- 1/3 cup sour cream
- 1/4 cup mayonnaise
- 1 tablespoon finely chopped fresh basil
- 2 teaspoons minced garlic
- 2 teaspoons balsamic vinegar
- 1/4 teaspoon salt

Grill the bell pepper over *Direct Medium* heat until the skin is blackened and blistered all over, 12 to 15 minutes, turning occasionally. Place the pepper in a small bowl and cover with plastic wrap to trap the steam. Set aside for at least 10 minutes, then remove the pepper from the bowl and peel away the charred skin. Cut off the top, remove the seeds, and roughly chop the pepper. Place in a food processor along with the remaining ingredients. Process until smooth. Cover with plastic wrap and refrigerate until about 20 minutes before you are ready to serve.

Makes about 2/3 cup

Rémoulade

- 1/2 cup mayonnaise
- 1 tablespoon capers, drained and minced
- 1 tablespoon sweet pickle relish
- 1 tablespoon finely chopped fresh tarragon
- 2 teaspoons minced shallot
- 1 teaspoon tarragon vinegar
- 1 teaspoon minced garlic
- 1/2 teaspoon Dijon mustard
- 1/4 teaspoon paprika
- 1/8 teaspoon kosher salt

In a medium bowl, whisk the ingredients. If not using right away, cover and refrigerate for as long as 24 hours.

Makes about 3/4 cup

Romesco Sauce

   2 medium red bell peppers
 1/4 cup whole almonds
   1 medium garlic clove
 1/2 cup loosely packed fresh
     Italian parsley leaves and
     tender stems
   2 teaspoons sherry wine
     vinegar
 1/2 teaspoon kosher salt
 1/8 teaspoon ground cayenne
     pepper
 1/4 cup extra virgin olive oil

Grill the bell peppers over
Direct Medium heat until they
are blackened and blistered all
over, 12 to 15 minutes, turning
occasionally. Place the peppers
in a small bowl and cover with
plastic wrap to trap the steam.
Set aside for at least 10 minutes,
then peel the skins from the
peppers and discard the skins,
stems, and seeds.

   In a small skillet over medium heat, toast the almonds until
their aroma is apparent, 3 to 5
minutes, stirring occasionally.
In a food processor, finely chop
the garlic. Add the almonds and
process until finely chopped.
Add the peppers, parsley, vinegar, salt, and cayenne. Process
to create a coarse paste. With
the motor running, slowly add
the oil and process until you
have a fairly smooth sauce.

Makes about 3/4 cup

Tomato Salsa

 1 1/2 cups finely diced ripe
     tomatoes
 1/2 cup finely diced white
     onion, rinsed in a sieve
     under cold water
   2 tablespoons finely chopped
     fresh cilantro
   1 tablespoon extra virgin
     olive oil
   2 teaspoons fresh lime juice
   1 teaspoon minced jalapeño
     chile pepper [with seeds]
 1/4 teaspoon dried oregano
 1/4 teaspoon kosher salt
 1/4 teaspoon freshly ground
     black pepper

In a medium bowl, mix the
ingredients. Allow salsa to stand
for about 1 hour at room temperature. Drain in a sieve just
before serving.

Makes about 2 cups

Roasted Tomatillo Salsa

   1 small yellow onion, cut
     crosswise into 1/2-inch
     slices
     Extra virgin olive oil
   8 medium tomatillos, about
     1/2 pound, husked and
     rinsed
   1 medium poblano chile
     pepper
 1/4 cup lightly packed fresh
     cilantro leaves and tender
     stems
   1 medium garlic clove,
     crushed
 1/2 teaspoon dark brown sugar
 1/2 teaspoon kosher salt

Lightly brush or spray the onion
slices on both sides with oil.
Grill the onions, tomatillos,
and chile over *Direct High* heat
until lightly charred all over,
6 to 8 minutes, turning once or
twice. Transfer the onions and
tomatillos to a blender or food
processor and place the chile
on a work surface. When the
chile is cool enough to handle,
remove and discard the skin,
stem, and seeds. Add the chile to
the onions and tomatillos, along
with the remaining ingredients.
Process until fairly smooth.
Taste and adjust the seasonings
if necessary.

Makes about 1 cup

Ten Essentials for Better Grilling

The heart of grilling lies in the fire, within the grill itself, and what separates the master grillers from the masses is that the master grillers understand how the fire flavors the food. They know what kind of heat is right for each meat, fish, and vegetable. They know how to control the fire and sear the food with rich tastes and textures. They know how to capture the aromatic smoke that develops when juices and fats drip into the grill. Sure, recipes are important, but techniques matter most. Here is my top-ten list of recommendations.

1. Lighter Fluid: No Way!

There is no reason, except maybe pyromania [and that's not a good one], to use lighter fluid anymore. It's a petroleum product, and who wants that and its foul chemical fumes under their food? Chimney starters and paraffin cubes are much cleaner and much more effective.

4. Oil the Food, Not the Grate

Oil prevents food from sticking. It adds flavor and moisture, too. Lightly brushing or spraying the food with oil works better than brushing the grate. You won't waste oil and you will avoid a potentially dangerous situation.

5. Know When to Be Direct

Direct heat [when the fire is directly below the food] is best for relatively small, tender pieces of food that cook in 20 minutes or less. Indirect heat [when the fire is on either side of the food] is best for larger, tougher foods that require more than 20 minutes of cooking.

8. Caramelization is Key

One of biggest reasons for the popularity of grilled food is its seared taste. To develop this taste for maximum effect, use the right level of heat and resist the temptation to turn food often. Your patience will allow for caramelization, or browning. That creates literally hundreds of flavors and aromas. As a general rule, turn food only once.

9. Tame the Flame

Flare-ups happen, which is good because they sear the surface of what you are grilling. But too many flare-ups can burn your food. If the flames are getting out of control, move the food over indirect heat temporarily, until they die down. Then move the food back. As always, keep the lid down as much as possible.

2. Preheat the Grill

Preheating your grill with the lid closed for 10 to 15 minutes prepares the cooking grate. With all the coals glowing red, or all the gas burners on high, the temperature under the lid should reach 500°F. The heat loosens any bits and pieces of food hanging onto the grate, making it easy to brush them off. A hot grate is also crucial for searing food properly.

3. Keep it Clean

When bits of food have stuck to your stainless steel or porcelain-enameled cooking grate, and the grate is hot, clean it with a brass-bristle brush. This step is not only for cleanliness. It also prevents your food from sticking. Note: Use a steel brush if you have a cast-iron cooking grate.

6. Keep the Air Flowing

A charcoal fire needs air. The lid should be closed as much as possible, but keep the vents on the lid and below the charcoal grate open. Remove the ashes on the bottom of the grill regularly to prevent them from blocking the vents. A gas fire needs air, too, which it gets from openings below the grill.

7. Put a Lid on It

For four important reasons, the lid should be closed as much as possible.
1. It keeps the grates hot enough to sear the food.
2. It speeds up the cooking time and prevents the food from drying out.
3. It traps the smokiness that develops when fat and juices vaporize in the grill.
4. It prevents flare-ups by limiting oxygen.

10. Watch the Time and Temperature

The recipes in this book have been tested at 70°F weather at average altitudes. If you are grilling in a colder climate or in a higher altitude, the cooking times will be longer. If the wind is blowing hard, it will lower a gas grill's temperature and raise a charcoal grill's temperature. Grilling is both art and science. Pay attention to each.

STARTERS

The Grilled Appetizer Party

There was a time when I was fresh out of culinary school and eager to exercise all that I had just learned. I threw overwrought parties that involved every pot, skillet, and sieve I owned. After an exhausting decathlon of planning, shopping, and prepping , I still had to juggle the final cooking of each dish so they were all perfectly done at the moment my guests sat down to eat. By the end of the night, I was hunched over the sink scrubbing roasting pans and thinking...what was I thinking!

Now a party at my house means a barbecue. Fun and simple. Virtually everything is cooked on the grill. No messy pots and pans. And I've adopted an easy approach I want to share with you. I make a meal out of appetizers. Rather than serving a big main course that requires a lot of work at once, I grill a series of smaller things. As the host, the advantage of this idea is that there is no make-it-or-break-it moment when the whole meal has to be juggled at once. Plus no one feels obligated to have the main course. Guests can pick whatever they want whenever they want it

Let me give you an example. Before people arrive, I make a couple appetizers that can sit at room temperature for an hour or so. They might be Roasted Eggplant Dip with Toasted Pita [page 53] and Grilled Shrimp Cocktail [page 49].

I put them on a buffet outside, along with a platter of prosciutto and other sliced meats, a couple wedges of cheese, and some crackers. As people get settled, I grill Chicken Wings with Orange-Mustard Glaze [page 44]. When those are ready, I put them on a platter and add them to the buffet. Then I move to something else like Thin-Crusted Pizzas with Grilled Red Onions and Black Olives [page 50].

I make a meal out of appetizers. Rather than serving a big main course that requires a lot of work at once, I grill a series of smaller things.

I love the fact that I am never rushed. And because my grill is so close to where people are gathering and eating, my guests can come over and cook with me anytime. We banter back and forth about what toppings to put the pizzas or when to add more coals. The informality puts everyone at ease. Eventually, I clear off the buffet and bring out a dessert that I made ahead, such as my Chocolate Brownie Cake [page 295]. If you are looking for casual, easy approach to entertaining, trust me, this one really works.

Grilling Pizza

Grilled pizzas have a definite "wow" factor that adds to their delicious appeal. They make great party food because they can be as big or small as you like and guests can choose their own toppings. Here's how to prepare the dough. Cut squares of parchment paper a little bigger than the rounds of dough you plan to make and lightly oil each sheet of paper on one side. Roll or press the dough flat on the oiled side of the paper. Then lightly oil the top side of the dough. [If you are preparing for a big party, you can stack the rounds of dough with their sheets of paper and store them in the refrigerator for up to two hours. Bring the dough to room temperature before grilling.] The paper keeps the rounds of dough in their shape as you move them to the grill.

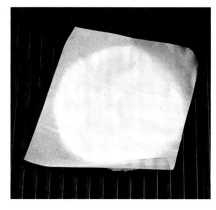

1. Lay the dough on the grate, with the paper side facing up.

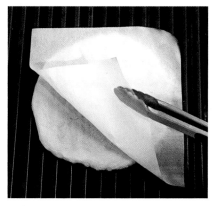

2. Grab one corner of the paper with tongs and peel it off.

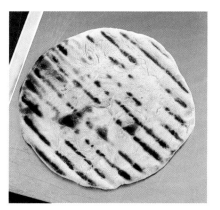

3. Flip the grilled dough onto a baking sheet. Pile on the toppings and slide the pizza back on the grill.

Grill-Roasting Bell Peppers

1. Grill over direct medium heat for 12 to 15 minutes until blackened and blistered. Turn every 3 to 5 minutes for even cooking.

2. Move the peppers to a bowl and cover with plastic wrap, or place them in a paper bag and seal it tightly. Let stand for 10 to 15 minutes. The steam trapped inside helps to release the skins.

3. When the peppers are cool enough to handle, remove and discard the stems and seeds. Then peel off the blackened skins and discard them. Cut or chop.

Grilled Chicken and Red Onion Quesadillas

PREP TIME: 15 MINUTES
MARINATING TIME: 3 TO 4 HOURS
GRILLING TIME: 12 TO 18 MINUTES

PASTE
- 2 large garlic cloves
- 1 jalapeño chile pepper, stem removed
- 1 cup tightly packed fresh cilantro leaves
- 3 tablespoons extra virgin olive oil
- 2 tablespoons sherry vinegar
- 1 teaspoon kosher salt
- ½ teaspoon dried oregano
- ½ teaspoon freshly ground black pepper

- 3 boneless, skinless chicken breast halves, about 8 ounces each
- 1 large red onion, cut crosswise into ½-inch slices
  Extra virgin olive oil
- 2 cups grated Monterey Jack cheese
- 4 flour tortillas [10 inches]
- 1 cup good-quality tomato salsa

1. To make the paste: In a food processor, mince the garlic and jalapeño. Add the remaining paste ingredients and process until smooth. Coat the chicken breasts on all sides with the paste. Cover and refrigerate for 3 to 4 hours.

2. Lightly brush or spray the onion slices with oil. Grill the chicken and onions over *Direct Medium* heat until the chicken is opaque in the center and the onions are tender, 8 to 12 minutes, turning once. Remove the chicken and onions from the grill and allow to cool. Cut the chicken crosswise into ⅛-inch slices and the onions into ¼-inch pieces.

3. Evenly divide the chicken, onions, and cheese over half of each tortilla. Fold the empty half of each tortilla over the filling, creating a half-circle, and press down firmly. Grill the quesadillas over *Direct Medium* heat until well marked and the cheese has melted, 4 to 6 minutes, turning carefully once. Allow the quesadillas to cool for a minute or two before cutting into wedges. Serve warm with the salsa.

MAKES 4 TO 6 SERVINGS

I make these quesadillas a lot for parties. If a big crowd is coming over, I fill and fold the tortillas a few hours ahead and stack them on a tray. As people arrive, I grill the quesadillas for about five minutes to melt the cheese and toast the tortillas. The warming rack is a convenient place to hold them once they have been grilled.

Chicken Wings
with Orange-Mustard Glaze

PREP TIME: 10 MINUTES
MARINATING TIME: 1 TO 2 HOURS
GRILLING TIME: 30 TO 40 MINUTES

SAUCE
²/₃ cup cider vinegar
¹/₃ cup Dijon mustard
¹/₃ cup orange marmalade
 1 teaspoon prepared chili powder
 1 teaspoon granulated garlic
 1 teaspoon kosher salt
 1 teaspoon dark sesame oil
¹/₂ teaspoon curry powder
¹/₂ teaspoon freshly ground black pepper
¹/₄ teaspoon ground ginger

 16 chicken wings, wing tips removed

1. To make the sauce: In a medium saucepan, whisk the sauce ingredients. Bring the sauce to a boil, then lower the heat and simmer for 10 to 15 minutes, stirring occasionally. Allow to cool to room temperature.
2. Place the chicken in a large, resealable plastic bag and pour in half of the sauce; reserve the other half. Press the air out of the bag and seal tightly. Turn the bag to coat the chicken, place the bag in a bowl, and refrigerate for 1 to 2 hours, turning the bag occasionally.
3. Remove the chicken from the bag and discard the sauce left in the bag. Grill over *Direct Low* heat until the meat is no longer pink at the bone, 30 to 40 minutes, brushing with the reserved sauce and turning occasionally. Serve warm.

MAKE 4 SERVINGS

Spicy Cayenne Chicken Wings

PREP TIME: 5 MINUTES
MARINATING TIME: 2 TO 3 HOURS
GRILLING TIME: 16 TO 18 MINUTES

MARINADE
¹/₄ cup extra virgin olive oil
 2 tablespoons fresh lemon juice
 1 tablespoon minced garlic
1¹/₂ teaspoons kosher salt
 2 teaspoons dried oregano
 2 teaspoons paprika
 1 teaspoon celery seed
 1 teaspoon ground cayenne pepper

 16 chicken wings, wing tips removed

1. To make the marinade: In a small bowl, whisk the marinade ingredients.
2. Place the chicken in a large, resealable plastic bag and pour in the marinade. Press the air out of the bag and seal tightly. Turn the bag to distribute the marinade, place the bag in a bowl, and refrigerate for 2 to 3 hours.
3. Remove the chicken from the bag and discard the marinade. Grill over *Direct Medium* heat until the meat is no longer pink at the bone, 16 to 18 minutes, turning occasionally. Serve warm.

MAKES 4 SERVINGS

Skillet Mussels and Clams
with Chorizo

PREP TIME: 10 MINUTES
GRILLING TIME: ABOUT 10 MINUTES

- $^1/_4$ pound chorizo sausage
- 2   tablespoons extra virgin olive oil
- 2   dozen mussels, about 1 pound, scrubbed and debearded
- 1   dozen littleneck clams, about 1 pound, scrubbed
- 1   tablespoon finely chopped garlic
- $^1/_4$ cup white wine
- 1   tablespoon finely chopped fresh parsley
- 1   tablespoon finely chopped fresh mint

1. Remove the sausage from the casing and break into pieces $^1/_4$ inch or smaller. In a 12-inch oven-proof skillet over *Direct High* heat, warm the olive oil and cook the sausage until the meat is no longer pink, about 3 minutes, stirring occasionally [be sure to wear a cooking mitt to protect your hand from the hot handle].
2. Add the mussels, clams, and garlic. Cook for 3 minutes, stirring gently once or twice. Add the wine. As the shells steam open, transfer them with tongs to a medium bowl [the clams will probably take longer to open]. Discard any mussels and clams that do not open within 10 minutes in the skillet. Return the opened shellfish to the skillet and add the parsley and mint. Stir gently to evenly distribute the ingredients. Serve warm.

MAKES 4 SERVINGS

Fire and Ice Oysters
with Horseradish Sauce

PREP TIME: 10 MINUTES
GRILLING TIME: 2 TO 4 MINUTES

SAUCE
- $^1/_2$ cup sour cream
- 2   tablespoons prepared horseradish
- 1   tablespoon fresh lemon juice
- 1   tablespoon finely chopped fresh chives
- $^1/_4$ teaspoon Worcestershire sauce
- $^1/_4$ teaspoon Tabasco® sauce
- $^1/_4$ teaspoon kosher salt
- $^1/_4$ teaspoon freshly ground black pepper

- 2   dozen fresh oysters

1. To make the sauce: In a small bowl, whisk the sauce ingredients. Cover with plastic wrap and refrigerate for 30 minutes, or until ready to serve.
2. Grip each oyster, flat side up, in a folded kitchen towel. Find the small opening between the shells near the hinge and pry open with an oyster knife. Try to keep the juices in the shell. Loosen the oyster from the shell by running the oyster knife carefully underneath the body. Discard the top, flatter shell, keeping the oyster and juices in the bottom, deeper shell.
3. Grill the oysters, shell side down, over *Direct High* heat until the juices around the oysters boil and almost completely evaporate, 2 to 4 minutes. Using tongs, carefully remove the oysters from the grill. Place the hot oysters on plates with small bowls of the sauce for dipping.

MAKES 4 TO 6 SERVINGS

Grilled Crab Cakes
with Mango Salsa

PREP TIME: 20 MINUTES
MARINATING TIME: 30 MINUTES TO 2 HOURS
GRILLING TIME: 6 TO 8 MINUTES

SALSA
- 1 ripe mango, about 1 pound, peeled, seeded, cut into ¼-inch dice
- 1 medium red onion, finely chopped
- 3 tablespoons finely chopped fresh basil
- 1 tablespoon fresh lime juice
- 1 tablespoon minced jalapeño chile pepper
- ½ teaspoon kosher salt

- ¾ pound fresh, frozen, or canned lump crabmeat
- 1 cup plain bread crumbs
- ¾ cup mayonnaise
- 1 egg, beaten
- 2 green onions, white and light green parts only, minced
- ½ teaspoon soy sauce
- ¼ teaspoon Tabasco® sauce
- ¼ teaspoon kosher salt
- ⅛ teaspoon freshly ground black pepper

1. To make the salsa: In a medium bowl, combine the salsa ingredients. Mix well and let stand at room temperature for 30 minutes to 2 hours, to let the flavors blend.

2. Drain the crabmeat in a sieve [if frozen, allow to defrost]. In a medium bowl, flake the meat with a fork and discard any shells or cartilage that might remain. Add the remaining ingredients, mixing gently but thoroughly. Shape into 16 small cakes, each about 2 inches in diameter and about ½ inch thick. Place the cakes on a plate, cover with plastic wrap, and refrigerate for 30 minutes or as long as 2 hours, so they will hold together on the grill.

3. Grill over *Direct High* heat until the bread crumbs are toasted, 6 to 8 minutes, turning once very carefully with a spatula. Serve warm with the salsa spooned on top.

MAKES 16 CRAB CAKES

Shrimp Satay
with Peanut Dipping Sauce

PREP TIME: 20 MINUTES
GRILLING TIME: 2 TO 4 MINUTES

SAUCE
- 1 tablespoon vegetable oil
- 1 tablespoon minced garlic
- 1 tablespoon minced ginger
- ¼ cup smooth peanut butter
- 1 tablespoon soy sauce
- ¼ teaspoon freshly ground black pepper
- ¼ teaspoon Tabasco® sauce
- 1 tablespoon fresh lime juice

- 20 large shrimp, about 1 pound, peeled and deveined
- 1 tablespoon vegetable oil
- ¼ teaspoon prepared chili powder
- ¼ teaspoon curry powder
- ¼ teaspoon freshly ground black pepper
- ⅛ teaspoon kosher salt

1. To make the sauce: In a small saucepan over medium-high heat, warm the oil. Add the garlic and ginger, and cook until fragrant, about 1 minute, stirring occasionally. Add ½ cup of water, followed by the peanut butter, soy sauce, pepper, and Tabasco sauce. Whisk until smooth. When the sauce comes to a simmer, remove the pan from the heat. Just before serving, reheat the sauce over medium heat and add the lime juice, plus 2 to 3 tablespoons of water, whisking vigorously to achieve a smooth consistency.

2. Lightly brush or spray the shrimp with oil. Season with the chili powder, curry powder, pepper, and salt. Thread the shrimp on skewers, either one per skewer for hors d'oeuvres or five per skewer for appetizers. Grill over *Direct High* heat until the shrimp are firm to the touch and just turning opaque in the center, 2 to 4 minutes, turning once. Serve warm with the peanut dipping sauce.

MAKES 4 TO 6 SERVINGS

Grilled Shrimp Cocktail

PREP TIME: 15 MINUTES
MARINATING TIME: 30 MINUTES TO 1 HOUR
GRILLING TIME: 2 TO 4 MINUTES

SAUCE
  1 bottle [12 ounces] mild chili sauce
  2 tablespoons fresh lemon juice
  1 tablespoon mayonnaise
  2 teaspoons prepared horseradish
  1 teaspoon Worcestershire sauce
  ¼ teaspoon Tabasco® sauce
  ¼ teaspoon kosher salt

  45 large shrimp, about 2 pounds,
     peeled and deveined
  1 tablespoon extra virgin olive oil
  1 tablespoon fresh lemon juice
  1 tablespoon minced garlic
  ¼ teaspoon kosher salt
  ¼ teaspoon freshly ground black pepper
  2 tablespoons finely chopped fresh dill

1. To make sauce: In a medium bowl, mix the sauce ingredients. Cover with plastic wrap and refrigerate until ready to use.
2. In a medium bowl, combine the shrimp with the remaining ingredients, except the dill. Toss gently to evenly coat the shrimp. Cover and refrigerate for 30 minutes to 1 hour.
3. Grill over *Direct High* heat until the shrimp are firm to the touch and just turning opaque in the center, 2 to 4 minutes, turning once. Place the shrimp in a medium bowl. Add the dill and toss to coat them evenly. Serve warm with the sauce.

MAKES 6 TO 8 SERVINGS

Thin-Crusted Pizzas

with Grilled Red Onions and Black Olives

PREP TIME: 45 MINUTES
GRILLING TIME: 15 TO 20 MINUTES

DOUGH
1 envelope active dry yeast
½ teaspoon granulated sugar
2½ cups all-purpose flour, plus more for rolling dough
Extra virgin olive oil
1 teaspoon kosher salt

SAUCE
2 tablespoons extra virgin olive oil
½ cup finely chopped red onion
2 teaspoons minced garlic
1 teaspoon dried oregano
1 can [28 ounces] whole tomatoes
½ teaspoon granulated sugar
½ teaspoon kosher salt
¼ teaspoon freshly ground black pepper

2 large red onions, cut crosswise into ⅓-inch slices
Extra virgin olive oil
½ cup Mediterranean black olives, pitted and cut in half
2 cups grated mozzarella cheese, about 8 ounces
1 to 2 tablespoons finely chopped fresh Italian parsley

1. To prepare the dough: In a medium bowl, combine the yeast and sugar with ¾ cup warm water [105°F to 115°F]. Stir once and let stand until foamy, 5 to 10 minutes. Add 2½ cups of the flour, 3 tablespoons of olive oil, and the salt. Stir until the dough holds together. Transfer to a lightly floured work surface and knead until smooth, 4 to 6 minutes. Shape into a ball and place in a lightly oiled bowl. Turn the ball to cover the surface with oil. Cover the bowl with plastic wrap and set aside in a warm place until the dough doubles in size, 1 to 1½ hours.

2. To make the sauce: In a medium saucepan over medium-high heat, warm the olive oil. Add the onions and cook until soft, about 5 minutes, stirring occasionally. Add the garlic and oregano, and cook until the garlic is light brown, about 1 minute, stirring occasionally. Add the tomatoes, including the juice. Use the back of a large spoon to crush the tomatoes. Season with the sugar, salt, and pepper. Bring the sauce to a boil, and then lower the heat to a simmer. Cook until you have 2 cups of sauce, 40 to 45 minutes, stirring occasionally. Let cool slightly and then purée in a food processor or blender. Allow to cool.

3. Brush or spray the onion slices with oil. Grill over *Direct Medium* heat until well marked, 10 to 12 minutes, turning once. Cut each slice in half.

4. Punch down the dough in the bowl. Transfer to a lightly floured surface and cut into 4 equal pieces. Cut parchment paper into 9-inch squares and lightly oil each sheet of paper on one side [see page 41]. Roll or press the dough flat on the oiled side of the paper into circles about 8 inches in diameter, leaving the dough a little thicker at the edge than in the middle. Then lightly oil the top side of the dough. Lay the dough on the grate, with the paper side facing up. Grab one corner of the paper with tongs and peel it off. Grill over *Direct Medium* heat until they are marked on the underside, 2 to 3 minutes, rotating the crusts occasionally for even cooking. Don't worry if the crusts bubble; they will deflate when turned over. Transfer the crusts from the cooking grate to the back of a baking sheet, with the grilled sides facing up.

5. Spread about ½ cup of the sauce across each pizza crust, leaving a ½-inch border around the edges. Arrange the onions and olives over the sauce. Sprinkle the cheese on top. Transfer the pizzas from the baking sheet to the cooking grate. Grill until the crusts are crisp and the cheese is melted, 4 to 5 minutes, rotating the crusts occasionally for even cooking. Transfer to a cutting board. Garnish with parsley. Cut into wedges. Serve warm.

MAKES 4 SMALL PIZZAS

Grilled Tuna Crostini

Grilled Spanish Toast

PREP TIME: 20 MINUTES
GRILLING TIME: ABOUT 10 MINUTES

TOPPING
  2 albacore tuna fillets, about 8 ounces each
     and 1 inch thick
     Extra virgin olive oil
  1 teaspoon ground fennel seed
     Kosher salt
     Freshly ground black pepper
$\frac{1}{2}$ cup mayonnaise
$\frac{1}{2}$ cup finely diced cucumber
  2 tablespoons finely chopped fresh dill
  2 tablespoons finely chopped black olives
  1 tablespoon capers, drained
  1 tablespoon fresh lemon juice

  1 loaf Italian or French bread
     Sliced tomatoes [optional]
     Lettuce leaves [optional]

1. To prepare the topping: Lightly brush or spray the tuna all over with oil. Season both sides with the fennel and salt and pepper to taste. Grill over *Direct Medium* heat until opaque throughout and firm to the touch, 8 to 10 minutes, turning once. Transfer to a cutting board and chop the tuna into $\frac{1}{4}$-inch pieces. In a medium bowl, combine the tuna along with the remaining topping ingredients. Gently stir to combine.
2. Cut the bread on the bias into $\frac{1}{3}$-inch slices. Lightly brush or spray both sides of the slices with olive oil and grill over *Direct Medium* heat until toasted, 1 to 2 minutes, turning once.
3. Spoon the topping on the toasted slices of bread, with sliced tomatoes and lettuce, if desired.

MAKES 15 TO 20 PIECES

PREP TIME: 15 MINUTES
GRILLING TIME: 10 MINUTES

  6 slices day-old French or Italian bread, each
     3 to 4 inches across and $\frac{3}{4}$ inch thick

TOPPING
  2 ripe plum tomatoes
  2 teaspoons minced garlic
$\frac{1}{2}$ teaspoon paprika
$\frac{1}{2}$ teaspoon kosher salt
$\frac{1}{4}$ teaspoon freshly ground black pepper

  6 tablespoons grated Spanish manchego cheese
  1 to 2 tablespoons extra virgin olive oil,
     preferably Spanish
  1 tablespoon roughly chopped fresh oregano

1. Spread the bread out on a baking sheet and allow to dry for a couple of hours.
2. To prepare the topping: Grill the tomatoes over *Direct Medium* heat until the skins begin to blister, about 5 minutes, turning once or twice. When cool enough to handle, remove and discard the core and skins. In a food processor or blender, process the tomatoes to an almost paste-like consistency, and then add the remaining topping ingredients and process until smooth.
3. Spread the topping over the entire surface of one side of each slice of bread. Gently press the topping into the bread as you work. Grill the bread, tomato side down first, over *Direct Medium* heat until well marked and toasted, 3 to 5 minutes, turning once. Watch carefully to prevent the bread from burning.
4. Transfer the toasts to a platter. Spread the cheese over the toasts, drizzle with the oil, and sprinkle with oregano. Serve warm.

MAKES 4 TO 6 SERVINGS

Roasted Eggplant Dip
with Toasted Pita

PREP TIME: 10 MINUTES
GRILLING TIME: 18 TO 25 MINUTES

DIP

- 2 globe eggplants, 14 to 16 ounces each
- 1 can [15 ounces] white cannellini beans, rinsed
- 1/2 cup lightly packed fresh Italian parsley leaves and tender stems
- 2 medium garlic cloves
- 2 anchovy fillets
- 2 tablespoons oil-packed, sun-dried tomatoes
- 2 tablespoons extra virgin olive oil
- 1 tablespoon fresh lemon juice
- 2 teaspoons red wine vinegar
- 1 teaspoon kosher salt
- 1/4 teaspoon freshly ground black pepper

- 6 pita bread pockets

1. To make the dip: Prick each eggplant all over with a fork. Grill over *Direct High* heat until the skins have collapsed and the flesh has softened, 15 to 20 minutes, turning every 5 minutes.
2. When cool enough to handle, cut each eggplant in half lengthwise, scoop out the flesh, and place in a food processor, leaving the skins and brownish liquid behind. Add the remaining dip ingredients and process until smooth.
3. Grill the pita over *Direct Medium* heat until lightly toasted, 3 to 5 minutes, turning occasionally. Cut each pita into wedges. Serve with the dip.

MAKES 4 TO 6 SERVINGS

Grilled Asparagus Soup

PREP TIME: 20 MINUTES
GRILLING TIME: 4 TO 6 MINUTES

- 2 pounds asparagus spears, tough ends removed
- 6 to 8 green onions, root ends trimmed
- 1/3 cup extra virgin olive oil
- 4 cups chicken broth
- 2 cups tightly packed baby spinach leaves
- 1/4 teaspoon freshly ground black pepper
- 1/4 cup heavy cream
- 2 teaspoons finely chopped fresh tarragon Kosher salt

1. Place the asparagus and green onions in a large bowl and coat with the olive oil. Grill them over *Direct Medium* heat until they are marked by the grill but not dark, 4 to 6 minutes, turning once. Transfer to a cutting board and cut into 2-inch lengths and place in a medium saucepan.
2. Add the chicken broth, spinach, and pepper to the saucepan. Bring the mixture to a boil over high heat, and then simmer for 4 to 5 minutes. Using a slotted spoon, transfer the vegetables to a food processor and purée them. Return the pureed vegetables to the saucepan and mix well. Whisk in the cream and tarragon. Simmer the soup for 3 to 5 minutes, but do not let it boil. Season with salt to taste. Serve warm.

MAKES 6 SERVINGS

Sweet Potato and Ginger Soup

PREP TIME: 20 MINUTES
GRILLING TIME: ABOUT 10 MINUTES

2 pounds sweet potatoes, peeled and
cut crosswise into $^1/_2$-inch slices
1 medium red onion, cut crosswise into
$^1/_2$-inch slices
1 section fresh ginger, about $1^1/_2$ inches by
$1^1/_2$ inches, peeled
Vegetable oil
Kosher salt
Freshly ground black pepper
6 cups low-sodium chicken or vegetable stock
$^1/_4$ teaspoon ground allspice
$^1/_8$ teaspoon ground cayenne pepper
$^1/_4$ cup half-and-half
2 tablespoons finely chopped fresh Italian parsley
1 tablespoon fresh lime juice

1. Lightly brush or spray the sweet potatoes, onion slices, and ginger on all sides with oil. Season with salt and pepper to taste. Grill over *Direct Medium* heat until the sweet potatoes, onions, and ginger are well marked, about 10 minutes, turning once. Finely chop the ginger. In a large saucepan, combine the sweet potatoes, onion, ginger, chicken stock, allspice, and cayenne. Bring to a boil, reduce heat, cover, and simmer for 30 minutes.

2. Allow the soup to cool for 10 to 15 minutes. In a blender or food processor and in at least two batches, carefully puree the soup. Return the soup to the pan. Add the half-and-half, parsley, lime juice, and heat to serving temperature. Taste and season with salt and pepper, if necessary. Serve hot.

MAKES ABOUT 8 CUPS

Grilled Tomato and Onion Soup
with Toasted Parmesan Croutons

PREP TIME: 20 MINUTES
GRILLING TIME: 12 TO 14 MINUTES

2½   pounds plum tomatoes, cored
4   medium yellow onions, cut into ½-inch slices
    Extra virgin olive oil
3   cups reduced-sodium chicken stock
1   tablespoon thinly sliced garlic
1   tablespoon finely chopped fresh thyme
    Kosher salt
    Freshly ground black pepper
½   cup grated Parmigiano-Reggiano cheese
1   baguette

1. Brush or spray the tomatoes and onions with oil. Grill over *Direct Medium* heat until the tomato skins begin to blister and the onions are tender, 8 to 10 minutes, turning once or twice. Transfer the tomatoes to a bowl and when cool enough to handle, peel away the skins and discard [work over the bowl to reserve all of the juices]. Place a sieve over a large saucepan and gently squeeze the tomatoes over the sieve to catch the seeds. Discard the seeds. Roughly chop the tomatoes and onions and add them to the saucepan along with the tomato juice from the bowl, the chicken stock, garlic, and thyme. Bring the soup to a boil then reduce the heat to a simmer. Season with salt and pepper to taste. Simmer the soup for 15 to 20 minutes, stirring occasionally.

2. To make the croutons: In a small bowl, blend ¼ cup of olive oil with the cheese. Slice the bread on the bias into twelve pieces, each about ½-inch thick. Spread the oil mixture over both sides of the bread. Press the mixture into the bread as you work. Grill the bread over *Direct Low* heat until golden, about 4 minutes, turning once.

3. To serve, ladle about 1 cup of soup into each serving bowl. Place two croutons on top.

MAKES 6 SERVINGS

Marinated Mushroom Bruschetta
with Pine Nuts and Goat Cheese

PREP TIME: 45 MINUTES
MARINATING TIME: 1 TO 2 HOURS
GRILLING TIME: 21 TO 27 MINUTES

MARINADE
½ cup dry white wine
¼ cup extra virgin olive oil
2 teaspoons minced garlic
2 teaspoons finely chopped fresh rosemary
½ teaspoon kosher salt
¼ teaspoon freshly ground black pepper

½ pound large shiitake mushrooms, stems removed
2 red bell peppers
20 slices good-quality French bread, each about 2 inches in diameter and ¼ inch thick
Extra virgin olive oil
¼ cup pine nuts
2 tablespoons finely chopped fresh Italian parsley
4 ounces goat cheese

1. To make the marinade: In a medium bowl, whisk the marinade ingredients. Place the mushrooms in a large, resealable plastic bag and pour in the marinade. Press the air out of the bag and seal tightly. Turn the bag several times to distribute the ingredients. Allow the mushrooms to marinate at room temperature for 1 to 2 hours, turning the bag occasionally.

2. Grill the bell peppers over *Direct Medium* heat until they are blackened and blistered all over, 12 to 15 minutes, turning occasionally. Place the peppers in a medium bowl and cover with plastic wrap to trap the steam. Set aside for at least 10 minutes, then peel the skins and discard the stems and seeds.

3. Shake any excess moisture from the mushrooms. Grill over *Direct Medium* heat until tender, 8 to 10 minutes, turning occasionally. Lightly brush or spray the slices of bread on both sides with olive oil. Grill over *Direct Medium* heat until lightly toasted, 1 to 2 minutes, turning once.

4. In a medium pan over medium heat, cook the pine nuts until lightly toasted, 5 to 10 minutes, shaking the pan occasionally.

5. Very finely chop the bell peppers, mushrooms, and pine nuts, and combine all of them in a medium bowl. Add the parsley and stir. Spread a very thin layer of goat cheese on one side of each slice of bread. Arrange about 1 tablespoon of mushroom mixture on top of each. Serve at room temperature.

MAKES ABOUT 20 BRUSCHETTA

Smoked Trout Bruschetta

PREP TIME: 20 MINUTES
GRILLING TIME: 27 TO 30 MINUTES

- 2 boneless or bone-in trout, gutted and cleaned, about 12 ounces each
  Extra virgin olive oil
  Sea salt
- 1/4 teaspoon freshly ground black pepper
- 1/2 lemon, thinly sliced
- 2 handfuls fresh dill sprigs
- 1 untreated cedar plank [about 16 inches by 8 inches], submerged in water for at least 1 hour
- 2 plum tomatoes, finely diced
  Juice of 1 lemon
- 2 medium baguettes, cut crosswise into 1/2-inch slices

1. Lightly brush or spray the trout with 2 tablespoons of olive oil and season, inside and out, with 1/2 teaspoon of sea salt and the pepper. Overlap the lemon slices inside the belly of each trout. Finely chop enough of the dill to have 2 tablespoons set aside for garnish. Use the remaining dill, including the stems, to fill the belly of each trout.

2. Put the cedar plank over *Direct Medium* heat and cook until the wood starts to smoke, 10 to 12 minutes. Arrange the trout on the plank and cook until the flesh is opaque throughout and begins to flake, about 15 minutes. Remove the trout from the grill and place on a cutting board. When the trout is cool enough to handle, peel the skin off both sides. Use the blade of a sharp knife to lift the boneless trout fillets to a bowl, or slide the smoked flesh away from the backbone and off the rib bones if using bone-in trout. Break the flesh into small pieces and check to see if there are any small bones still hidden in the flesh. Add the diced tomatoes to the bowl and drizzle with a little lemon juice and olive oil. Season with the reserved dill and sea salt to taste. Mix gently.

3. Lightly brush or spray the slices of bread on each side with olive oil. Grill over *Direct Medium* heat until lightly toasted, 1 to 2 minutes, turning once. Arrange pieces of the smoked trout mixture on top of the bread. Serve at room temperature.

MAKES 6 TO 8 SERVINGS

Eggplant, Prosciutto, and Mozzarella "Sandwiches"

2 medium red bell peppers
Extra virgin olive oil
1 teaspoon kosher salt
1/4 teaspoon freshly ground black pepper
2 globe eggplants, about 1 pound each, trimmed
8 thin slices Prosciutto di Parma
8 slices mozzarella, each 1/4 inch thick
8 medium fresh basil leaves

1. Grill the bell peppers over *Direct Medium* heat until they are blackened and blistered all over, 12 to 15 minutes, turning occasionally. Place the peppers in a medium bowl and cover with plastic to trap the steam. Set aside for at least 10 minutes, then peel the skin and discard the stems and seeds. Place the peppers in a food processor with 1 tablespoon oil, and the salt and pepper. Process until smooth, scraping down the sides as needed.

2. Cut each eggplant crosswise into 8 slices, each about 1/2 inch thick. Lightly brush or spray both sides with oil. Grill over *Direct Medium* heat until the underside is well marked, 3 to 4 minutes. Transfer half of the slices to a tray, with the grilled sides facing up. Turn the remaining slices over and grill until well marked on both sides, 3 to 4 minutes more.

3. Place a tablespoon of the red pepper mixture in the center of the grilled side of each eggplant slice on the tray. Place a slice of prosciutto [folded to fit], a slice of the mozzarella, and a basil leaf on top of the red pepper mixture. Top each "sandwich" with a slice of the eggplant that has been grilled on both sides. Use a wide spatula to place the "sandwiches" on the cooking grate, uncooked side down, and grill over *Direct Medium* heat until the cheese is softened and the sandwiches are heated through, 2 to 3 minutes. Serve warm with the remaining pepper mixture spooned, if desired.

Makes 8 appetizer or side dish servings or 4 lunch servings

▲▲▲

Great grilled eggplant starts with great eggplant. Look for firm ones without any bruises or wrinkles. For this recipe, I like the big globe eggplant, but not the ones with wide curves like a wine bottle that give you slices with very different diameters. Buy ones shaped more like a cylinder.

▼▼▼

Meatballs on a Stick

PREP TIME: 15 MINUTES
GRILLING TIME: 6 TO 8 MINUTES

MEATBALLS
3/4   pound ground beef
1/2   pound ground pork
1/3   cup bread crumbs
  3   tablespoons whole milk
  3   tablespoons finely chopped fresh Italian parsley
  1   egg, beaten
  2   teaspoons Dijon mustard
1/2   teaspoon finely chopped fresh thyme
1/2   teaspoon granulated onion
1/2   teaspoon kosher salt
1/4   teaspoon freshly ground black pepper
1/4   teaspoon Tabasco® sauce

SAUCE
1/3   cup ketchup
  2   tablespoons mayonnaise
1/2   teaspoon red wine vinegar
1/8   teaspoon kosher salt

      Extra virgin olive oil

1. To make the meatballs: In a medium bowl, combine the meatball ingredients. Using your hands, gently mix until the ingredients are evenly distributed. Wet your hands with cold water and shape the meat into balls, each about 1 inch in diameter. Be careful not to overwork the meat. Cover with plastic wrap and refrigerate for about 45 minutes, or until very cold.
2. To make the sauce: In a small bowl, whisk together the sauce ingredients.
3. Lightly brush or spray the meatballs with oil. Grill over *Direct High* heat until the meat is thoroughly cooked but not dry, 6 to 8 minutes, gently turning occasionally. Arrange the meatballs on a serving platter with toothpicks. Serve warm with the sauce.

MAKES 25 TO 30 SMALL MEATBALLS

Pulled Pork Tostadas
with Guacamole

PREP TIME: 20 MINUTES
GRILLING TIME: 3½ TO 4 HOURS

RUB
- 1 tablespoon kosher salt
- 1 tablespoon paprika
- 1 tablespoon brown sugar
- 1 teaspoon prepared chili powder

- 1 boneless pork shoulder roast [Boston Butt], about 4 pounds

GUACAMOLE
- 8 ripe Hass avocados
- ⅓ cup fresh lime juice
- 2 teaspoons kosher salt
- ½ cup finely chopped fresh cilantro

- 1½ cups good-quality spicy tomato salsa
- 1 large bag sturdy tortilla chips

1. To make the rub: In a small bowl, mix the rub ingredients with your fingertips.

2. Coat the roast thoroughly on all sides with the rub. Allow the roast to stand at room temperature for 20 to 30 minutes before grilling.

3. Grill the roast over *Indirect Medium* heat until the internal temperature reaches 185°F to 190°F, 3½ to 4 hours. Adjust the grill's temperature so it stays about 325°F. The meat should be so tender it pulls apart easily. Remove the roast from the grill, place it on a cutting board, and loosely cover with foil. Let rest for about 20 minutes.

4. Meanwhile, make the guacamole: Scoop the avocado flesh into a medium bowl. Add the lime juice and salt and, using the back of a fork, mash the guacamole together. Stir in the cilantro. Cover the surface with plastic wrap to prevent browning.

5. Using two forks, pull the pork apart into shreds, discarding any pockets of fat. If desired, finely chop the pork with a knife. Place the shredded pork in a large saucepan over medium heat and moisten with the salsa.

6. To serve, place about one tablespoon of pork on each tortilla chip. Top with about half as much guacamole. Serve while the pork is warm.

MAKES ABOUT 100 PIECES

RED MEAT

A Griller's Rite of Passage

Fortunately a lot has changed since the 1970s, when I grilled my first steak. I think it was a bottom round steak, a big hunk of sinewy meat from the tail end of a cow. I tossed it on the grill and cooked it until the meat was black and the edges curled up like a hammock. There was no trace of red left inside, and the texture felt like rope. My family choked it down with milk but demanded I try another approach.

I have been grilling my way to better steak ever since. Thin ones, thick ones. Using direct heat, indirect heat, an open lid, a closed lid...I've tried every combination. When I finally put the elements together in the right way and sat down to a tender steak with a seared, caramelized surface and a rosy red interior where specks of milky fat had melted into the juicy meat...man, I thought I was *it* [see

The secret to success begins with matching the cut of meat to the method.

page 78 for the recipe].

The secret to success begins with matching the cut of meat to the method. Small, tender cuts of red meat are ideal for grilling over direct high heat. As the cuts get bigger and tougher, they are better suited for searing over high or medium heat and then grill-roasting over indirect heat. Some of the really tough cuts call for slow barbecuing, which breaks down the sinew in meat over hours. On page 66 is a listing of popular cuts grouped by the method that's best for each one. Find your favorite ones and let's cook.

Types of Red Meat for the Grill

Tender Cuts for Grilling	Moderately Tender Cuts for Grilling	Bigger Cuts for Searing and Grill-Roasting	Tougher Cuts for Barbecuing
Beef Tenderloin (Filet Mignon) Steak	Beef Top Sirloin	Beef Whole Tenderloin	Baby Back Ribs
Beef Rib Steak/Rib-Eye Steak	Beef Flank Steak	Beef Tri-Tip Roast	Spareribs
Beef Porterhouse Steak	Beef Hanger Steak	Beef Standing Rib Roast (Prime Rib)	Shoulder (Boston butt)
Beef T-bone Steak	Beef Skirt Steak	Beef Strip Loin	
New York Strip	Beef Flatiron Steak	Rack of Veal	
Lamb Loin Chop	Veal Shoulder Blade Chop	Rack of Lamb	
Lamb Sirloin Chop	Lamb Shoulder Blade Chop	Leg of Lamb	
Veal Loin Chop	Lamb Sirloin Chop		

What to Look For in Beef

We are all looking for taste and tenderness in beef. Tenderness is pretty easy to find, as ranchers get better and better at selective breeding. But many of these tender breeds are also quite lean, much leaner than twenty years ago. As anyone who has eaten a well-marbled strip steak will tell you, the bits of fat running through the meat are crucial to its taste. Very lean meat just doesn't satisfy, so buy with an eye for flavor.

Marbling: Beef should have a coarse marbling of milky white fat running through it. If the marbling is minimal or if the fat has a brown or yellow tint [a sign of old, dry meat], avoid it. Also avoid meat with large clumps of fat within the flesh. The thin marbling will melt and

give the flesh richness and juiciness; the large clumps can be greasy and cause flare-ups.

Color: The flesh should have a rich pink or light cherry appearance. If it has a deep red or other dark color, there's a good chance it came from a dairy cow and the meat will be bland and tough.

Moisture: The surface should be moist, but not wet or sticky.

A cut of meat that has been individually wrapped should not have much liquid in the package. That would indicate that the meat has been frozen and thawed.

Do Grades Matter? Well, yes. Meat producers pay the United States Department of Agriculture [USDA] to grade their beef if they believe the quality is high enough. Only about two percent of beef gets the very top grade, Prime, and most of that is sold to restaurants. The second highest grade is Choice, which reflects generous marbling and tender meat. If you see a grade of Select or no grade at all, maybe you should grill chicken that day. The beef is likely to be dry and chewy.

Brown is Better

Whichever cut of meat you choose, and whatever its grade might be, you'll get the most flavor from it when the surface is cooked to a deep brown color. When sugars and proteins in the meat are heated by the grill, they produce literally hundreds of flavors and aromas. That's why so many recipes in this chapter involve searing over direct heat.

A lot of people will tell you that searing seals in moisture, but that theory has been debunked. Instead, searing develops a layer of incredible flavor and also some nice texture.

Wet meat doesn't sear, it steams, so be sure to pat the surface dry with paper towels before grilling.

Salt can also affect searing. I recommend waiting to salt red meat until 5 to 10 minutes before grilling because, over a longer period of time, salt pulls blood and juices from inside the meat, making the surface wet. Salt does, however, need to go on before grilling. Salt added afterwards doesn't penetrate very well.

1. A thickness somewhere between 1 and 1¼ inches is great. If the steak has more than about ¼-inch of fat on the outside, trim it off, to avoid flare-ups. Allow the steak to "stand" at room temperature for 20 to 30 minutes before grilling.

2. Pat the steak dry. Lightly brush or spray with oil on both sides and season with kosher salt and black pepper 5 to 10 before grilling. Sear the steak over direct high heat for 2 minutes.

3. Be sure to close the lid. If flare-ups occur at any time, move the steak over indirect high heat temporarily [about 10 seconds]; the marks will be blurred, but you'll save your steak from the flames. To create cross-hatch marks, rotate the steak 90° and sear for 2 minutes more, with the lid closed. If you don't want cross-hatch marks, just sear the steak for 4 minutes total in the previous position.

4. Turn the steak over and continue to cook over direct high heat with the lid closed, until it reaches the desired doneness, 2 to 4 minutes for medium-rare [see page 70 for tips on doneness]. Transfer the steak to a cutting board or serving plate and "let it rest" for 3 to 5 minutes. This allows the juices that have been driven to the center to ease back into place. Now have at it!

Flank Steak

The fancy cuts of steak get all the attention. Sure, it's easy to love a succulent rib-eye steak cut from the center of a standing prime rib. That is the stuff that great steakhouses are made of. But if bigger flavor is your thing, spend some time with some of the unsung steaks from the chest and side of a cow. They are a little chewier, but with that chew comes more taste than a rib-eye could ever deliver. I am a big fan of skirt steaks, flatiron steaks, hanger steaks, and flank steaks. A marinated flank steak was the original London broil, before chefs started using the relatively flavorless top sirloin for that classic recipe.

A flank steak has a long grain running from the top to the bottom.

By cutting a flank steak against the grain, in thin slices, you shorten the length of the grain, making the steak tender for chewing.

Hamburger

Some days nothing is better than a hamburger. It combines the intensely beefy flavor of chuck meat with the magic that only a grill provides. Chuck meat comes from the shoulder of a steer, an area that gets a lot of exercise, so it is tough, too tough for direct grilling. Unless, of course, the meat is finely ground and shaped into patties. Some people make burgers from ground sirloin, but I think that meat is bland by comparison. I like eighty percent lean chuck, which means it is twenty percent fat. That's just enough to keep the burgers moist when they are cooked to medium doneness. Because ground beef has so much surface area and it gets handled so much, it is more susceptible to bacterial growth than larger cuts of beef, so you need to cook it to 160°F.

Before shaping the patties, season the meat in a bowl with salt and pepper. A dash of Worcestershire sauce improves the flavor throughout. For me, 6 ounces is a good size for a hamburger. I like them about 4½ inches across and ¾ inch thick.

To get beautifully grilled burgers, put a dimple in the middle of each raw patty with your fingertips or the back of a spoon. When a hamburger cooks, it shrinks from the outside in, and the middle puffs up. The dimple compensates for the puffing, and you get nice, flat burgers—perfect for piling on the toppings.

Direct high heat [450° to 550°F on the grill's thermometer] gives the surface excellent grill marks. Resist the temptation to flip the burgers over and over. The more you flip the less flavor you will develop. Once is enough, really. Keep the lid closed as much as possible and don't press down on the burgers with a spatula. You'll squeeze out all kinds of good juices.

Grill them for 4 to 5 minutes per side. Add your favorite toppings. That's it. What could be easier or more satisfying? It hits you where you live.

Lamb: The Other Red Meat

When buying lamb, look for meat that is light red [not too dark] and finely grained [not coarse]. The fat should be white [not yellow]. I like lamb served rare or medium-rare, so I suggest buying chops and roasts that are at least ¾ inch thick. Thinner meat just cooks too quickly.

Favorite Cuts

Rib chops are the most tender of all...whether they are cut into individual servings or left as a whole rack of lamb. They come from the rib section, predictably, which gets very little exercise. Loin chops are cut from a section a little farther toward the legs of the sheep. You can spot them by the T in each one, like a small version of a beef T-bone steak. Another lamb chop to seriously consider is the shoulder chop from, you guessed it, the shoulder. Meat from the shoulder of a cow is quite tough, but on a sheep, it is tender enough to grill over direct heat. Lamb shoulder chops are considerably less expensive than the rib and loin chops.

The leg of lamb opens up lots of possibilities. You can cook the whole leg, with or without the bone, on a rotisserie. You can grill sirloin chops from the top end of the leg. You can sear a boneless leg of lamb, then grill-roast it over indirect heat. Or you can cut the meat in cubes and make shish kabobs.

If you decide to sear the boneless leg and grill-roast it, make sure to remove the excess fat and sinew first. Also, to help the meat cook as evenly as possible, cut the meat to an even thickness. See below.

Preparing Boneless Leg of Lamb

1. Begin with the fattier side facing up. Using a sharp, thin knife, remove some, but not all, of the surface fat, to prevent flare-ups.

2. Turn the leg over. Cut away any large clumps of fat.

3. Slide the tip of your knife under the large areas of sinew and carefully work the knife between the sinew and meat.

4. For slightly thicker sections of the leg, make an angled cut at the thickness you want and spread the meat open like a book.

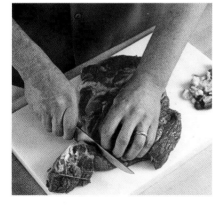

5. If one section of the leg is considerably thicker than the rest, cut it off and grill it separately.

6. In the end, you should have a leg of lamb with a relatively even thickness and 1 or 2 small sections to grill separately.

When is it Done?

Recognizing the moment when a big piece of red meat has reached the degree of doneness you want is actually quite simple. Stick the probe of an instant-read thermometer into the thickest part of the meat. When the internal temperature is 5 to 10 degrees below what you ultimately want to eat, take the meat off the grill. That's because larger pieces of meat, such as a beef strip loin or a leg of lamb, retain quite a bit of heat as they "rest" at room temperature. They continue to cook.

For optimal safety, the USDA recommends cooking red meat to 145°F [final temperature] and ground red meat to 160°F. The USDA believes that 145°F is medium-rare, but virtually all chefs today believe medium-rare is closer to 130°F. The chart below compares chef standards with USDA recommendations. Ultimately, it is up to you what doneness you choose.

Checking for the doneness of steaks and chops is a little more difficult with an instant-read thermometer because you need to position the sensing "dimple" of the probe right in the center of the meat. It's easy to miss the center and get an inaccurate reading, so I recommend peeking inside one of the steaks or chops. Take it off the grill and put in on a cutting board, with the best-looking side [presentation side] facing down. With the tip of a sharp knife, make a little cut in the middle so you can see the color of the meat inside. If the color is still too pink, put it back on the grill. Otherwise, get the rest of the meat off the grill and pat yourself on the back.

Doneness	Chef Standards	USDA Recommendations
Rare	120° to 125°F	n/a
Medium-Rare	125° to 135°F	145°F
Medium	135° to 145°F	160°F
Medium-Well	145° to 155°F	n/a
Well-Done	155°F+	170°F

Making a Compound Butter

1. A compound butter is a flavored butter that can work well as a rich finishing sauce to melt on red meat. Begin by softening butter and combining it with herbs, spices, lemon juice, lemon zest, and spices [see page 84 for a recipe].

2. Use the back of a fork to mash the ingredients and distribute them evenly.

3. At this point the butter is ready to use. Or you can wrap it in plastic wrap and shape it into a cylinder. Refrigerate it and slice off as much as you need.

Grilling Guide for Red Meat

BEEF	Thickness/Weight	Approximate Grilling Time
Steak*	¾ inch thick	**4 to 6 minutes** Direct High
	1 inch thick	**6 to 8 minutes** Direct High
	1¼ inches thick	**8 to 10 minutes** Direct High
	1½ inches thick	**12 to 16 minutes;** sear 8 to 10 minutes Direct High, grill 4 to 6 minutes Indirect High
	2 inches thick	**18 to 22 minutes;** sear 8 to 10 minutes Direct High, grill 10 to 12 minutes Indirect High
Skirt steak	¼ to ½ inch thick	**4 to 6 minutes** Direct High
Flank steak	1½ to 2 pounds, ¾ inch thick	**8 to 10 minutes** Direct High
Kabob	1 to 1½ inch cubes	**7 to 8 minutes** Direct High
Tenderloin, whole	3½ to 4 pounds	**35 to 50 minutes;** sear 15 minutes Direct Medium, grill 20 to 30 minutes Indirect Medium
Ground beef patty	¾ inch thick	**8 to 10 minutes** Direct High
Rib roast (prime rib), boneless	5 to 6 pounds	**1¼ to 1¾ hours** Indirect Medium
Rib roast (prime rib), with bone	5 to 6 pounds	**1½ to 2 hours** Indirect Medium
Strip loin roast, boneless	4 to 5 pounds	**45 to 60 minutes;** sear 2 to 4 minutes Direct High, grill 45 to 60 minutes Indirect Medium
Tri-tip roast	2 to 2½ pounds	**30 to 40 minutes;** sear 10 minutes Direct Medium, grill 20 to 30 minutes Indirect Medium
Veal loin chop	1 inch thick	**6 to 8 minutes** Direct High

includes New York, porterhouse, rib-eye, T-bone, and tenderloin

LAMB	Thickness/Weight	Approximate Grilling Time
Chop: loin, rib, shoulder, or sirloin	¾ to 1¼ inches thick	**8 to 12 minutes** Direct Medium
Leg of lamb roast, boneless	5 to 7 pounds	**1¼ to 1¾ hours** Indirect Medium
Leg of lamb, butterflied	3 to 3½ pounds	**1¼ to 1½ hours;** sear 10 to 15 minutes Direct Medium, grill 1 to 1¼ hours Indirect Medium
Rib crown roast	3 to 4 pounds	**1 to 1¼ hours** Indirect Medium
Ground lamb patty	¾ inch thick	**8 to 10 minutes** Direct Medium
Rack of lamb	1 to 1½ pounds	**20 to 30 minutes** Direct Medium

Note: All cooking times are for medium-rare doneness, except ground beef and ground lamb (medium).

New York Strip Steaks

with Crushed Garlic and Tennessee Barbecue Sauce

PREP TIME: 10 MINUTES
GRILLING TIME: 6 TO 8 MINUTES

SAUCE
 ¹/₂ cup ketchup
 2 tablespoons Jack Daniel's® whiskey
 1 tablespoon steak sauce
 1 tablespoon dark brown sugar
 2 teaspoons Worcestershire sauce
 ¹/₄ teaspoon granulated garlic
 ¹/₄ teaspoon kosher salt
 ¹/₄ teaspoon freshly ground black pepper

 4 New York strip steaks, about 8 ounces each
    and 1 inch thick
 3 medium garlic cloves
 ¹/₂ teaspoon kosher salt
 3 tablespoons extra virgin olive oil
 1 tablespoon finely chopped fresh rosemary
 2 teaspoons coarsely ground black pepper

1. To make the sauce: In a small heavy-bottom saucepan, whisk the sauce ingredients with ¹/₂ cup of water. Bring to a simmer over medium-high heat, then reduce the heat and simmer for 10 minutes, stirring occasionally.

2. Trim most of the exterior fat from the steaks. Allow to stand at room temperature 20 to 30 minutes before grilling.

3. Roughly chop the garlic, and then sprinkle the salt on top. Using both the sharp edge and the flat side of the knife blade, crush the garlic and salt together to create a paste. In a small bowl, mix the garlic paste with the oil, rosemary, and pepper. Smear the mixture evenly all over the steaks.

4. Grill over *Direct High* heat until cooked to desired doneness, 6 to 8 minutes for medium-rare, turning once [if flare-ups occur, move the steaks temporarily over *Indirect High* heat]. Remove from the grill and let rest for 3 to 5 minutes. Serve warm with the sauce on the side.

MAKES 4 SERVINGS

By crushing and smearing garlic and kosher salt together, you create a smooth paste that can evenly cover a steak, and as it cooks, it melts into the surface of the meat. Use it on pork chops, chicken pieces, and fish fillets, too.

New York Steaks
with Rosemary and Roasted Garlic Pesto

PREP TIME: 15 MINUTES
MARINATING TIME: 2 TO 4 HOURS
GRILLING TIME: ABOUT 1 HOUR

2 medium heads garlic
Extra virgin olive oil

PESTO
1/3 cup lightly packed rosemary leaves
2/3 cup lightly packed Italian parsley leaves
1/2 cup pine nuts
2 serrano chile peppers, stemmed and
roughly chopped
2 teaspoons freshly grated lime zest
1 teaspoon kosher salt
1/2 teaspoon freshly ground black pepper

4 New York strip steaks, about 8 ounces each
and 1 inch thick

1. Remove the loose, papery outer skin from the
heads of garlic. Using a sharp knife, cut about 1/2
inch off the top to expose the cloves. Place each
garlic head on a large square of heavy-duty aluminum foil and drizzle 1 tablespoon of the olive oil
over the top of the cloves. Fold up the foil sides

and seal to make a packet, leaving a little room for
the expansion of steam. Grill over *Indirect Medium*
heat until the cloves are soft, 45 minutes to 1 hour.
Set aside to cool.
2. To make the pesto: Place the rosemary, parsley,
pine nuts, and chile peppers in a food processor.
Process until the herbs are finely chopped. Squeeze
out the garlic cloves into the food processor, being
careful not to add any of the papery skin. Process
just to incorporate the garlic. Transfer the mixture
to a medium bowl and add 1/4 cup olive oil, the
lime zest, salt, and pepper. Mix well to create a
paste.
3. Spread the paste evenly on both sides of the
steaks. Cover with plastic wrap and refrigerate for 2
to 4 hours. Allow the steaks to stand at room temperature for 20 to 30 minutes before grilling.
4. Grill over *Direct High* heat until cooked to
desired doneness, 6 to 8 minutes for medium-rare,
turning once [if flare-ups occur, move the steaks
temporarily over *Indirect High* heat]. Remove from
the grill and let rest for about 5 minutes. Serve
warm.

MAKES 4 SERVINGS

Paprika-Rubbed Steaks
with Pickled Onions

PREP TIME: 10 MINUTES
MARINATING TIME: 3 HOURS
GRILLING TIME: 6 TO 8 MINUTES

ONION
- 1   small red or sweet yellow onion
- 2   tablespoons fresh lemon juice
- 2   tablespoons red wine vinegar
- 2   teaspoons granulated sugar
- 1   teaspoon kosher salt
- 1/4   teaspoon dry mustard

- 4   New York strip steaks, about 8 ounces each and 1 inch thick
-   Extra virgin olive oil
- 1   teaspoon paprika
- 1/2   teaspoon light brown sugar
- 1/2   teaspoon kosher salt
- 1/2   teaspoon freshly ground black pepper

1. To prepare the onion: Cut the peeled onion in half lengthwise through the root end. Trim off the ends. With a very sharp knife, cut the onion into paper-thin slices and place in a shallow dish, such as a glass pie plate. Add the remaining onion ingredients and toss to dissolve the salt and sugar. Set aside at room temperature for about 3 hours, stirring the onions occasionally.

2. Allow the steaks to stand at room temperature for 20 to 30 minutes before grilling. Lightly brush or spray both sides of the steaks with oil. In a small bowl, mix the paprika, brown sugar, salt, and pepper together and then press the seasonings into both sides of the steaks. Grill over *Direct High* heat until cooked to desired doneness, 6 to 8 minutes for medium-rare, turning once [if flare-ups occur, move the steaks temporarily over *Indirect High* heat]. Remove from the grill and let rest for 3 to 5 minutes. Strain the onions in a sieve. Serve the steaks warm with the pickled onions on top.

MAKES 4 SERVINGS

New York Steaks
with Avocado and Grilled Corn Salsa

PREP TIME: 15 MINUTES
GRILLING TIME: 16 TO 23 MINUTES

SALSA
  2 ears of sweet corn, shucked
     Extra virgin olive oil
  1 large clove garlic
  1 ripe Hass avocado, roughly chopped
  ¼ cup finely chopped fresh basil
  6 green onions, white and light green parts only,
     finely chopped
  3 tablespoons fresh lime juice
  ¼ teaspoon kosher salt
  ¼ teaspoon freshly ground black pepper

  4 New York strip steaks, about 8 ounces each
     and 1 inch thick

RUB
  1 teaspoon paprika
  ½ teaspoon pure chile powder
  ½ teaspoon granulated garlic
  ½ teaspoon kosher salt
  ¼ teaspoon dried oregano
  ¼ teaspoon freshly ground black pepper

1. To make the salsa: Lightly brush or spray the corn with oil. Grill over *Direct Medium* heat until browned in spots and tender, 10 to 15 minutes, turning occasionally. Allow to cool. Cut the kernels off the cobs and place in a medium bowl. Scrape the cobs with the back of a knife to release the milky juices. In a food processor, purée half the kernels, all of the milky juices, and the garlic, and then transfer the mixture back to the bowl with the remaining corn kernels. Add the rest of the salsa ingredients. Stir to combine.

2. Allow the steaks to stand at room temperature for 20 to 30 minutes before grilling. Lightly brush or spray the steaks on both sides with oil.

3. To make the rub: In a small bowl, combine the rub ingredients. Season the steaks on both sides with the rub. Grill over *Direct High* heat until cooked to desired doneness, 6 to 8 minutes for medium-rare, turning once [if flare-ups occur, move the steaks temporarily over *Indirect High* heat]. Remove from the grill and let rest for about 5 minutes before serving with the salsa on top.

MAKES 4 SERVINGS

New York Steaks
with Roquefort Butter

PREP TIME: 10 MINUTES
GRILLING TIME: 6 TO 8 MINUTES

BUTTER
- 4 tablespoons [½ stick] unsalted butter, at room temperature
- 2 ounces [about ⅓ cup] crumbled blue cheese, such as Roquefort
- ¼ teaspoon granulated garlic
- ¼ teaspoon freshly ground black pepper

- 4 New York strip steaks, about 8 ounces each and 1 inch thick
  Extra virgin olive oil
  Kosher salt
  Freshly ground black pepper
- 4 lemon wedges

1. To make the butter: In a small bowl, combine the butter ingredients. With the back of a fork, mash the butter mixture together until evenly distributed.
2. Trim most of the exterior fat from the steaks. Allow to stand at room temperature for 20 to 30 minutes before grilling. Lightly brush or spray both sides of the steaks with olive oil and season with salt and pepper to taste. Grill over *Direct High* heat until cooked to desired doneness, 6 to 8 minutes for medium-rare, turning once [if flare-ups occur, move the steaks temporarily over *Indirect High* heat]. Remove from the grill and let rest for 3 to 5 minutes. Serve warm with the butter smeared over the top and lemon wedges served on the side.

MAKES 4 SERVINGS

Last Minute Rib-Eye Steaks

PREP TIME: 5 MINUTES
GRILLING TIME: 6 TO 8 MINUTES

RUB
- 1 teaspoon granulated garlic
- 1 teaspoon kosher salt
- ½ teaspoon ground cumin
- ½ teaspoon pure chile powder
- ¼ teaspoon freshly ground black pepper

- 4 rib-eye steaks, about 12 ounces each and 1 inch thick
  Extra virgin olive oil

1. To make the rub: In a small bowl, mix the rub ingredients.
2. Allow the steaks to stand at room temperature for 20 to 30 minutes before grilling. Lightly brush or spray the steaks with the oil. Season the steaks with the rub, pressing the spices into the meat. Grill over *Direct High* heat until cooked to desired doneness, 6 to 8 minutes for medium-rare, turning once [if flare-ups occur, move the steaks temporarily over *Indirect High* heat]. Let rest for 3 to 5 minutes. Serve warm.

MAKES 4 TO 6 SERVINGS

Bourbon-Barbecued Rib-Eye Steaks

PREP TIME: 15 MINUTES
MARINATING TIME: 1½ TO 2 HOURS
GRILLING TIME: 8 TO 10 MINUTES

MARINADE
½ cup bourbon
¼ cup ketchup
2 tablespoons extra virgin olive oil
2 tablespoons soy sauce
1 tablespoon white wine vinegar
2 teaspoons minced garlic
½ teaspoon Tabasco® sauce
½ teaspoon freshly ground black pepper

2 bone-in rib-eye steaks, about 1¼ pounds each
   and 1 to 1¼ inches thick
2 tablespoons extra virgin olive oil
1 teaspoon paprika
½ teaspoon kosher salt
¼ teaspoon freshly ground black pepper
1 tablespoon finely chopped fresh Italian parsley

1. To make the marinade: In a medium bowl, whisk the marinade ingredients. Place the steaks in a large, plastic resealable bag and pour in the marinade. Press out the air, seal the bag, and turn several times to coat the meat. Place the bag in a bowl and refrigerate for 1½ to 2 hours, turning the bag occasionally.

2. Allow the steaks to stand at room temperature for 20 to 30 minutes before grilling. Remove the steaks from the bag and discard the marinade. Pat the steaks dry with paper towels. Brush or spray both sides with olive oil.

3. In a small bowl, mix the paprika, salt, and pepper. Press the seasonings into both sides of the meat. Grill over *Direct High* heat until cooked to your desired doneness, 8 to 10 minutes for medium-rare, turning once [if flare-ups occur, move the steaks temporarily over *Indirect High* heat]. Transfer to a cutting board and let rest for 3 to 5 minutes. Carve the meat from the bone and cut the steak across the grain into ¼-inch slices, discarding any large pieces of fat. Arrange the slices on a platter or individual plates. Drizzle any juices collected on the cutting board over the slices. Garnish with parsley. Serve warm.

MAKES 4 SERVINGS

There are two things to remember here. After you have marinated the steaks, pat them dry on both sides. Wet steaks don't sear; they steam. Also, resist the temptation to lift the lid and turn them over and over. You develop the richest flavors in steaks when you leave them alone as much as possible, turning them just once or twice.

Bone-In Rib-Eye Steaks
with Herbed Potato Salad

PREP TIME: 15 MINUTES
GRILLING TIME: ABOUT 30 MINUTES

  2 pounds small new red potatoes, each about
      1 inch in diameter

DRESSING
  ¼ cup extra virgin olive oil
  3 tablespoons finely chopped fresh Italian parsley
  3 tablespoons finely chopped fresh dill
  1 tablespoon finely chopped shallots
  1 tablespoon white wine vinegar
  1 tablespoon whole grain mustard
  1 teaspoon kosher salt
  ½ teaspoon granulated sugar
  ¼ teaspoon freshly ground black pepper

  4 bone-in rib-eye steaks, about 12 ounces each
      and 1 inch thick
      Extra virgin olive oil
  1 teaspoon celery seed
  1 teaspoon kosher salt
  ½ teaspoon freshly ground black pepper

1. Grill the potatoes over *Direct Medium* heat until tender, 20 to 25 minutes, turning occasionally. When cool enough to handle, cut in half.
2. To make the dressing: In a medium bowl, whisk the dressing ingredients. Add the potatoes and gently toss to combine with dressing while they are still warm.
3. Allow the steaks to stand at room temperature for 20 to 30 minutes before grilling. Lightly brush or spray the steaks with the oil and season with the celery seed, salt, and pepper. Grill over *Direct High* heat until cooked to desired doneness, 8 to 10 minutes for medium-rare, turning once [if flare-ups occur, move the steaks temporarily over *Indirect High heat*]. Remove the steaks from the grill and let rest for 3 to 5 minutes. Serve warm with the potato salad.

MAKES 4 TO 6 SERVINGS

Rib-Eye Steaks
with Tomato Harissa

PREP TIME: 20 MINUTES
GRILLING TIME: 18 TO 23 MINUTES

SAUCE

- 1 large red bell pepper
- 1 teaspoon coriander seed
- 1 teaspoon mustard seed
- 1 teaspoon cumin seed
- 1 medium garlic clove
- 1/4 cup extra virgin olive oil
- 1/4 cup tightly packed fresh mint leaves
- 2 tablespoons red wine vinegar
- 1 tablespoon tomato paste
- 1/2 teaspoon kosher salt
- 1/4 teaspoon ground cayenne pepper

- 4 rib-eye steaks, 8 to 10 ounces each and 1 inch thick
  Extra virgin olive oil
- 3/4 teaspoon kosher salt
- 1/2 teaspoon freshly ground black pepper

1. To make the sauce: Grill the bell pepper over *Direct Medium* heat until it is blackened and blistered all over, 12 to 15 minutes, turning occasionally. Place the pepper in a small bowl and cover with plastic wrap to trap the steam. Set aside for at least 10 minutes, then peel the skin from the pepper, discard the stem and seeds, and roughly chop the pepper.

2. In a small skillet over medium heat, toast the coriander, mustard, and cumin seeds until the aromas of the spices are apparent, 3 to 5 minutes, stirring occasionally. Pulverize the spices in a spice/coffee grinder. In a food processor, finely chop the garlic. Add the chopped bell peppers, pulverized spices, and the remaining sauce ingredients. Process until completely smooth.

3. Allow the steaks to stand at room temperature for 20 to 30 minutes before grilling. Lightly brush or spray both sides of the steaks with oil, and season them with salt and pepper. Grill over *Direct High* heat until cooked to desired doneness, 6 to 8 minutes for medium-rare, turning once [if flare-ups occur, move the steaks temporarily over *Indirect High* heat]. Remove from the grill and let rest for 3 to 5 minutes. Serve warm with the sauce on the side.

MAKES 4 SERVINGS

Rib-Eye Steaks
with Mexican Barbecue Sauce

PREP TIME: 45 MINUTES
GRILLING TIME: 14 TO 18 MINUTES

SAUCE
- 1 large ancho chile pepper, about ½ ounce, stem and seeds removed
- 3 plum tomatoes, cored and cut in half lengthwise
- 2 slices red onion, each about ½ inch thick
  Extra virgin olive oil
- 2 medium garlic cloves, smashed
- 3 tablespoons cider vinegar
- 2 teaspoons light brown sugar
- 1 teaspoon dried oregano
- 1 teaspoon kosher salt
- ½ teaspoon ground cumin
- ½ teaspoon freshly ground black pepper
- ¼ teaspoon ground allspice
- ⅛ teaspoon ground cloves

- 4 rib-eye steaks, about 12 ounces each and 1 inch thick
- 1 teaspoon paprika
- 1 teaspoon kosher salt
- ½ teaspoon light brown sugar
- ½ teaspoon freshly ground black pepper

1. To make the sauce: In a small bowl, cover the ancho chile with ¾ cup boiling water and allow the chile to soften for 20 to 30 minutes, turning occasionally. Lightly brush or spray the tomatoes and onions with oil. Grill over *Direct High* heat until slightly charred, 8 to 10 minutes, turning once. Place the chile and soaking water, tomatoes, and onions in a blender or food processor. Add the remaining sauce ingredients and process until completely smooth, about 1 minute. Pour the sauce into a medium saucepan. Bring to a boil over high heat, then lower the heat to a simmer and cook for 5 to 10 minutes. Remove from the heat. Pour half of the sauce into a small bowl to brush on the steaks as they grill; reserve the rest to serve with the steaks.
2. Allow the steaks to stand at room temperature for 20 to 30 minutes before grilling. In a small bowl, combine the paprika, salt, brown sugar, and pepper. Lightly brush or spray the steaks on both sides with oil; season with the spice mixture. Grill the steaks over *Direct High* heat until cooked to desired doneness, 6 to 8 minutes for medium-rare, brushing with sauce and turning once [if flare-ups occur, move the steaks temporarily over *Indirect High* heat]. Remove from the grill and let rest for 3 to 5 minutes. Serve warm with the reserved sauce.

MAKES 4 SERVINGS

T-Bone Steaks
with Eggplant Caponata

PREP TIME: 40 MINUTES
GRILLING TIME: 16 TO 22 MINUTES

CAPONATA
- 1 medium eggplant
- 1 small yellow onion
  Extra virgin olive oil
- 1 large ripe tomato
- 16 Kalamata olives, pitted and cut in half
- ¼ cup finely chopped fresh basil
- 1 tablespoon capers, drained
- 2 teaspoons balsamic vinegar
- 2 teaspoons minced garlic
  Kosher salt
  Freshly ground black pepper

- 4 T-bone steaks, about 16 ounces each and 1 inch thick
- 4 teaspoons herbes de Provence

1. To make the caponata: Trim the ends from the eggplant and then cut the eggplant crosswise into ½-inch thick slices. Cut the onion crosswise into ½-inch thick slices. Brush or spray both sides of the eggplant and onions with oil. Grill over *Direct Medium* heat until well marked and tender, 8 to 12 minutes. Transfer to a cutting board and when cool enough to handle, cut into ½-inch dice and combine them in a medium bowl. Core and cut the tomato into ½-inch dice, and add to the bowl. Add the remaining caponata ingredients including 2 tablespoons of oil and salt and pepper to taste. Mix well. The caponata is best made a few hours before serving and left at room temperature.

2. Allow the steaks to stand at room temperature for 20 to 30 minutes before grilling. Lightly brush or spray both sides of the steaks with oil and season with the herbes de Provence, and salt and pepper to taste. Grill over *Direct High* heat until cooked to desired doneness, 8 to 10 minutes for medium-rare, turning once [if flare-ups occur, move the steaks temporarily over *Indirect High* heat]. Transfer to a cutting board and let rest for 3 to 5 minutes. Slice and serve warm with the caponata.

MAKES 4 TO 6 SERVINGS

Giant T-Bone Steaks
with Lone Star Rub

PREP TIME: 5 MINUTES
GRILLING TIME: 8 TO 10 MINUTES

RUB
  2 teaspoons kosher salt
  1½ teaspoons pure chile powder
  1½ teaspoons granulated onion
  ¾ teaspoon granulated garlic
  ½ teaspoon paprika
  ½ teaspoon dried marjoram
  ¼ teaspoon ground cumin
  ¼ teaspoon freshly ground black pepper
  ⅛ teaspoon ground cinnamon

  4 T-bone steaks, 12 to 16 ounces each
    and 1 inch thick
  2 tablespoons extra virgin olive oil
  2 limes, cut into wedges [optional]

1. To make the rub: In a small bowl, combine the rub ingredients.
2. Allow the steaks to stand at room temperature for 20 to 30 minutes before grilling. Lightly brush or spray both sides of the steaks with the oil and then evenly coat with the rub, gently pressing the spices into the meat. Grill over *Direct High* heat until cooked to desired doneness, 8 to 10 minutes for medium-rare, turning once [if flare-ups occur, move the steaks temporarily over *Indirect High* heat]. Transfer the steaks to a work surface and let rest for 3 to 5 minutes before carving. Serve warm with the lime wedges, if desired.

MAKES 4 GENEROUS SERVINGS

Filet Mignon
with Lemon-Parsley Butter

PREP TIME: 10 MINUTES
GRILLING TIME: 8 TO 10 MINUTES

BUTTER
  4 tablespoons unsalted butter, softened
  1 tablespoon finely chopped fresh Italian parsley
  ¼ teaspoon grated lemon zest
  1 teaspoon fresh lemon juice
  ¼ teaspoon kosher salt
  ¼ teaspoon freshly ground black pepper

  4 filets mignons, about 8 ounces each
    and 1¼ inches thick
    Extra virgin olive oil
  ½ teaspoon kosher salt
  ½ teaspoon freshly ground black pepper

1. To make the butter: In a small bowl, combine the butter ingredients. Using the back of a fork, mash and stir until evenly distributed. Cover and refrigerate until ready to serve.
2. Allow the filets mignons to stand at room temperature for 20 to 30 minutes before grilling. Lightly brush or spray both sides with oil. Season evenly with the salt and pepper. Grill over *Direct High* heat until cooked to your desired doneness, 8 to 10 minutes for medium-rare, turning once. Transfer each filet to a serving plate and place a tablespoon of the butter on top to melt. Serve warm.

MAKES 4 SERVINGS

Porterhouse Steaks
with Sun-Dried Tomato Pesto

PREP TIME: 10 MINUTES
GRILLING TIME: 8 TO 10 MINUTES

PESTO
$^1/_4$ cup pine nuts
  1 cup loosely packed fresh basil leaves
$^1/_3$ cup oil-packed, sun-dried tomatoes, drained
$^1/_4$ cup freshly grated Parmigiano-Reggiano cheese
  1 medium garlic clove
$^1/_2$ teaspoon kosher salt
$^1/_4$ cup extra virgin olive oil

  4 porterhouse steaks, 12 to 16 ounces each
     and 1 inch thick
  2 tablespoons extra virgin olive oil
  1 teaspoon kosher salt
$^1/_2$ teaspoon freshly ground black pepper

1. To make the pesto: In a medium skillet over medium heat, spread the pine nuts in a single layer and cook until lightly browned and toasted, about 5 minutes, stirring occasionally. Put the nuts in a food processor. Add all the remaining pesto ingredients except the oil. Pulse to create a coarse cornmeal consistency. Slowly add the oil and pulse until it is incorporated. For a slightly looser consistency, add 1 to 2 tablespoons warm water as you pulse. The finished pesto should have all the ingredients blended but not puréed.

2. Allow the steaks to stand at room temperature for 20 to 30 minutes before grilling. Lightly brush or spray both sides of the steaks with the oil and then season with salt and pepper, pressing the seasonings into the meat. Grill over *Direct High* heat until cooked to desired doneness, 8 to 10 minutes for medium-rare, turning once or twice [if flare-ups occur, move the steaks temporarily over *Indirect High* heat]. Remove the steaks from the grill and let rest for 3 to 5 minutes. Serve each steak with a generous dollop of pesto on top.

MAKES 4 GENEROUS SERVINGS

Carne Asada Fajitas

PREP TIME: 30 MINUTES
GRILLING TIME: 18 TO 23 MINUTES

GUACAMOLE
2 ripe Hass avocados
1 tablespoon finely chopped fresh cilantro
2 teaspoons fresh lime juice
1 teaspoon minced garlic
1/2 teaspoon kosher salt
1/4 teaspoon freshly ground black pepper

RUB
1 teaspoon paprika
1/2 teaspoon dark brown sugar
1/2 teaspoon pure chile powder
1/2 teaspoon kosher salt
1/4 teaspoon freshly ground black pepper
1/4 teaspoon ground cumin

1 flank steak, about 1 pound and 3/4 inch thick,
   trimmed of any surface fat
   Extra virgin olive oil
1 medium red onion, cut crosswise into
   1/3-inch slices
2 medium red or green bell peppers, seeded and
   cut into flat sections
4 flour tortillas [10 inches]
   Tabasco® sauce

1. To make the guacamole: Scoop the avocado flesh into a medium bowl. Add the remaining guacamole ingredients and stir with a fork until thoroughly combined. Cover the surface with plastic wrap to prevent browning.
2. To make the rub: In a small bowl, combine all the rub ingredients. Lightly brush or spray the flank steak on both sides with oil and then season evenly with the rub. Allow the steak to stand at room temperature for 20 to 30 minutes before grilling.
3. Lightly brush or spray the onion and bell peppers on both sides with oil. Grill over *Direct Medium* heat until tender, turning once. The onion will take 8 to 10 minutes and the bell peppers will take 6 to 8 minutes. Cut the onion and bell peppers into bite-sized pieces. Grill the flank steak over *Direct High* heat until cooked to desired doneness, 8 to 10 minutes for medium-rare, turning once. Remove from the grill and let rest for 3 to 5 minutes. Wrap the tortillas in a foil package. Grill the package over *Direct Medium* heat to warm the tortillas, 2 to 3 minutes, turning once.
4. To serve, cut the flank steak against the grain into 1/4-inch slices. Place the warm tortillas, sliced meat, onions, peppers, and guacamole in separate serving dishes. Let each person make their own fajita by placing the fillings down the center of each tortilla and adding Tabasco sauce to taste. Wrap and serve warm.

MAKES 4 SERVINGS

Flank Steak
with Dried Mushroom Magic

PREP TIME: 10 MINUTES
GRILLING TIME: 8 TO 10 MINUTES

- ¼ ounce dried shiitake mushrooms [about 6 medium]
- 1 teaspoon whole black peppercorns
- 3 tablespoons peanut oil
- 1 flank steak, 1½ to 2 pounds, trimmed of any surface fat

SAUCE
- 2 tablespoons soy sauce
- 2 teaspoons granulated sugar
- 2 teaspoons rice vinegar

1. In a spice grinder or coffee mill, grind the mushrooms and peppercorns to a powder. Transfer the powder to a small bowl, add the oil, and stir to create a paste. Smear the paste evenly over both sides of the flank steak. Allow the flank steak to stand at room temperature for 20 to 30 minutes before grilling.
2. To make the sauce: In a small bowl, whisk the sauce ingredients.
3. Grill the steak over *Direct High* heat until cooked to desired doneness, 8 to 10 minutes for medium-rare, turning once. Remove from the grill and let rest for 3 to 5 minutes. Cut across the grain into thin strips. Place the strips in a medium bowl. Pour the sauce over the strips. Toss to evenly coat. Serve warm.

MAKES 4 TO 6 SERVINGS

Pacific Island Skirt Steaks

PREP TIME: 10 MINUTES
MARINATING TIME: 1 HOUR
GRILLING TIME: 4 TO 6 MINUTES

MARINADE
- 1 small yellow onion, roughly chopped
- ⅓ cup soy sauce
- ¼ cup fresh lemon juice
- ¼ cup vegetable oil
- 2 tablespoons dark brown sugar
- 2 tablespoons minced garlic
- ½ teaspoon ground allspice

- 2 skirt steaks, about 1 pound each and ½ inch thick
  Vegetable oil
  Freshly ground black pepper

1. To make the marinade: In a medium bowl, whisk the marinade ingredients.
2. Cut each skirt steak into 8- to 10-inch pieces. Place the steaks in a large, resealable plastic bag and pour in the marinade. Press the air out of the bag and seal tightly. Refrigerate for 1 hour, turning occasionally.
3. Remove the steaks from the bag and discard the marinade. Pat the steaks dry with paper towels and allow the steaks to stand at room temperature for 20 to 30 minutes. Lightly brush or spray both sides of the steaks with oil and season with pepper to taste. Grill over *Direct High* heat until cooked to desired doneness, 4 to 6 minutes for medium-rare, turning once. Remove from the grill and let rest for 2 to 3 minutes. Slice thinly. Serve warm.

MAKES 4 TO 6 SERVINGS

Grilled Mandarin Skirt Steaks

PREP TIME: 15 MINUTES
MARINATING TIME: 1 TO 2 HOURS
GRILLING TIME: 4 TO 6 MINUTES

MARINADE
 Zest and juice of 4 large tangerines or
 small oranges [about ⅔ cup]
¼ cup soy sauce
2 tablespoons vegetable oil
2 tablespoons minced fresh ginger
2 teaspoons minced garlic
2 teaspoons hot chili-garlic sauce,
 such as sriracha

2 skirt steaks, about 1 pound each
 and ½ inch thick

1. To make the marinade: In a small bowl, whisk the marinade ingredients.
2. Cut each skirt steak into 8- to 10-inch pieces. Place the steaks in a large, resealable plastic bag and pour in the marinade. Press the air out of the bag and seal tightly. Turn the bag several times to distribute the marinade. Refrigerate for 1 to 2 hours.
3. Allow the steaks to stand at room temperature for 20 to 30 minutes before grilling. Remove the steaks from the bag and discard the marinade. Lightly pat the steaks dry with paper towels. Grill the steaks over *Direct High* heat until cooked to desired doneness, 4 to 6 minutes for medium-rare, turning once. Remove from the grill and let rest for 2 to 3 minutes. Cut crosswise into ¼-inch slices. Serve warm.

MAKES 4 TO 6 SERVINGS

Chicago-Style Hot Dogs

PREP TIME: 10 MINUTES
GRILLING TIME: 4 TO 5 MINUTES

2 medium ripe tomatoes, cut crosswise into
 ¼-inch slices
8 beef hot dogs
8 hot dog buns, preferably poppy seed
16 pepperoncini peppers
2 dill pickles, cut into spears
½ cup finely chopped yellow onion
½ cup sweet pickle relish
 Yellow mustard
 Celery salt

1. Cut each tomato slice in half to make half moons.
2. Grill the hot dogs over *Direct Medium* heat until browned, 4 to 5 minutes, turning once. During the last 30 seconds, grill the hot dog buns, cut side down. Place a grilled hot dog in each bun with two tomato slices, two peppers, a pickle spear, chopped onion, pickle relish, and mustard. Finish with a generous dash of celery salt. Serve warm.

MAKES 8 SERVINGS

Chile-Rubbed Flatiron Steaks
with Chipotle-Red Pepper Sauce

PREP TIME: 30 MINUTES
GRILLING TIME: ABOUT 20 MINUTES

SAUCE
- 2 large red bell peppers
- 2 large garlic cloves
- 2 tablespoons balsamic vinegar
- 1 tablespoon extra virgin olive oil
- 1 canned chipotle chile pepper
- 1 teaspoon dried oregano
- ½ teaspoon kosher salt
- ¼ teaspoon freshly ground black pepper

- 2 flatiron steaks, about 1 pound each and ½ inch thick
- 2 tablespoons extra virgin olive oil
- 2 teaspoons prepared chili powder
- 1 teaspoon kosher salt
- ¼ teaspoon freshly ground black pepper

1. To make the sauce: Grill the bell peppers over *Direct High* heat until they are blackened and blistered all over, 12 to 15 minutes, turning occasionally. Place the peppers in a large bowl and cover with plastic to trap the steam. Set aside for at least 10 minutes, then remove the peppers from the bowl and peel away the charred skins. Cut off the tops and remove the seeds. Place the peppers in a food processor or blender along with the remaining sauce ingredients. Process until smooth. Transfer to a small serving bowl.

2. Allow the steaks to stand at room temperature for 20 to 30 minutes before grilling. Lightly brush or spray the steaks all over with oil and season with the chili powder, salt, and pepper. Grill over *Direct High* heat until cooked to desired doneness, 4 to 6 minutes for medium-rare, turning once. Remove from the grill and let rest for 3 to 5 minutes before cutting into ¼-inch slices. Serve warm with the sauce.

MAKES 4 TO 6 SERVINGS

Flatiron Steaks

with Little Italy Relish

PREP TIME: 20 MINUTES
GRILLING TIME: 4 TO 6 MINUTES

RELISH
- 1 cup finely diced roasted red bell peppers
- 1 cup finely diced ripe tomato
- ½ cup pitted green olives, quartered lengthwise
- ½ cup pitted black olives, quartered lengthwise
- ½ cup finely diced celery, preferably from the tender inside stalks
- ¼ cup extra virgin olive oil
- 2 tablespoons roughly chopped fresh Italian parsley
- 1 tablespoon red wine vinegar
- 1 teaspoon minced garlic
- 1 teaspoon kosher salt
- ½ teaspoon dried oregano
- ½ teaspoon crushed red pepper flakes

- 2 flatiron steaks, about 1 pound each and ½ inch thick
  Extra virgin olive oil
- 1 teaspoon kosher salt
- ½ teaspoon freshly ground black pepper

1. To make the relish: In a medium bowl, mix the relish ingredients. Set aside at room temperature for 2 hours before serving to release juices and blend the flavors.

2. Allow the steaks to stand at room temperature for 20 to 30 minutes before grilling. Lightly brush or spray the steaks with oil and season with the salt and pepper. Grill over *Direct High* heat until cooked to desired doneness, 4 to 6 minutes for medium-rare, turning once. Remove from the grill and let rest for 2 to 3 minutes. Cut across the grain into ½-inch slices and serve warm with the relish spooned over the top.

MAKES 4 SERVINGS

A flatiron steak comes from the shoulder, a well-exercised area of the cow, so it tends to be a little tougher than a rib-eye or strip steak, but it also has deeper flavors. Just before grilling, I remove the thin line of gristle running down the center of flatiron steaks. They take their name from the shape of the meat before it is cut into steaks, which resembles an old-fashioned iron.

Bacon and Swiss Burgers

PREP TIME: 20 MINUTES
GRILLING TIME: 8 TO 10 MINUTES

    3   slices bacon
    1   cup finely chopped yellow onion
    1   tablespoon minced garlic
    1   tablespoon minced fresh thyme
 1½   pounds ground chuck [80% lean]
    1   teaspoon Worcestershire sauce
  ½   teaspoon kosher salt
  ½   teaspoon freshly ground black pepper
  ¼   teaspoon Tabasco® sauce
    4   thin slices Swiss cheese
    4   hamburger buns
    8   medium slices ripe tomato

1. In a medium skillet over medium heat, cook the bacon until crispy, about 10 minutes, turning occasionally. Drain the bacon on paper towels, reserving the fat in the skillet. Cook the onion in the fat over medium heat until tender, about 5 minutes, stirring occasionally. Add the garlic and thyme. Continue to cook until the garlic has softened, about 2 minutes, stirring occasionally. Transfer the onion mixture to a small bowl and let cool. Finely chop the bacon.

2. In a medium bowl, mix the ground chuck with the Worcestershire, salt, pepper, Tabasco, the onion mixture, and the bacon. Shape into 4 patties, each about ¾ inch thick.

3. Grill the patties over *Direct High* heat until medium, 8 to 10 minutes, turning once. During the last minute of grilling place a slice of cheese on each patty to melt, and grill the hamburger buns, cut side down, until toasted. Serve warm, with tomatoes, ketchup, and/or mustard.

MAKES 4 SERVINGS

Cheeseburger of Champions

PREP TIME: 10 MINUTES
GRILLING TIME: 8 TO 10 MINUTES

 1½   pounds ground chuck [80% lean]
    1   tablespoon ketchup
    1   teaspoon dried basil
  ½   teaspoon dried thyme
  ½   teaspoon kosher salt
  ½   teaspoon Worcestershire sauce
  ½   teaspoon Tabasco® sauce
  ¼   teaspoon freshly ground black pepper
    4   thin slices Monterey Jack cheese
    4   hamburger buns
    4   lettuce leaves
    4   tomato slices

1. In a medium bowl, using your hands, gently combine the ground chuck with the ketchup, basil, thyme, salt, Worcestershire, Tabasco, and pepper. Gently shape into 4 patties, each about ¾ inch thick.

2. Grill the patties over *Direct High* heat until medium, 8 to 10 minutes, turning once. During the last minute of grilling place a slice of cheese on each patty to melt, and grill the hamburger buns, cut side down, until toasted. Assemble the cheeseburgers with lettuce, tomato, and ketchup and/or mustard, if desired. Serve warm.

MAKES 4 SERVINGS

Double-Decker Mushroom Beef Burgers

PREP TIME: 10 MINUTES
GRILLING TIME: 12 TO 15 MINUTES

4   portabello mushrooms, 3 to 4 inches across
1/3 cup extra virgin olive oil
2   tablespoons Dijon mustard
2   tablespoons soy sauce
1/2 teaspoon freshly ground black pepper
1 1/2 pounds ground chuck [80% lean]
1   teaspoon soy sauce
1/2 teaspoon granulated onion
1/4 teaspoon freshly ground pepper
1/2 teaspoon kosher salt
4   hamburger buns
2   tablespoons unsalted butter, melted
4   lettuce leaves
    Ketchup

1. Remove mushroom stems and discard; wipe mushroom caps with a damp paper towel. Scrape out the dark gills with a teaspoon and discard. In a small bowl, whisk together the oil, mustard, soy sauce, and pepper. Brush the mushrooms generously on both sides with this mixture.
2. In a medium bowl, gently mix the ground chuck, soy sauce, granulated onion, pepper, and salt. Shape into 4 patties, each about 3/4 inch thick.
3. Grill the mushrooms over *Direct High* heat until tender, 12 to 15 minutes, turning and basting occasionally with the oil mixture. Grill the patties over *Direct High* heat until medium, 8 to 10 minutes, turning once. Brush the cut sides of the hamburger buns with melted butter and grill over *Direct Medium* heat until toasted, about 30 seconds. Build the burgers on the buns with mushrooms, lettuce, and ketchup. Serve warm.

MAKES 4 SERVINGS

Hollywood Cheeseburgers
with Mushrooms and Brie

PREP TIME: 10 MINUTES
GRILLING TIME: 8 TO 10 MINUTES

BURGERS
1   ounce dried mushrooms, such as shiitake
1 1/2 pounds ground chuck [80% lean]
1   tablespoon extra virgin olive oil
1   tablespoon dried tarragon
1   teaspoon kosher salt
1/2 teaspoon freshly ground black pepper
1/2 teaspoon granulated garlic
1/2 teaspoon Worcestershire sauce

2   ounces brie cheese, thinly sliced
8   slices sourdough bread, each 1/2 inch thick
4   lettuce leaves
    Whole grain mustard

1. To prepare the burgers: In a medium bowl, cover mushrooms with boiling water and allow them to soak until soft, about 45 minutes. Drain the mushrooms and squeeze out the excess water. Blot the mushrooms with paper towels, cut out the tough stems and discard. In a food processor, process the mushrooms until finely chopped and place them in a medium bowl. Add the remaining burger ingredients and gently mix with your hands. Shape into 4 patties, each about 3/4 inch thick.
2. Grill the patties over *Direct High* heat until medium, 8 to 10 minutes, turning once. During the last 30 seconds, top the burgers with the brie and grill the bread until lightly toasted. Serve the burgers hot on the toasted bread with the lettuce and mustard.

MAKES 4 SERVINGS

Mount Olympus Meatball Kabobs

PREP TIME: 15 MINUTES
MARINATING TIME: 2 TO 8 HOURS
GRILLING TIME: 8 TO 10 MINUTES

MEATBALLS
 2 medium garlic cloves
 1 small red onion, roughly chopped [about
   1 cup]
 1/4 cup lightly packed fresh mint leaves
 3/4 pound ground lamb
 3/4 pound ground beef
 1 tablespoon red wine vinegar
 1 1/2 teaspoons kosher salt
 1 teaspoon freshly ground black pepper
 1 teaspoon dried oregano
 1/2 teaspoon paprika

SAUCE
 4 ounces English cucumber
 1 cup plain yogurt
 2 tablespoons extra virgin olive oil
 2 tablespoons finely chopped fresh dill
 1/2 teaspoon kosher salt
 1/4 teaspoon freshly ground black pepper
 1/8 teaspoon Tabasco® sauce

 Extra virgin olive oil

1. To prepare the meatballs: In a food processor, finely chop the garlic, onion, and mint. In a medium bowl, combine the contents of the food processor with the remaining meatball ingredients. Blend and squeeze the mixture with your hands until it is well combined. Lightly wet your hands with cold water, then shape the mixture into meatballs about 1 1/2 inches in diameter [you should have 20 to 25 meatballs]. Thread long, wide skewers through the center of the meatballs, about 4 to 5 meatballs per skewer, leaving a little room between each meatball. Place the kabobs on a baking sheet, cover, and refrigerate for 2 hours, or as long as 8 hours.
2. To make the sauce: Grate the cucumber. Drain in a colander and squeeze out most of the moisture. In a medium bowl, whisk together cucumber and remaining sauce ingredients. Cover and refrigerate until ready to serve.
3. Lightly brush or spray the kabobs on all sides with oil. Grill over *Direct Medium* heat until fully cooked, 8 to 10 minutes, gently rotating meatballs 2 or 3 times during grilling. Serve warm with the sauce.

MAKES 4 TO 6 SERVINGS

Sirloin Steak
with Pizzaiola Sauce

PREP TIME: 15 MINUTES
GRILLING TIME: 15 TO 21 MINUTES

SAUCE
2½ pounds plum tomatoes
2 tablespoons extra virgin olive oil
1 tablespoon thinly sliced garlic
¼ cup thinly sliced oil-packed sun-dried tomatoes
¼ teaspoon crushed red pepper flakes
Kosher salt
Freshly ground black pepper
2 tablespoons finely chopped fresh oregano

1 top sirloin steak, 1½ to 2 pounds and about
1½ inches thick
Extra virgin olive oil

1. To make the sauce: Grill the tomatoes over *Direct High* heat until lightly charred on both sides, 3 to 5 minutes. When cool enough to handle, peel away the skin, halve the tomatoes crosswise, remove the cores, squeeze out the seeds, and then rough chop the tomatoes.

2. In a medium saucepan over medium heat, warm the oil and cook the garlic until golden brown, 1 to 2 minutes, stirring occasionally. Add the tomatoes, sun-dried tomatoes, and pepper flakes. Reduce the heat and simmer for 15 to 20 minutes. Season to taste with salt and pepper, then stir in the oregano.

3. Allow the steak to stand at room temperature for 20 to 30 minutes before grilling. Brush or spray both sides of the steak with oil. Season with salt and pepper, rubbing the seasonings into the meat. Sear over *Direct High* heat for 8 to 10 minutes, turning once, and then grill over *Indirect High* heat until cooked to desired doneness, 4 to 6 minutes for medium-rare. Remove from the grill and let rest for 3 to 5 minutes. Reheat the sauce over medium heat. Cut the steak into thick slices and serve over a pool of the sauce.

MAKES 4 SERVINGS

King-Size Beef Kabobs
with Salsa Verde

PREP TIME: 20 MINUTES
MARINATING TIME: 1 HOUR
GRILLING TIME: 7 TO 8 MINUTES

SAUCE
1 cup lightly packed Italian parsley leaves, with some stems attached
1 tablespoon capers, rinsed and drained
2 anchovy fillets, coarsely chopped
2 hard-cooked egg yolks
6 tablespoons extra virgin olive oil
2 teaspoons red wine vinegar
1/4 teaspoon kosher salt
1/4 teaspoon freshly cracked black pepper

2 pounds top sirloin, about 1½ inches thick
1/2 teaspoon freshly ground black pepper
1/2 teaspoon granulated garlic
2 tablespoons extra virgin olive oil
1/2 teaspoon kosher salt
12 slices ripe tomato [optional]

1. To make the sauce: In a food processor, finely chop the parsley, capers, anchovy fillets, and egg yolks. With the machine running add the oil in a steady stream, then add the vinegar, salt, and pepper. The sauce can be made up to one day in advance and kept, covered, in the refrigerator. Stir sauce just before serving.

2. Trim the sirloin of any excess fat and cut into 1½-inch cubes. Season with the pepper and granulated garlic, pressing the spices into the meat. Place the meat in a medium bowl, cover with plastic wrap and refrigerate for about 1 hour.

3. Allow the meat to stand at room temperature for 20 to 30 minutes before grilling. Add the oil to the bowl, toss to coat the meat evenly, and then thread the meat onto skewers. Sprinkle with the salt.

4. Grill the kabobs on all four sides over *Direct High* heat until cooked to desired doneness, 7 to 8 minutes for medium-rare, turning four times. Serve warm with the sauce on the side and sliced tomatoes, if desired.

MAKES 4 TO 6 SERVINGS

▲▲▲

King-size is key here. The cubes of beef need to be big enough that the centers don't overcook while you are searing the outsides. It is a good idea to allow the meat to stand at room temperature for 20 to 30 minutes and to use a really hot grill. By taking the chill off the meat and grilling it fast, you will make these kabobs tender and juicy.

▼▼▼

Argentine Beef Tenderloin Sandwiches
with Roasted Peppers and Sweet Onions

PREP TIME: 30 MINUTES
GRILLING TIME: 50 MINUTES TO 1 HOUR

- 4 red bell peppers
- 2 teaspoons minced garlic
- 2 medium yellow onions, cut into ½-inch slices
  Extra virgin olive oil
- 1 center-cut beef tenderloin, about 2½ pounds
- 1 teaspoon kosher salt
- 2 teaspoons freshly ground black pepper
- 8 large French rolls, split open
- 4 hardboiled eggs, sliced crosswise
- 8 large lettuce leaves
- 1 cup good-quality mayonnaise

1. Grill the bell peppers over *Direct Medium* heat until the skins are blackened and blistered all over, 12 to 15 minutes, turning occasionally. Place the peppers in a small bowl and cover with plastic wrap to trap the steam. Set aside for at least 10 minutes, then remove the peppers from the bowl and peel away the charred skins. Cut off the tops and remove the seeds and cut lengthwise into ½-inch wide strips. In a large bowl, mix the peppers and the garlic.

2. Lightly brush or spray the onion slices with oil. Grill over *Direct Medium* heat until nicely marked and tender, 8 to 10 minutes, turning once. Cut the onion slices in half and add to the bowl with the peppers and garlic.

3. Trim the tenderloin of any excess fat and silver skin and allow to stand at room temperature for 20 to 30 minutes before grilling. Lightly brush with oil and rub the salt and pepper into the meat. Sear over *Direct Medium* heat until well marked, about 15 minutes, turning a quarter turn every 3 to 4 minutes. Move the tenderloin over *Indirect Medium* heat and grill until cooked to desired doneness, 15 to 20 minutes longer for medium-rare, turning once. Remove from the grill and let rest 5 to 10 minutes. Cut into thin slices and place on a warm platter.

4. Grill the rolls, cut sides down, over *Direct Medium* heat until lightly toasted, about 30 seconds. Allow guests to assemble sandwiches with beef, peppers, onions, eggs, lettuce, and mayonnaise.

MAKES 8 SERVINGS

Hot Tenderloin Sandwiches

PREP TIME: 20 MINUTES
GRILLING TIME: 30 TO 35 MINUTES

  1 cup sour cream
  2 tablespoons prepared horseradish
  1 teaspoon Dijon mustard

  1 center-cut beef tenderloin, 2 to 2½ pounds
     Extra virgin olive oil
  1 teaspoon kosher salt
 ½ teaspoon freshly ground black pepper

  1 large baguette, cut in half lengthwise
  1 bunch arugula, washed and dried
  1 cup grated Fontina cheese

1. In a small bowl, mix the sour cream, horseradish, and mustard. Set aside.

2. Trim the tenderloin of any excess fat and silver skin and allow to stand at room temperature for 20 to 30 minutes before grilling. Lightly brush or spray with oil and season with salt and pepper. Sear over *Direct Medium* heat until well marked, about 15 minutes, turning a quarter turn every 3 to 4 minutes. Continue grilling over *Indirect Medium* heat until cooked to desired doneness, 15 to 20 minutes longer for medium-rare, turning once. Remove from the grill and let rest for 5 to 10 minutes. Cut into ⅛-inch slices.

3. Lightly brush the cut side of the baguette with oil and grill, cut side down, over *Direct Medium* heat until lightly toasted, about 30 seconds.

4. Spread the baguette with the sour cream mixture, layer with arugula and sliced tenderloin, then top with the grated cheese. Cut crosswise into individual sandwiches.

MAKES 6 SERVINGS

Spinach-Stuffed Beef Tenderloin
with Horseradish Sauce

PREP TIME: 30 MINUTES
GRILLING TIME: 35 TO 45 MINUTES

SAUCE
- ¹/₂ cup sour cream
- ¹/₃ cup mayonnaise
- 3 tablespoons prepared horseradish
- 2 tablespoons finely chopped fresh dill
- 1 tablespoon fresh lemon juice
- 1 teaspoon minced garlic
- ¹/₄ teaspoon kosher salt
- ¹/₄ teaspoon freshly ground black pepper

- 6 slices bacon
- 1 tablespoon minced garlic
- ¹/₂ pound fresh baby spinach
- 3 tablespoons raisins
  Freshly ground black pepper
- 1 center-cut beef tenderloin, 3 to 3¹/₂ pounds
- 2 tablespoons finely chopped fresh dill
  Kosher salt

1. To make the sauce: In a medium bowl, whisk the sauce ingredients. Cover and refrigerate until about 20 minutes before serving.

2. In a large skillet, cook the bacon over medium heat until crispy, about 10 minutes, turning occasionally. Drain the bacon on paper towels. Pour off [and reserve] all but 2 tablespoons of the bacon fat in the skillet. Add the garlic to the pan; cook for about 30 seconds, stirring occasionally. Add the spinach; cook until the spinach is wilted, 1 to 2 minutes, stirring constantly. Place the spinach mixture in a medium bowl. Add the raisins and ¹/₈ teaspoon of pepper. Finely chop the bacon and add it to the bowl. Stir the mixture and allow it to cool to room temperature.

3. Trim the tenderloin of any excess fat and silver skin and allow to stand at room temperature for 20 to 30 minutes before grilling. Using a long, narrow knife, make a hole in the center than runs the full length of the tenderloin. Turn the knife over and cut to expand the opening. Stuff the spinach mixture into the hole from both ends using the handle of a spatula or wooden spoon. Using kitchen string, tie the beef into a compact, even cylinder. Lightly brush the beef all over with some of the reserved bacon fat [or olive oil]. Season with the dill and salt and pepper to taste.

4. Sear over *Direct Medium* heat for 15 minutes, turning a quarter turn once every 3 to 4 minutes. Continue to grill over *Indirect Medium* heat until cooked to desired doneness, 20 to 30 minutes longer for medium-rare, turning once. Remove from the grill and let rest for 5 to 10 minutes. Carefully cut into 1-inch slices. Serve warm with the sauce.

MAKES 6 TO 8 SERVINGS

Tapenade-Coated Beef Tenderloin
with Herb Salad

PREP TIME: 20 MINUTES
MARINATING TIME: 4 HOURS TO OVERNIGHT
GRILLING TIME: 35 TO 40 MINUTES

1   center-cut beef tenderloin, about 2 pounds
1   jar [8 ounces] black olive tapenade

SALAD
½   cup fresh basil leaves
½   cup fresh mint leaves
¼   cup fresh tarragon leaves
1   cup fresh Italian parsley leaves
½   cup fresh chives, cut in 1-inch pieces
8   cups mixed baby greens, about 6 ounces
4   tablespoons extra virgin olive oil
2   to 4 tablespoons fresh lemon juice
    Kosher salt
    Freshly ground black pepper

1. Trim the tenderloin of any excess fat and silver skin. Place on a large sheet of plastic wrap on a work surface. Reserve 2 tablespoons of the tapenade and spread the remaining tapenade in a thin layer on all sides of the tenderloin. Pull up sides and ends of plastic wrap over the meat to seal tightly. Place on a plate and refrigerate 4 hours or overnight.
2. Remove the tenderloin from the refrigerator and allow to stand at room temperature 20 to 30 minutes before grilling. Grill over *Direct Medium* heat until cooked to desired doneness, 35 to 40 minutes for medium-rare, turning a quarter turn every 10 minutes. [Some of the olive coating will stick to the grates.] Remove from the grill and let rest 5 to 10 minutes.
3. Meanwhile make the herb salad: Tear the basil and mint leaves and combine them with the remaining herbs and greens in a salad bowl. In a small bowl, whisk together the oil, lemon juice, and salt and pepper to taste. Pour over the salad and toss to combine.
4. Cut the tenderloin into ½-inch-thick slices, top with a dollop of the reserved tapenade, and serve warm with the salad.

MAKES 4 TO 6 SERVINGS

Barbecued Meatloaf
with Shiitake Mushrooms

PREP TIME: 20 MINUTES
GRILLING TIME: ABOUT 1½ HOURS

MEATLOAF
12 shiitake mushrooms, about 6 ounces total,
    each 1½ to 2 inches across
    Extra virgin olive oil
1   cup bread crumbs
¼   cup milk
2   pounds ground chuck [80% lean]
1   egg, lightly beaten
2   tablespoons Dijon mustard
1   tablespoon Worcestershire sauce
1   tablespoon minced garlic
1   teaspoon dried thyme
1   teaspoon kosher salt
½   teaspoon finely ground fresh black pepper

⅓   cup barbecue sauce

1. To prepare the meatloaf: Remove and discard the tough stems from the mushrooms and then generously brush or spray them with oil. Grill over *Direct Medium* heat until barely tender, 6 to 7 minutes, turning once or twice. When cool enough to handle, cut the mushrooms into ¼-inch pieces.
2. In a medium bowl combine the bread crumbs and milk, mix well, and let stand while combining the rest of the ingredients. In a large bowl, combine the meatloaf ingredients, including the mushrooms and soaked bread crumbs. Using your hands, mix the ingredients thoroughly but do not overwork. Form into a loaf about 9 inches long and 5 inches wide. Place the loaf in the middle of a disposable aluminum pan. Grill over *Indirect Medium* heat for 45 minutes.
3. After 45 minutes of grilling, brush the barbecue sauce over the top and sides of the meatloaf and continue to grill until the internal temperature reaches 160°F, 40 to 45 minutes more. Let rest for 5 to 10 minutes. Cut into 1-inch slices and serve warm.

MAKES 6 TO 8 SERVINGS

Texas Beef Ribs
in Tomato-Jalapeño Sauce

PREP TIME: 10 MINUTES
GRILLING TIME: ABOUT 2 HOURS

SAUCE
- 2 cups tomato sauce
- ½ cup dry red wine
- ½ cup jalapeño jelly
- 1 tablespoon cider vinegar
- 2 teaspoons prepared chili powder

- 1 rack beef ribs, 4 to 5 pounds, cut into 3 or 4 sections to fit inside the pan
- 2 teaspoons kosher salt
- 1 teaspoon freshly ground black pepper

1. To make the sauce: In a small saucepan, combine the sauce ingredients and bring to a boil, stirring until the jelly dissolves. Remove the pan from the heat.

2. Allow the ribs to stand at room temperature for 20 to 30 minutes before grilling. Season the ribs on both sides with the salt and pepper. Sear the ribs over *Direct Medium* heat until nicely browned, 8 to 10 minutes, turning occasionally [watch for flare-ups]. Place the ribs, meaty side down, in a deep 10x13-inch baking dish [not aluminum or cast-iron]. Bring the sauce back to a boil and pour over the ribs. Cover the baking dish tightly with aluminum foil. Grill over *Indirect Medium* heat for 1 hour. Remove the foil and continue grilling until the meat has pulled away easily from the bone, 45 to 60 minutes, turning the ribs occasionally. Remove the ribs from the sauce. Cut into individual ribs. Serve warm with some sauce drizzled over the top.

MAKES 4 SERVINGS

Prime Rib

with Garlic and Blue Cheese Dressing

PREP TIME: 20 MINUTES
GRILLING TIME: 1½ TO 2 HOURS

    1   bone-in standing prime rib roast,
        5 to 6 pounds, trimmed of excess fat
    6   large garlic cloves
    ¼   cup lightly packed fresh rosemary leaves
    ¼   cup lightly packed fresh basil leaves
    2   teaspoons kosher salt
    2   teaspoons freshly ground black pepper
    3   tablespoons Dijon mustard
    3   tablespoons extra virgin olive oil

DRESSING
    ¾   cup heavy cream
    1   medium garlic clove, thinly sliced
    6   ounces blue cheese, crumbled
        Freshly ground black pepper

1. Allow the roast to stand at room temperature 30 to 45 minutes before grilling.

2. In a food processor finely mince the garlic, rosemary, basil, salt, and pepper. Add the mustard and olive oil, and process to form a paste. Smear the paste all over the top and sides of the roast. Grill, bone side down, over *Indirect Medium* heat until cooked to desired doneness, 1½ to 2 hours for medium-rare. Transfer the roast to a cutting board and remove the bones. Loosely cover the roast with aluminum foil and let rest for 20 to 30 minutes. The internal temperature will rise 5°F to 10°F during this time.

3. Meanwhile, make the dressing: Place the cream and garlic in a medium saucepan. Bring the cream to a boil over medium-high heat, then lower the heat to a simmer and cook until the cream coats the back of a spoon, 5 to 10 minutes. Remove the pan from the heat. Add the cheese, stirring to help it blend into the cream. Season with pepper to taste. Carve meat into slices. Serve warm with the dressing.

MAKES 6 TO 8 SERVINGS

If ever there was a reason for buying an instant-read thermometer, this is it. After spending a big chunk of change on prime rib, the cost of a thermometer is negligible, and that little tool almost guarantees that the meat will be grilled precisely to the doneness you like.

Herb-Crusted Prime Rib
with Red Wine Sauce

PREP TIME: 30 MINUTES
GRILLING TIME: 1½ TO 1¾ HOURS

SAUCE
  2 tablespoons extra virgin olive oil
  1 medium carrot, roughly chopped
  2 stalks celery, roughly chopped
  1 medium yellow onion, roughly chopped
  5 medium garlic cloves, crushed
  2 tablespoons tomato paste
  3 cups beef broth
  1 cup dry red wine
  ¼ cup balsamic vinegar
  2 bay leaves
  1 tablespoon finely chopped fresh rosemary
     Freshly ground black pepper
  4 tablespoons unsalted butter
     Kosher salt

  1 boneless rib roast, about 5 pounds, trimmed of
     excess fat
     Extra virgin olive oil
  2 tablespoons herbes de Provence

1. To make the sauce: In a large saucepan over high heat, warm the olive oil. Add the carrot, celery, and onion, and cook until the vegetables begin to brown, 6 to 8 minutes, stirring occasionally. Add the garlic and cook for about 2 more minutes, stirring occasionally. Reduce the heat to medium, add the tomato paste, and cook for about 2 more minutes, stirring occasionally. Add the broth, wine, vinegar, bay leaves, rosemary, and ½ teaspoon of pepper. Mix well. Bring to a boil over high heat, then reduce the heat and let simmer for 45 minutes.

2. Strain the sauce through a sieve into a medium saucepan, pressing down on the solids with the back of a spoon. Continue to simmer until about ¾ cup of liquid remains, about 45 more minutes. Add the butter 1 tablespoon at a time, whisking to melt them. Season with salt and pepper to taste. Remove the sauce from the heat.

3. Allow the beef to stand at room temperature 30 to 45 minutes before grilling. Lightly brush or spray the roast all over with oil and season with the herbes de Provence, and salt and pepper to taste.

4. Grill the beef over *Indirect Medium* heat until cooked to desired doneness, 1½ to 1¾ hours for medium-rare, but start checking with an instant-read thermometer after 1¼ hours. Transfer the beef to a cutting board, loosely cover with aluminum foil, and let rest for 10 to 20 minutes. Meanwhile warm the sauce over medium heat. Carve the beef and serve warm with the sauce.

MAKES 6 TO 8 SERVINGS

Strip Loin Roast
with Creamy Watercress and Tarragon Sauce

PREP TIME: 30 MINUTES
GRILLING TIME: 45 MINUTES TO ABOUT 1 HOUR

SAUCE
- 4 large garlic cloves
- 1 large bunch watercress, about 3 ounces
- 1 large bunch tarragon, leaves only
- ½ cup mayonnaise
- ½ cup sour cream
- 1 tablespoon grated lemon zest
- 1 tablespoon fresh lemon juice
- ½ teaspoon kosher salt
- ½ teaspoon freshly ground black pepper

- 1 boneless strip loin roast, 4 to 5 pounds
- 2 tablespoon herbes de Provence
- 2 tablespoons extra virgin olive oil
- 2 teaspoons kosher salt
- 1 teaspoon freshly ground black pepper

1. To make the sauce: In a food processor, mince the garlic. Add the watercress and tarragon and process until finely chopped. Add the mayonnaise and sour cream and process until smooth. Add the remaining sauce ingredients and process until evenly distributed. Cover the sauce and refrigerate until about 20 minutes before serving.

2. Trim the roast of any excess fat, leaving a ¼-inch layer of fat on the top. Allow to stand at room temperature for 20 to 30 minutes before grilling.

3. In a small bowl, mix together the herbes de Provence, oil, salt, and pepper. Smear the seasonings evenly over the outside of the roast. Sear over *Direct High* heat until lightly browned, 2 to 4 minutes, turning once [watch for flare-ups]. Move the roast over *Indirect Medium* heat [keep your grill at 325°F] and cook until it reaches the desired doneness, 45 minutes to 1 hour for medium-rare. Remove from the grill and let rest for 5 to 10 minutes. Cut into thin slices. Serve warm with the sauce.

MAKES 8 TO 10 SERVINGS

Tri-Tip Roast

with Tomato Red Barbecue Sauce

PREP TIME: 20 MINUTES
GRILLING TIME: 30 TO 40 MINUTES

SAUCE
- ½ cup ketchup
- 2 tablespoons white wine vinegar
- 1 tablespoon Worcestershire sauce
- 2 teaspoons molasses
- 1 teaspoon soy sauce
- ½ teaspoon prepared chili powder
- ½ teaspoon granulated garlic
- ¼ teaspoon celery salt
- ¼ teaspoon liquid hickory smoke

RUB
- ½ teaspoon kosher salt
- ½ teaspoon celery salt
- ¼ teaspoon freshly ground black pepper
- ¼ teaspoon granulated garlic

- 1 tri-tip roast, about 2 pounds and 1½ inches thick
- 2 tablespoons extra virgin olive oil

1. To make the sauce: In a medium saucepan, combine the sauce ingredients with 2 tablespoons of water. Bring to a simmer over medium heat and cook for about 1 minute, stirring occasionally. Set aside half of the sauce for dipping.
2. To make the rub: In a small bowl, thoroughly mix the rub ingredients with your fingertips.
3. Allow the roast to stand at room temperature 20 to 30 minutes before grilling. Lightly coat the meat with the oil and season with the rub, pressing the spices into the meat. Grill over *Direct Medium* heat until well marked on both sides, about 10 minutes, turning once. Move the roast over *Indirect Medium* heat and cook to the desired doneness, 20 to 30 minutes more for medium-rare, brushing the meat with the remaining half of the sauce on both sides and turning it over every 5 minutes or so. Remove from the grill and let rest for 5 to 10 minutes. Cut the meat across the grain into very thin slices. Serve warm with the dipping sauce.

MAKES 6 SERVINGS

▲▲▲

Here you have it, an easy, delicious barbecue sauce with all the fundamental flavors in place. Sweet, sour, spicy, and salty. I leave it to you to add the "x" factor, if you want. That little something-something is what makes a barbecue sauce your own. See page 32 for ideas.

▼▼▼

Tri-Tip Roast
with Chimichurri Sauce

PREP TIME: 15 MINUTES
MARINATING TIME: 4 TO 6 HOURS
GRILLING TIME: 30 TO 40 MINUTES

MARINADE AND SAUCE
- 4 large garlic cloves
- 1 cup loosely packed fresh Italian parsley leaves
- 1 cup loosely packed fresh cilantro leaves
- 1/2 cup loosely packed fresh basil leaves
- 3/4 cup extra virgin olive oil
- 1/4 cup rice vinegar
- 1 teaspoon kosher salt
- 1/2 teaspoon freshly ground black pepper
- 1/2 teaspoon Tabasco® sauce

- 1 tri-tip roast, about 2 pounds and 1½ inches thick

1. To make the marinade and sauce: In a food processor, mince the garlic. Add the parsley, cilantro, and basil. Pulse to finely chop the herbs. With the processor running, slowly add the oil in a thin stream, and then add the remaining ingredients for the marinade and sauce. Pour about half of the mixture into a large, resealable plastic bag and set the other half aside for sauce. Add the roast to the bag. Press out the air and seal tightly. Turn the bag to distribute the marinade, place in a bowl, and refrigerate for 4 to 6 hours.

2. Remove the roast from the bag, discard the marinade in the bag, and allow to stand at room temperature for 20 to 30 minutes before grilling. Grill over *Direct Medium* heat until well marked on both sides, about 10 minutes, turning once. Move the meat over *Indirect Medium* heat and cook to the desired doneness, 20 to 30 minutes more for medium-rare. Remove from the grill and let rest for 5 to 10 minutes. Cut into thin slices and serve warm with the reserved sauce.

MAKES 4 TO 6 SERVINGS

Whiskey and Onion-Marinated Brisket

PREP TIME: 20 MINUTES
MARINATING TIME: 4 HOURS
GRILLING TIME: 4 HOURS

RUB
- 1 tablespoon granulated onion
- 2 teaspoons celery salt
- 1 teaspoon dried dill
- 1/2 teaspoon kosher salt
- 1/2 teaspoon freshly ground black pepper

- 1 beef brisket, about 3 pounds, trimmed of surface fat
  Extra virgin olive oil
- 1/2 cup whiskey
- 1 can [15 ounces] beef or vegetable stock
- 1 1/2 pounds small red potatoes
- 1 teaspoon kosher salt, divided
- 1/2 teaspoon finely ground fresh black pepper, divided
- 1 bag [10 ounces] small white onions, peeled
- 1 bag [16 ounces] peeled baby carrots

1. To make the rub: In a small bowl, mix the rub ingredients.
2. Press the rub into the brisket and place in a disposable 13x9-inch aluminum pan. Cover with plastic wrap and refrigerate for 4 hours.

3. Remove the brisket from the refrigerator and allow to stand at room temperature for about 30 minutes before grilling. Generously brush or spray the brisket with olive oil. Sear over *Direct High* heat until browned, about 8 minutes, turning once. Transfer the brisket to the aluminum pan. Pour in the whiskey and beef stock, and cover the pan with aluminum foil. Grill over *Indirect Low* heat for 2 hours, keeping the grill temperature about 300°F.
4. Cut the small potatoes in half [if the potatoes are larger than 2 1/2 inches in diameter, cut them into quarters]. In a medium bowl combine the potatoes, 1/2 teaspoon of the salt, and 1/4 teaspoon of the pepper. In another medium bowl combine the onions, carrots, and the remaining 1/2 teaspoon of salt and 1/4 teaspoon pepper.
5. After the 2 hours of grilling, uncover the meat, turn it over, place the potatoes around the edges, and place onions and carrots on top. Cover the meat again and continue to cook for 2 hours more, or longer if not fork tender.
6. Remove the brisket and vegetables from the grill. Place the brisket on a cutting board and cut across the grain into thin, diagonal slices. If desired, skim fat from the pan juices. Place on serving tray, top with pan juices, and surround with the vegetables.

MAKES 4 TO 6 SERVINGS

Grilled Veal Chops
with Red Pepper Sauce

PREP TIME: 15 MINUTES
GRILLING TIME: 24 TO 30 MINUTES

SAUCE
1 large red bell pepper
⅓ cup sour cream
¼ cup mayonnaise
1 tablespoon finely chopped fresh basil
2 teaspoons minced garlic
2 teaspoons balsamic vinegar
¼ teaspoon kosher salt

RUB
1 teaspoon pure chile powder
1 teaspoon minced garlic
¾ teaspoon kosher salt
½ teaspoon paprika
½ teaspoon dried thyme
¼ teaspoon dry mustard
¼ teaspoon freshly ground black pepper

4 veal rib chops, about 12 ounces each
and 1½ inches thick
Extra virgin olive oil

1. To make the sauce: Grill the bell pepper over *Direct Medium* heat until the skin is blackened and blistered all over, 12 to 15 minutes, turning occasionally. Place the pepper in a small bowl and cover with plastic wrap to trap the steam. Set aside for at least 10 minutes, then remove the pepper from the bowl and peel away the charred skin. Cut off the top, remove the seeds, and roughly chop the pepper. Place in a food processor along with the remaining sauce ingredients. Process until smooth. Cover and refrigerate until about 20 minutes before you are ready to serve.

2. To make the rub: In a small bowl, combine the rub ingredients and then crush the spices between your fingertips to release their flavors.

3. Trim the chops of any excess fat and allow to stand at room temperature for 20 to 30 minutes before grilling. Lightly brush or spray the chops with oil and then divide the rub evenly over both sides of the veal chops. Grill over *Direct Medium* heat until just slightly pink in the center, 12 to 15 minutes, turning once. Remove from the grill and let rest for 3 to 5 minutes. Serve warm with the sauce.

MAKES 4 SERVINGS

Veal Chops
with Pancetta and Garlic

PREP TIME: 15 MINUTES
GRILLING TIME: 6 TO 8 MINUTES

4 ounces pancetta, cut into ¼-inch dice
3 teaspoons minced fresh rosemary, divided
1 teaspoon minced garlic
1 tablespoon fresh lemon juice
4 veal rib chops, each about 1¼ inches thick
Extra virgin olive oil
¼ teaspoon freshly ground black pepper

1. In a medium skillet over medium heat, cook the pancetta until crispy, 5 to 10 minutes, stirring occasionally. Add 2 teaspoons of the rosemary and the garlic and cook until the garlic is golden brown, about 1 minute, stirring occasionally. Remove the skillet from the heat and add the lemon juice. Mix well.

2. Allow the chops to stand at room temperature for 20 to 30 minutes before grilling. Trim the chops of any excess fat and cut a pocket halfway up the side of each chop all the way to the bone. Spread the pancetta mixture inside the pockets and close them by pressing on the top with the palm of your hand. Lightly brush or spray the chops with oil and season both sides with the pepper and the remaining 1 teaspoon of rosemary. Grill over *Direct High* heat until cooked to desired doneness, 6 to 8 for medium-rare, turning once [watch for flare-ups]. Remove from the grill and let rest for 3 to 5 minutes. Serve warm.

MAKES 4 SERVINGS

Lamb Chops
with Toasted Curry

PREP TIME: 10 MINUTES
GRILLING TIME: 5 TO 8 MINUTES

CURRY

½	teaspoon ground coriander
½	teaspoon ground cumin
½	teaspoon freshly ground black pepper
¼	teaspoon ground ginger
⅛	teaspoon ground cayenne pepper
⅛	teaspoon ground cinnamon
	Pinch ground cloves
¼	teaspoon ground turmeric
¼	teaspoon kosher salt

16	rib lamb chops, each about ¾ inch thick
	Vegetable oil

1. To prepare the curry: In a small skillet over medium heat, combine the coriander, cumin, pepper, ginger, cayenne, cinnamon, and cloves. Toast the spices until the aromas are apparent, about 2 to 3 minutes, stirring occasionally. Transfer the mixture to a small bowl and add the turmeric and salt. Blend thoroughly.
2. Trim the chops of excess fat. Lightly brush or spray the chops on both sides with vegetable oil and season on both sides with the curry. Grill over *Direct Medium* heat until cooked to desired doneness, 5 to 8 minutes for medium-rare, turning once. Serve warm.

MAKES 4 SERVINGS

Rosemary Lamb Chops
with Grill-Roasted Potatoes

PREP TIME: 20 MINUTES
GRILLING TIME: 19 TO 26 MINUTES

SEASONING

1	tablespoon finely chopped garlic
1	teaspoon kosher salt
1	tablespoon finely chopped fresh rosemary
2	teaspoons finely chopped fresh thyme
¾	teaspoon freshly ground black pepper

2	pounds new potatoes, about 1½ inches in diameter, washed and quartered
	Extra virgin olive oil
8	loin lamb chops, about 4 ounces each and 1¼ inches thick, trimmed of excess fat

1. To make the seasoning: Roughly chop the garlic, and then sprinkle the salt on top. Using both the sharp edge and the flat side of the knife blade, crush the garlic and salt together to create a paste. Add the remaining seasoning ingredients and chop them together.
2. Place the cut potatoes in a medium bowl. Drizzle 2 tablespoons of oil over the top and add about half of the seasoning mixture. Mix well. Grill the potatoes over *Direct Medium* heat until tender, 10 to 15 minutes, turning occasionally. Keep the potatoes warm while you grill the lamb.
3. Lightly brush or spray the chops on both sides with oil. Spread the remaining half of the seasoning mixture on both sides of the chops. Grill over *Direct Medium* heat until cooked to desired doneness, 9 to 11 minutes for medium-rare, turning once. Serve warm with the potatoes.

MAKES 4 SERVINGS

Mongolian Lamb Barbecue

PREP TIME: 15 MINUTES
MARINATING TIME: 1 TO 2 HOURS
GRILLING TIME: 8 MINUTES

MARINADE
1/3 cup hoisin sauce
2 tablespoons oyster sauce
2 tablespoons soy sauce
2 tablespoons dry sherry
2 tablespoons rice vinegar
2 tablespoons canola oil
1 tablespoon honey
1 tablespoon minced ginger
1 tablespoon minced garlic
1/2 teaspoon crushed red pepper flakes [optional]

1 boneless leg of lamb, about 2 pounds, trimmed of excess fat, cut into 1 1/2-inch cubes
3 red or yellow bell peppers, cut into 1-inch squares

1. To make the marinade: In a medium bowl, whisk the marinade ingredients.
2. Place the lamb in a large, resealable plastic bag and pour in the marinade. Press the air out of the bag and seal tightly. Turn the bag to distribute the marinade, place in a bowl, and refrigerate for 1 to 2 hours, turning occasionally. Allow the lamb to stand at room temperature for 20 to 30 minutes before grilling.
3. Remove the lamb from the bag and discard the marinade. Skewer the lamb alternately with the bell pepper squares. Grill the skewers over *Direct Medium* heat until cooked to desired doneness, about 8 minutes for medium-rare, turning occasionally. Serve warm.

MAKES 4 TO 6 SERVINGS

Lamb and Pepper Kabobs
Marinated with Lemon and Fennel

PREP TIME: 20 MINUTES
MARINATING TIME: 20 TO 30 MINUTES
GRILLING TIME: 6 TO 7 MINUTES

MARINADE
2 medium garlic cloves
1 tablespoon slivered almonds
1 tablespoon fresh bread crumbs
6 tablespoons extra virgin olive oil
1/4 cup lightly packed fresh parsley leaves
2 tablespoons fresh lemon juice
1 teaspoon whole fennel seed
1/2 teaspoon kosher salt
1/4 teaspoon freshly ground black pepper

1 boneless leg of lamb, about 1 1/2 pounds, trimmed of excess fat, cut into 1 1/2-inch cubes
2 medium green, red, or yellow bell peppers
1 lemon, thinly sliced

1. To make the marinade: In a food processor, mince the garlic, almonds, and bread crumbs. Add the remaining marinade ingredients and process until smooth.
2. Remove the stem and seeds from the bell peppers. Cut the peppers into 1-inch strips. In a medium bowl, mix the lamb and peppers with the marinade. Marinate at room temperature for 20 to 30 minutes.
3. Thread the lemon slices with the lamb alternately on skewers. Grill the pepper over *Direct High* heat until well marked and tender, 4 to 6 minutes, turning once. Cut the peppers into 1/4-inch strips or 1-inch pieces. Grill the skewers over *Direct High* heat until the meat cooked to the desired doneness, 6 to 7 minutes for medium-rare, turning once. Serve the skewers hot on top of the peppers.

MAKES 4 SERVINGS

Lamb Burgers
with Oregano, Mint, and Cucumber-Garlic Sauce

PREP TIME: 15 MINUTES
GRILLING TIME: 8 TO 10 MINUTES

SAUCE

- 4 ounces English cucumber
- 2 teaspoons minced garlic
- 8 tablespoons finely chopped fresh mint, divided
- ½ cup plain yogurt
- ½ teaspoon kosher salt
  Few drops Tabasco® sauce

BURGERS

- 2 pounds ground lamb
- ⅔ cup crumbled feta cheese
- ⅓ cup minced yellow onion
- 3 tablespoons finely chopped fresh oregano
- 1½ teaspoons kosher salt
- ½ teaspoon freshly ground black pepper

- 6 onion or Kaiser rolls
- 6 slices ripe tomato

1. To make the sauce: Peel and grate the cucumber. Drain in a colander while preparing the rest of the ingredients. In a small bowl, stir the garlic, 2 tablespoons of the mint, the drained cucumber, and the remaining sauce ingredients. Cover and refrigerate until ready to serve.

2. To prepare the burgers: In a large bowl, gently mix the burger ingredients, including the remaining 6 tablespoons of mint. Shape the meat into 6 patties of equal size, about ¾-inch thick. Refrigerate for at least 15 minutes before grilling. Grill the burgers over *Direct High* heat until cooked through, 8 to 10 minutes, turning once. During the last 30 seconds, toast the buns, cut side down, over *Direct High* heat.

3. Serve the lamb burgers on the toasted buns with the tomato slices and cucumber sauce.

MAKES 6 SERVINGS

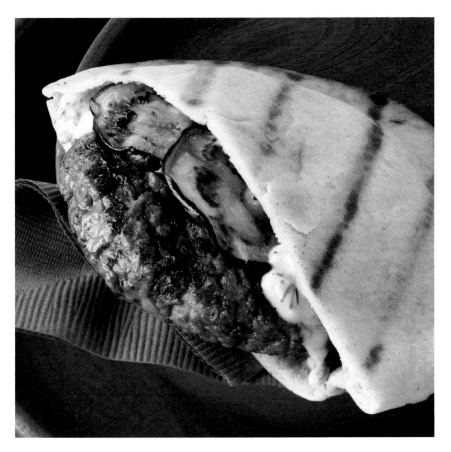

Lamb Burgers

with Sun-Dried Tomatoes, Grilled Eggplant, and Tzatziki Sauce

PREP TIME: 20 MINUTES
GRILLING TIME: 10 TO 12 MINUTES

SAUCE

³/₄	cup plain yogurt
2	tablespoons finely chopped red onion
1	tablespoon finely chopped fresh dill
1	tablespoon finely chopped fresh mint
1	tablespoon fresh lime juice
1	tablespoon extra virgin olive oil
¹/₂	teaspoon freshly ground black pepper
¹/₄	teaspoon kosher salt

¹/₂	cup tightly packed fresh dill
2	large garlic cloves
¹/₄	cup oil-packed sun-dried tomatoes, about 8 whole pieces
1	tablespoon oil from the jar of sun-dried tomatoes
³/₄	teaspoon kosher salt, divided
¹/₂	teaspoon freshly ground black pepper, divided
1¹/₄	pounds ground lamb
8	eggplant slices, each about ¹/₃-inch thick and 4 inches across
	Extra virgin olive oil
¹/₂	teaspoon granulated onion
4	pita pockets

1. To make the sauce: In a small bowl, whisk the sauce ingredients. Cover and refrigerate until ready to serve.

2. In a food processor, finely chop the dill and garlic. Add the tomatoes, 1 tablespoon of oil from the jar of tomatoes, ¹/₂ teaspoon of the salt, and ¹/₄ teaspoon of the pepper. Process until the tomatoes are finely chopped. In a medium bowl, combine the lamb with the chopped tomato mixture. Using your hands, gently mix the ingredients to distribute them evenly. Gently shape the meat into 4 patties, each about ³/₄-inch thick.

3. Generously brush or spray the eggplant on both sides with olive oil; season with the granulated onion, and the remaining ¹/₄ teaspoon salt and ¹/₄ teaspoon pepper.

4. Grill the lamb patties and eggplant slices over *Direct Medium* heat for 10 to 12 minutes, turning once. The lamb patties should be medium and the eggplant slices should be tender. Assemble the burgers with a lamb patty, 2 eggplant slices, and some tzatziki sauce inside each pita. Serve warm.

MAKES 4 SERVINGS

Leg of Lamb

with Roasted Garlic and Mint

PREP TIME: 15 MINUTES
GRILLING TIME: 2 TO 2¹/₂ HOURS

PASTE

    2   medium heads garlic
    3   tablespoons extra virgin olive oil, divided
    2   tablespoons finely chopped fresh rosemary
    2   tablespoons finely chopped fresh mint
    1   tablespoon balsamic vinegar
 1¹/₂   teaspoons kosher salt
  ¹/₂   teaspoon freshly ground black pepper

    1   boneless leg of lamb, 3 to 3¹/₂ pounds, butterflied

1. To make the paste: Remove the loose, papery outer skin from the heads of garlic. Using a sharp knife, cut about ¹/₂ inch off the top to expose the cloves. Place each garlic head on a large square of heavy-duty aluminum foil and drizzle 1 tablespoon of olive oil over the top of the cloves. Fold up the foil sides and seal to make a packet, leaving a little room for the expansion of steam. Grill over *Indirect Medium* heat until the cloves are soft, 45 minutes to 1 hour. When cool enough to handle, squeeze out the garlic cloves into a medium bowl. Add the remaining paste ingredients, including the remaining 1 tablespoon of oil. Using the back of a fork, or a mortar and pestle, thoroughly combine the ingredients to create a paste.

2. Carefully remove any excess fat and sinew from both sides of the lamb and lay it, skin side down, on a flat surface. It should be 1 to 1¹/₂ inches thick. Spread half of the paste over one side of the lamb and roll the lamb tightly into a long cylinder. Using twine, tie the lamb at 2-inch intervals. Trim off the loose ends of twine. Spread the remaining half of the paste over the outside of the lamb. If not grilling immediately, cover and refrigerate. Allow the lamb to stand at room temperature 30 to 40 minutes before grilling.

3. Sear the lamb over *Direct Medium* heat until brown all both sides, 10 to 15 minutes, turning as necessary [if flare-ups occur, move the lamb temporarily over *Indirect Medium* heat]. Move the lamb over *Indirect Medium* heat and continue grilling to desired doneness, 1 to 1¹/₄ hours more for medium-rare. Remove from the grill and let rest for 5 to 10 minutes. Remove the twine. Cut the lamb crosswise into ¹/₄-inch slices and serve warm.

MAKES 6 SERVINGS

▲▲

You really don't need a butcher to tie a leg of lamb. Just wrap the twine around and around, and from end to end, until the meat has a relatively even thickness throughout [more like a shoebox than like a football].

▼▼

Rack of Lamb
with Javanese Peanut Sauce

PREP TIME: 20 MINUTES
GRILLING TIME: 20 TO 30 MINUTES

SAUCE
- 1 tablespoon peanut oil
- 1 teaspoon minced fresh ginger
- 1 teaspoon minced garlic
- ¾ cup coconut milk
- ⅓ cup smooth peanut butter
- 2 tablespoons rice vinegar
- 1 tablespoon finely chopped fresh cilantro
- 1 teaspoon soy sauce
- ½ teaspoon curry powder
  Pinch of ground cayenne pepper

- 2 racks of lamb, 1 to 1½ pounds each, frenched
- 2 teaspoons garam masala
- 1 teaspoon kosher salt
- ½ teaspoon freshly ground black pepper
- 2 tablespoons peanut oil

1. To make the sauce: In a small saucepan, warm the oil over medium-high heat. Add the ginger and garlic and cook until the garlic begins to brown, 1 to 2 minutes, stirring occasionally. Add the remaining sauce ingredients. Whisk to create a smooth texture. Bring the sauce to a boil, and then remove it from the heat.

2. Trim any excess fat from the lamb. Allow to stand at room temperature for 20 to 30 minutes before grilling. In a small bowl, mix the garam masala, salt, pepper, and oil to form a thin paste. Spread the paste over the meat. Loosely cover the bones with aluminum foil to keep them from burning. Grill the lamb over *Direct Medium* heat until cooked to desired doneness, 20 to 30 minutes for medium-rare, turning once [watch for flare-ups]. Remove from the grill and let rest for 5 minutes before cutting into chops. Meanwhile reheat the sauce. Serve the lamb warm with the sauce.

MAKES 4 SERVINGS

Rack of Lamb
with Roasted-Shallot Vinaigrette

PREP TIME: 15 MINUTES
GRILLING TIME: 17 TO 19 MINUTES

VINAIGRETTE
- 1 large shallot, about 1 ounce, unpeeled
- ¼ cup extra virgin olive oil, divided
- 1 tablespoon balsamic vinegar
- 1 teaspoon Dijon mustard
- 1 teaspoon finely chopped fresh thyme
- ½ teaspoon kosher salt
- ¼ teaspoon freshly ground black pepper

- 2 racks of lamb, 1 to 1½ pounds each, frenched
  Extra virgin olive oil
- 2 tablespoons finely chopped fresh thyme
- ½ teaspoon kosher salt
- ½ teaspoon freshly ground black pepper

1. To make the vinaigrette: Lightly brush or spray the shallot all over with a bit of the olive oil. Grill over *Direct Medium* heat until it is blackened in spots and very soft throughout, about 15 minutes, turning once. Remove the shallot from the grill and allow to cool. Remove and discard the peel. Finely chop the shallot and put it in a medium bowl along with the remaining vinaigrette ingredients, whisking in the rest of the olive oil to create a smooth dressing.

2. Trim any excess fat from the lamb. Allow to stand at room temperature 20 to 30 minutes before grilling. Lightly brush or spray the lamb with oil and season with the thyme, salt, and pepper. Loosely cover the bones with aluminum foil to keep them from burning. Sear, bone side down first, over *Direct Medium* heat until lightly browned, 2 to 4 minutes, turning once [flare-ups might occur]. Move the lamb over *Indirect Medium* heat and grill to desired doneness, about 15 minutes more for medium-rare. Remove from the grill and let rest for 5 minutes before cutting into chops. Serve warm with the vinaigrette.

MAKES 4 SERVINGS

PORK

America's Own

Almost every kind of food we eat today, whether it's pizza from Italy or spring rolls from Vietnam, belongs to another part of the world. We Americans have certainly put our own spin on foods from other places, but is there anything we can truly call our own? Absolutely. Barbecued pork.

Back in the fifteenth century, Indians in the Caribbean used the word barbocoa for a frame of sticks that held meat and fish over a wood-burning fire. When British colonists got a taste, they devoured this alternative to their usual fare of meat boiled in iron pots, and they improved on it by bringing domesticated pigs to the party. The term evolved into barbecue. Of course, many of those British colonists became America's first citizens. Before long the practice of slow-roasting whole hogs over smoldering wood became a favorite choice for outdoor shindigs, attracting large crowds and no small amount of revelry. In George Washington's diary, he recorded one barbecue he attended in Alexandria, Virginia, that lasted three entire days. During the twentieth century, many of the best pit masters in the south [often freed slaves] moved north and west, bringing their talent and new recipes to the big cities across the land.

Today many of the best barbecue restaurants stake their reputations on pork. In places like Memphis and Kansas City, ribs rule. In the Carolinas and other parts of the South, pulled pork is the specialty. You will find barbecued or grilled pork dishes in just about every great restaurant in America. The reason goes beyond patriotism. Pork just tastes great on the grill. It is inherently juicy and tender but, of course, not every cut of pork should be grilled the same way. As with any meat, the method depends on the particular size and texture. The following pages outline my specific recommendations for making the most of good ole American pork.

Pork just tastes great on the grill. It is inherently juicy and tender but, of course, not every cut of pork should be grilled the same way.

Types of Pork for the Grill

Tender Cuts for Grilling	Moderately Tender Cuts for Grilling	Bigger Cuts for Searing and Grill-Roasting	Tougher Cuts for Barbecuing
Rib Chop	Sirloin Chop	Rack of Pork	Baby Back Ribs
Loin Chop	Shoulder Blade Steak	Sirloin Loin Roast	Spareribs
Center-Cut Chop,	Ham Steak	Center Rib Roast	Shoulder (Boston butt)
Tenderloin (whole or		Center Loin Roast	
in medallions)		Cured Ham	
		Country Style Ribs	

What to Look For in Pork

The color and firmness of the meat are the best indicators of quality. Look for light to reddish pink meat. Avoid anything really pale or grayish. The fat should be creamy white and smooth. The texture should be firm to the touch, with a fine, smooth grain. If it is soft or watery, reject it. If the pork is packaged, it should not have much moisture in the package. Any liquid there should be clear, not cloudy.

Preparing a Pork Tenderloin

REAL GRILLING 101

1. The first step is to remove the sinewy layer on the surface called silver skin.

2. Slip the tip of a sharp, thin knife under one end of the silver skin.

3. Grab the loosened end with your fingertips. Then slide the knife away from you just underneath the silver skin.

4. Continue cutting away from you, with the knife blade angled slightly upwards.

5. The "cleaned" tenderloins should have hardly any visible silver skin or surface fat.

6. For great flavor, make a paste of oil, garlic, herbs, lemon zest, and spices. Press it into the meat before grilling.

Peeling Pork Ribs

Spareribs and baby back ribs [shown here] have a thin, tough membrane attached to the bone side. Use a blunt tool, such as a flathead screwdriver, to get under the membrane and remove it so seasonings and sauces can penetrate. Slide the tool under the membrane right over one of the bones. Gradually work the tool down the bone.

When the tool is about half-way down the bone, stretch the membrane up to open up a flap. It's okay if the membrane breaks at this point. Use a paper towel to get a good grip and then peel the membrane off the ribs.

When Is It Done? Think Pink!

The USDA recommends that pork is cooked to well-done [170°F], but most chefs today cook it to 150°F or 160°F, when it still has some pink in the center and all the juices haven't been driven out. Of course, the doneness you choose is entirely up to you.

The pork chop on the left, with raw meat in the center, is clearly undercooked. The chop on the right, with a dry, gray appearance, is overcooked. The chop in the middle, with a little bit of pink in the center, is cooked to 150°F [just right]. See how the meat gives a little under pressure.

Grilling Guide for Pork

Type	Thickness/Weight	Approximate Grilling Time
Bratwurst, fresh		**20 to 25 minutes** Direct Medium
Bratwurst, pre-cooked		**10 to 12 minutes** Direct Medium
Pork chop, boneless or bone-in	½ inch thick	**5 to 7 minutes** Direct High
	¾ inch thick	**6 to 8 minutes** Direct High
	1 inch thick	**8 to 10 minutes** Direct Medium
	1¼ to 1½ inches thick	**10 to 12 minutes;** sear **6 minutes** Direct High, grill **4 to 6 minutes** Indirect Medium
Loin roast, boneless	2½ pounds	**40 to 45 minutes** Direct Medium
Loin roast, bone-in	3 to 5 pounds	**1¼ to 1¾ hours** Indirect Medium
Pork shoulder (Boston Butt), boneless	5 to 6 pounds	**3½ to 4 hours** Direct Low
Pork, ground	½ inch thick	**8 to 10 minutes** Direct Medium
Ribs, baby back	1½ to 2 pounds	**1½ to 2 hours** Indirect Low
Ribs, spareribs	3 to 5 pounds	**2½ to 3 hours** Indirect Low
Ribs, country-style, boneless	1½ to 2 pounds	**12 to 15 minutes** Direct Medium
Ribs, country-style, bone-in	3 to 4 pounds	**1½ to 2 hours** Indirect Medium
Tenderloin, whole	¾ to 1 pound	**15 to 20 minutes** Direct Medium

Pork Rib Chops

with Memphis Dry Rub and Sassy Barbecue Sauce

PREP TIME: 15 MINUTES
GRILLING TIME: 8 TO 10 MINUTES

SAUCE

- ½ cup ketchup
- 2 tablespoons molasses
- 1 tablespoon white wine vinegar
- 1 tablespoon Dijon mustard
- 1 tablespoon light brown sugar
- 2 teaspoons Worcestershire sauce
- ½ teaspoon kosher salt
- ¼ teaspoon Tabasco® sauce
- ¼ teaspoon granulated garlic
- ¼ teaspoon freshly ground black pepper

RUB

- 1½ teaspoons whole black peppercorns
- 1½ teaspoons mustard seed
- 1½ teaspoons paprika
- 1½ teaspoons light brown sugar
- 1½ teaspoons kosher salt
- 1 teaspoon granulated garlic
- 1 teaspoon granulated onion
- ¼ teaspoon ground cayenne pepper

- 6 bone-in pork rib chops, 10 to 12 ounces each and about 1 inch thick
  Canola oil

1. To make the sauce: In a small heavy-bottom saucepan, whisk the sauce ingredients with ½ cup water. Bring to boil over medium heat, then reduce the heat and simmer for 10 minutes, stirring occasionally.
2. To make the rub: In a spice grinder, pulse the peppercorns and the mustard seed until coarsely ground. Place in a small bowl and add the remaining rub ingredients, mixing well.
3. Allow the chops to stand at room temperature for 20 to 30 minutes before grilling. Lightly brush or spray the chops on both sides with oil and season with the rub, pressing the spices into the meat. Grill over *Direct Medium* heat until barely pink in the center of the meat, 8 to 10 minutes, turning once. Remove from the grill and let rest for 3 to 5 minutes. Serve warm with the sauce on the side.

MAKES 6 SERVINGS

You could substitute boneless pork chops here, but you will get more flavor from bone-in chops. The cooked bone adds its own richness, plus the meat along the bone is naturally sweeter and juicier.

White Wine-Marinated Rib Chops
with Roasted Corn and Red Peppers

PREP TIME: 15 MINUTES
MARINATING TIME: 2 HOURS
GRILLING TIME: 18 TO 23 MINUTES

MARINADE
- ½ cup dry white wine
- ¼ cup extra virgin olive oil
- ¼ cup roughly chopped fresh thyme
- 1 tablespoon minced garlic
- 2 teaspoons kosher salt
- 1 teaspoon freshly ground black pepper

- 4 bone-in pork rib chops, each about ¾ inch thick

SALSA
- 2 medium red bell peppers
- 2 medium ears corn
  Extra virgin olive oil
- 2 tablespoons finely chopped fresh Italian parsley
- 2 teaspoons sherry vinegar
- ¼ teaspoon kosher salt
- ⅛ teaspoon freshly ground black pepper

1. To make the marinade: In a medium bowl, whisk the marinade ingredients.
2. Put the chops in a large, resealable plastic bag and pour in the marinade. Press the air out of the bag, seal it tightly, and turn several times to evenly distribute the marinade. Put the bag on a large plate and refrigerate for 2 hours, turning once or twice.
3. To make the salsa: Grill the bell peppers over *Direct Medium* heat until they are blackened and blistered all over, 12 to 15 minutes, turning occasionally. At the same time, lightly brush or spray the corn with oil and grill over *Direct Medium* heat until browned in spots, 10 to 12 minutes, turning occasionally. Place the peppers in a medium bowl and cover with plastic to trap the steam. Set aside for at least 10 minutes, then peel the skins from the peppers, discard the stems and seeds, and cut into ¼-inch dice. When the corn is cool enough to handle, use a sharp knife to cut the kernels off the cobs. In a medium bowl, mix the peppers and corn with the remaining salsa ingredients.
4. Allow the chops to stand at room temperature for 20 to 30 minutes before grilling. Remove the chops from the bag, wipe off most of the marinade with paper towels, and discard the marinade. Grill over *Direct High* heat until barely pink in the center of the meat, 6 to 8 minutes, turning once. Let rest for 3 to 5 minutes. Serve warm with the salsa.

MAKES 4 SERVINGS

Brined Rosemary Pork Chops

Texas Two-Step Pork Chops

PREP TIME: 10 MINUTES
MARINATING TIME: 4 TO 6 HOURS
GRILLING TIME: 8 TO 10 MINUTES

BRINE
- 3 tablespoons kosher salt
- 3 tablespoons light brown sugar
- 3 whole branches fresh rosemary
- 2 tablespoons extra virgin olive oil
- 2 tablespoons balsamic vinegar
- 1 teaspoon freshly ground black pepper

- 4 bone-in pork rib chops, each about 1 inch thick
  Extra virgin olive oil

1. To make the brine: In a medium bowl, combine the salt and sugar. Pour 1 cup of hot water into the bowl and whisk to dissolve the salt and sugar. Add 2 cups of cold water along with the remaining brine ingredients.
2. Place the chops in a large, resealable plastic bag and pour in the brine. Press the air out of the bag and seal tightly. Turn the bag to distribute the brine, place the bag in a bowl, and refrigerate for 4 to 6 hours.
3. Remove the pork chops from the bag and pat dry with paper towels. Discard the brine. Allow to stand at room temperature for 20 to 30 minutes before grilling. Lightly brush or spray both sides of the chops with oil. Grill over *Direct Medium* heat until barely pink in the center of the meat, 8 to 10 minutes, turning once. Let rest for 3 to 5 minutes. Serve warm.

MAKES 4 SERVINGS

PREP TIME: 10 MINUTES
MARINATING TIME: 2 TO 4 HOURS
GRILLING TIME: 8 TO 10 MINUTES

MARINADE
- 1/4 cup ketchup
- 2 tablespoons apple juice
- 2 tablespoons extra virgin olive oil
- 2 tablespoons red wine vinegar
- 1 tablespoon Worcestershire sauce
- 2 teaspoons minced garlic
- 1 teaspoon Tabasco® sauce
- 1 teaspoon prepared chili powder
- 1/2 teaspoon kosher salt

- 6 bone-in pork rib chops, each about 1 inch thick

1. To make the marinade: In a medium bowl, whisk the marinade ingredients.
2. Place the chops in a large, resealable plastic bag and pour in the marinade. Press the air out of the bag and seal it tightly. Turn the bag several times to distribute the marinade, and refrigerate for 2 to 4 hours.
3. Remove the chops from the bag and discard the marinade. Allow the chops to stand at room temperature for 20 to 30 minutes before grilling. Grill over *Direct Medium* heat until barely pink in the center of the meat, 8 to 10 minutes, turning once. Let rest for 3 to 5 minutes. Serve warm.

MAKES 6 SERVINGS

West Indies Pork Chops
with Black Bean-Mango Salsa

PREP TIME: 15 MINUTES
MARINATING TIME: 1 TO 2 HOURS
GRILLING TIME: 6 TO 8 MINUTES

SALSA
- 1 cup canned black beans, rinsed
- 1 large mango, about 1 pound, cut into ¼-inch dice
- ¼ cup thinly sliced scallions, white and light green parts only
- 3 tablespoons finely chopped fresh basil
- 1 tablespoon extra virgin olive oil
- 2 teaspoons fresh lime juice
- ¼ teaspoon kosher salt
- ⅛ teaspoon freshly ground black pepper
- ⅛ teaspoon ground cumin
- ⅛ teaspoon pure chile powder

RUB
- 1 teaspoon light brown sugar
- 1 teaspoon granulated garlic
- 1 teaspoon dried thyme
- ¾ teaspoon kosher salt
- ¼ teaspoon freshly ground black pepper
- ¼ teaspoon ground allspice

- 4 bone-in pork rib chops, about 8 ounces each and ¾ inch thick
  Extra virgin olive oil

1. To make the salsa: In a medium bowl, mix the salsa ingredients. Let stand at room temperature for 1 to 2 hours.

2. To make the rub: In a small bowl, mix the rub ingredients with your fingertips. Allow the chops to stand at room temperature for 20 to 30 minutes before grilling. Lightly brush or spray the chops on both sides with oil and season with the rub. Grill over *Direct High* heat until barely pink in the center of the meat, 6 to 8 minutes, turning once or twice. Remove from the grill and let rest for 3 to 5 minutes. Serve warm with the salsa.

MAKES 4 SERVINGS

Hoisin-Glazed Pork Chops
with Plum Sauce

PREP TIME: 15 MINUTES
MARINATING TIME: 4 TO 6 HOURS
GRILLING TIME: 8 TO 10 MINUTES

MARINADE
- ½ cup hoisin sauce
- 2 tablespoons red wine vinegar
- 1 tablespoon canola oil
- 2 teaspoons minced garlic
- 1 teaspoon grated ginger
- 1 teaspoon Tabasco® sauce
- 1 teaspoon dark sesame oil

- 4 bone-in pork rib chops, each about 1 inch thick

SAUCE
- ¼ cup plum sauce
- 1 tablespoon Dijon mustard
- 2 teaspoons granulated sugar

1. To make the marinade: In a medium bowl, whisk the marinade ingredients.
2. Place the chops in a large, resealable plastic bag and pour in the marinade. Press the air out of the bag and seal it tightly. Turn the bag several times to distribute the marinade, and refrigerate for 4 to 6 hours.
3. To make the sauce: In a small bowl, whisk the sauce ingredients along with 2 tablespoons of water.
4. Allow the chops to stand at room temperature for 20 to 30 minutes before grilling. Remove the chops from the bag and discard the marinade. Grill over *Direct Medium* heat until barely pink in the center of the meat, 8 to 10 minutes, turning once. Remove from grill and let rest 3 to 5 minutes. Serve warm with the sauce on the side for dipping.

MAKES 4 SERVINGS

Coffee-Crusted Pork Chops
with Bourbon Cream Sauce

PREP TIME: 15 MINUTES
GRILLING TIME: 8 TO 10 MINUTES

SAUCE
  1 tablespoon butter
  1/4 cup finely chopped yellow onion
  1 teaspoon minced garlic
  1/4 cup bourbon
  1 cup low-sodium beef stock
  6 tablespoons heavy cream
  1 teaspoon finely chopped fresh thyme
     Kosher salt
     Freshly ground black pepper

RUB
  1 teaspoon finely ground dark-roasted coffee
  1 teaspoon finely chopped fresh thyme
  1 teaspoon kosher salt
  1/2 teaspoon freshly ground black pepper

  4 boneless pork loin chops, about 1 inch thick
     Extra virgin olive oil

1. To make the sauce: In a medium saucepan over medium-high heat, melt the butter. Add the onion and cook until tender, about 3 minutes, stirring occasionally to prevent browning. Add the garlic and cook for 1 minute more, stirring occasionally. Remove the saucepan from the heat, carefully add the bourbon, and return the saucepan to the heat [watch out; it might flame]. Once the flame subsides, reduce the heat to medium and add the beef stock and cream. Simmer until about 1/3 cup liquid remains, 15 to 20 minutes, stirring occasionally [times will vary depending on the diameter of your pan]. Add the thyme. Season with salt and pepper to taste.

2. To make the rub: In a small bowl, mix the rub ingredients with your fingertips.

3. Allow the chops to stand at room temperature for 20 to 30 minutes before grilling. Lightly brush or spray both sides of the chops with oil and season evenly with the rub, pressing the spices into the meat. Grill over *Direct Medium* heat until barely pink in the center of the meat, 8 to 10 minutes, turning once. Remove from the grill and let rest 3 to 5 minutes. Bring the sauce to a simmer and serve warm with the chops.

MAKES 4 SERVINGS

Pita Sandwiches with Pork Cutlets
and Tahini Sauce

PREP TIME: 15 MINUTES
GRILLING TIME: 2 MINUTES

SAUCE
- ¹/₃ cup tahini
- 2 tablespoons fresh lemon juice
- 2 tablespoons finely chopped fresh basil
- 1 teaspoon honey
- ¹/₂ teaspoon dried oregano
- ¹/₂ teaspoon kosher salt
- ¹/₄ teaspoon granulated garlic
- ¹/₄ teaspoon freshly ground black pepper

RUB
- ¹/₂ teaspoon pure chile powder
- ¹/₂ teaspoon freshly ground black pepper
- ¹/₂ teaspoon kosher salt
- ¹/₂ teaspoon ground cumin
- ¹/₂ teaspoon dried oregano
- ¹/₄ teaspoon granulated garlic

- 4 boneless pork loin chops, 5 to 6 ounces each
  Extra virgin olive oil
- 4 pitas [6 inches], cut in half
- 2 cups thinly sliced Romaine lettuce
- 1 cup roughly chopped ripe tomato
- 1 cup thinly sliced cucumber

1. To make the sauce: In a medium bowl, mix the sauce ingredients with ¹/₃ cup water until smooth.
2. To make the rub: In a small bowl, mix the rub ingredients with your fingertips.
3. Place the chops between two large sheets of plastic wrap. Using a mallet or rolling pin, lightly pound the chops into ¹/₄-inch-thick cutlets. Allow the cutlets to stand at room temperature for 20 to 30 minutes before grilling. Lightly brush or spray both sides of the cutlets with oil and season with the rub. Grill over *Direct High* heat for 2 minutes, turning once. Transfer the cutlets to a cutting board and cut each in half. Fill each pita half with pork, lettuce, tomatoes, and cucumber. Spoon the sauce inside. Serve warm.

MAKES 4 SERVINGS

Grilled Pork Burritos
with Fresh Tomato Salsa

PREP TIME: 30 MINUTES
GRILLING TIME: 5 TO 7 MINUTES

SALSA
½ cup finely diced white onion
1½ cups finely diced ripe tomatoes
2 tablespoons finely chopped fresh cilantro
1 tablespoon extra virgin olive oil
2 teaspoons fresh lime juice
1 teaspoon minced jalapeño chile pepper
¼ teaspoon dried oregano
¼ teaspoon kosher salt
¼ teaspoon freshly ground black pepper

RUB
½ teaspoon pure chile powder
½ teaspoon granulated garlic
½ teaspoon paprika
½ teaspoon kosher salt
¼ teaspoon ground coriander
¼ teaspoon ground cumin
¼ teaspoon freshly ground black pepper

2 pounds bone-in pork shoulder steaks, each about ½ inch thick
Extra virgin olive oil
1 can [16 ounces] refried beans
4 flour tortillas [10 inches]
⅓ cup sour cream

1. To make the salsa: Rinse the onion in a sieve under cold water. In a medium bowl, mix the onions with the remaining salsa ingredients. Allow salsa to stand at room temperature and drain in a sieve just before serving.

2. To make the rub: In a small bowl, mix the rub ingredients. Allow the pork to stand at room temperature for 20 to 30 minutes before grilling. Lightly brush or spray with oil and season with the rub.

3. In a medium saucepan over low heat, warm the beans for about 10 minutes, stirring occasionally.

4. Grill the pork over *Direct Medium* heat until the meat is firm and no longer pink in the center, 5 to 7 minutes, turning once. Cut into thin strips. Grill the tortillas over *Direct Medium* heat until lightly marked and warm, about 30 seconds per side. Lay the tortillas on a work surface. Spoon the refried beans in the center of each tortilla, spreading them to within 1 inch of the edge. Evenly divide the pork and salsa over the beans. Spoon some sour cream on top. Fold the bottom edge of each tortilla up and over the filling. Fold in the opposite sides just until they meet in the center. Roll up from the bottom. Serve warm.

MAKES 4 SERVINGS

▲▲▲

If I had just one meat to eat for the rest of my life, it would be pork. If I had to pick just one cut of pork, I'd probably say shoulder steaks, which are also called blade steaks. When they are grilled right, the meat is amazingly rich and succulent. Oh, by the way, these steaks are really inexpensive.

▼▼▼

Beer-Bathed Brats
with Sauerkraut and Apples

PREP TIME: 10 MINUTES
GRILLING TIME: ABOUT 25 MINUTES

 5 fresh bratwurst, preferably Johnsonville®
 1 small yellow onion
 1 small Granny Smith apple
 ½ pound sauerkraut, rinsed and drained
 1 bottle [12 ounces] beer, at room temperature
 3 tablespoons spicy brown mustard
 1 teaspoon caraway seed [optional]
 5 hot dog buns

1. In a heavy-duty foil pan, arrange the bratwurst in a single layer. Peel the onion and trim off the ends. Cut the onion in half lengthwise, then cut each half lengthwise into ⅛-inch slices. Core and quarter the apple, and cut lengthwise into ⅛-inch slices. Scatter the onions, apples, and sauerkraut over the bratwurst.
2. In a medium bowl, mix the beer, mustard, and caraway seed, if using. Add the beer mixture to the pan. Grill over *Direct Medium* heat for about 20 minutes, turning the bratwurst 2 or 3 times. Remove the bratwurst from the pan but leave the pan where it is to continue to cook the sauerkraut mixture. Grill the bratwurst over *Direct Medium* heat until nicely browned, 2 to 3 minutes, turning once. Serve the bratwurst warm in hot dog buns with the sauerkraut mixture. Serve more mustard on top, if desired.

MAKES 5 SERVINGS

Brats
with Glazed Red Onions

PREP TIME: 5 MINUTES
MARINATING TIME: 2 TO 4 HOURS
GRILLING TIME: 10 TO 12 MINUTES

 1 tablespoon extra virgin olive oil
 1 tablespoon balsamic vinegar
 ½ teaspoon dried thyme
 ½ teaspoon kosher salt
 ¼ teaspoon freshly ground black pepper
 2 medium red onions, cut crosswise into
   ½-inch slices
 5 smoked and pre-cooked bratwurst, preferably Johnsonville®
 5 hot dog rolls
   Mustard

1. In a large dish or platter, mix the oil, vinegar, thyme, salt, and pepper. Add the onions and gently turn the slices over in the oil mixture, being careful to keep them from falling apart. Set aside to marinate at room temperature for 2 to 4 hours.
2. Grill the onions and brats over *Direct Medium* heat until the onions are tender and the brats are browned, 10 to 12 minutes, turning occasionally. Serve the brats warm inside the rolls and arrange the onions on top. Pass the mustard.

MAKES 5 SERVINGS

Skewered Pork
and Peppers

PREP TIME: 10 MINUTES
GRILLING TIME: 4 TO 6 MINUTES

PASTE
  2 tablespoons extra virgin olive oil
  2 teaspoons Dijon mustard
  1 teaspoon paprika
  ½ teaspoon granulated garlic
  ½ teaspoon light brown sugar
  ½ teaspoon kosher salt
  ¼ teaspoon freshly ground black pepper

1¼ pounds boneless pork sirloin, cut into
      ¾-inch cubes
  2 large red bell peppers, cut into ¾-inch squares

1. To make the paste: In a medium bowl, combine
the paste ingredients and mix until smooth. Add
the pork to the bowl and stir to coat evenly. Allow
to stand at room temperature for 10 to 15 minutes
before grilling.
2. Thread the pork and peppers on skewers, alternating the ingredients. Grill over *Direct High* heat
until the pork is barely pink in the center, 4 to 6
minutes, turning once. Serve warm.

MAKES 4 TO 6 SERVINGS

Southwest Pork Kabobs
with Grape Tomatoes

PREP TIME: 20 MINUTES
MARINATING TIME: 1 HOUR
GRILLING TIME: 6 TO 8 MINUTES

MARINADE
  ½ cup fresh orange juice
  3 tablespoons extra virgin olive oil
  2 tablespoons red wine vinegar
  1 tablespoon minced garlic
  2 teaspoons pure chile powder
1½ teaspoons dried oregano
  1 teaspoon ground cumin
  1 teaspoon kosher salt
  ½ teaspoon freshly ground black pepper
  ½ teaspoon ground cinnamon

  2 pounds boneless pork sirloin, cut into
      1-inch cubes
  1 pint [12 to 16] grape or cherry tomatoes
  1 lime, cut into quarters
  2 tablespoons finely chopped fresh cilantro

1. To make the marinade: In a medium bowl, whisk
the marinade ingredients.
2. Put the pork in a large, resealable plastic bag and
pour in the marinade. Press the air out of the bag
and seal tightly. Turn the bag to distribute the marinade, place in a bowl, and refrigerate for 1 hour.
3. Remove the pork from the bag and discard the
marinade. Thread the pork and tomatoes onto
skewers, alternating the ingredients. Grill over
Direct High heat until the pork is barely pink in
the center and the tomatoes are very soft, 6 to 8
minutes, turning once or twice. Top with a squeeze
of lime juice and the cilantro. Serve warm.

MAKES 4 SERVINGS

Pork and Mango Skewers
with Vietnamese Dipping Sauce

PREP TIME: 20 MINUTES
GRILLING TIME: 8 TO 10 MINUTES

SAUCE
- 3 tablespoons fresh lime juice
- 2 tablespoons fish sauce
- 2 tablespoons granulated sugar
- 1 teaspoon freshly grated ginger
- 1 teaspoon hot chili-garlic sauce, such as sriracha

RUB
- 1 teaspoon ground cumin
- 1 teaspoon kosher salt
- ½ teaspoon ground coriander
- ½ teaspoon granulated sugar
- ¼ teaspoon five-spice powder
- ¼ teaspoon ground cayenne pepper

- 1½ pounds boneless pork sirloin, cut into 1½-inch cubes
- 1 tablespoon vegetable oil
- 4 ripe mangoes, cut into 1-inch chunks
- 6 green onions, white and light green parts only, cut into 1-inch lengths

1. To make the sauce: In a small bowl, whisk the sauce ingredients.

2. To make the rub: In a medium bowl, mix the rub ingredients with your fingertips. Add the pork and mix well to coat the pork thoroughly. Add the oil to lightly coat the pork. Allow to stand at room temperature for 10 to 15 minutes before grilling.

3. Thread the pork, mangoes, and green onions alternately on skewers, leaving a little room between the ingredients. Grill over *Direct High* heat until the pork is barely pink in the center, 8 to 10 minutes, turning once. Place the skewers on a platter and spoon about half the sauce over the top. Serve warm with the remaining sauce on the side.

MAKES 4 SERVINGS

Scallop and Hot Italian Sausage Kabobs

PREP TIME: 20 MINUTES
GRILLING TIME: 4 TO 6 MINUTES

- 4 hot Italian sausage links, about ¾ pound
- 1 medium red onion
- 2 tablespoons extra virgin olive oil, divided
- 2 tablespoons white wine vinegar
- ½ teaspoon dried oregano
- ¼ teaspoon kosher salt
- ⅛ teaspoon freshly ground black pepper
- 16 large sea scallops, about 1 pound

1. Use a fork to pierce the sausages in several places and put them in a large skillet. Cut the onion in quarters through the stem end. Cut each quarter in half crosswise. Add the onions to the skillet along with 1 tablespoon of the oil and ¼ cup of water. Bring the water to a boil over high heat. Lower the heat to medium and cook until the water has evaporated and the juices from the sausages are browning in the skillet, 10 to 12 minutes, turning the sausages and onions occasionally. Remove the sausages and onions. Add the vinegar to the skillet and stir to scrape up the brown bits. Pour the brown bits and vinegar into a medium bowl. Add the remaining 1 tablespoon of oil, the oregano, salt, and pepper.

2. Rinse the scallops and pat dry. Remove the small, tough side muscle from any scallops that still have it. Add the scallops to the vinegar mixture and toss to coat. Cut the sausages into 1-inch pieces. Thread the scallops and sausages through their sides onto skewers, alternating them with pieces of onion.

3. Grill the kabobs over *Direct Medium* heat until the scallops and sausages are browned and cooked through, 4 to 6 minutes, turning once. Serve warm.

MAKES 4 SERVINGS

Linguine with Hot Italian Sausages

PREP TIME: 15 MINUTES
GRILLING TIME: 6 TO 10 MINUTES

SAUCE
2 tablespoons extra virgin olive oil
½ medium yellow onion, finely chopped
2 medium garlic cloves, thinly sliced
¼ cup shredded carrot
1 teaspoon dried oregano
1 can [28 ounces] peeled whole tomatoes
½ teaspoon kosher salt
¼ teaspoon freshly ground black pepper
4 hot Italian sausages, about 4 ounces each and 1 inch thick
¼ cup finely chopped fresh basil

1 pound linguine

1 cup toasted bread crumbs [optional]

1. To make the sauce: In a medium saucepan over medium heat, warm the oil. Add the onion and garlic. Cook for 5 minutes, stirring occasionally. Add the carrot and oregano. Cook for 5 more minutes, stirring occasionally. Over a large bowl, crush the tomatoes in your hands and add them, along with all the juices, to the saucepan. Season with the salt and pepper. Simmer for 10 minutes, stirring occasionally to break apart any large pieces of tomato.
2. Grill the sausages over *Direct Medium* heat until no longer pink in the center, 6 to 10 minutes, turning occasionally. Slice them thinly crosswise and then roughly chop them. Add the sausages and basil to the saucepan. Stir. Keep warm.
3. In a large pot of boiling salted water, cook the linguine until barely tender. Drain the linguine and return it to the pot. Add the sauce. Stir to combine. Cover the pot for 1 minute to allow the pasta to absorb some sauce. Sprinkle toasted bread crumbs on top, if desired. Serve warm.

MAKES 4 TO 6 SERVINGS

Sausage, Pepper, and Onion Hero Sandwiches

PREP TIME: 10 MINUTES
GRILLING TIME: 14 TO 20 MINUTES

DRESSING
- ⅓ cup extra virgin olive oil
- 3 tablespoons red wine vinegar
- 1 tablespoon finely chopped fresh oregano
- 1 teaspoon minced garlic
- 1 teaspoon kosher salt
- ¼ teaspoon freshly ground black pepper

- 4 large Italian frying peppers [also called Cuban peppers]
- 1 large yellow onion
- 4 large sweet or hot Italian sausage links, about 1¼ pounds total, slit down one side and opened like a book
- 4 long hero rolls

1. To make the dressing: In a large bowl, whisk the dressing ingredients.
2. Cut each pepper in half lengthwise. Remove and discard the seeds and stems. Cut the onion crosswise into ½-inch thick slices. Lightly brush the peppers and onions with the dressing. Grill over *Direct Medium* heat until tender, 8 to 12 minutes, turning occasionally.
3. When the onions are cool enough to handle, cut each slice into quarters, separating the rings. Remove and discard the large pieces of blackened skin from the peppers. Cut the peppers into 2- to 3-inch pieces. Add the peppers and onion rings to the remaining dressing and toss to coat.
4. Grill the sausages over *Direct Medium* heat until golden brown and fully cooked, 6 to 8 minutes, turning occasionally. Grill the rolls until lightly toasted, 30 to 60 seconds.
5. Place a sausage on one side of each roll. Top with peppers and onions, distributing them equally. Drizzle any remaining dressing on the other side of each roll. Serve warm.

MAKES 4 SERVINGS

Honey-Dijon Glazed Ham
and Pineapple Brochettes

PREP TIME: 10 MINUTES
GRILLING TIME: 10 TO 12 MINUTES

GLAZE
- 1 tablespoon honey
- 1 tablespoon Dijon mustard
- 2 teaspoons fresh lemon juice
- 2 tablespoons extra virgin olive oil

- 1 center-cut smoked ham steak, about 1¼ pounds and 1 inch thick
- 5 slices fresh pineapple, cut to the same thickness as the ham
- ½ teaspoon kosher salt
- ¼ teaspoon ground cayenne pepper
- 2 green onions, white and some light green parts only, thinly sliced on the bias

1. To make the glaze: In a small bowl, whisk the honey, mustard, and lemon juice. In a steady stream whisk in the olive oil and then 1 teaspoon of lukewarm water.
2. Cut the ham into 1-inch cubes [you should have about 24 pieces]. Cut each slice of pineapple into quarters and trim the tough core from each piece. Sprinkle the pineapple with the salt. Thread the ham and pineapple alternately on skewers. Season both sides of the brochettes with the cayenne. Grill over *Direct Medium* heat until well marked and warm, 10 to 12 minutes, turning once. Spoon the glaze over the brochettes and garnish with the green onions. Serve warm.

MAKES 6 SERVINGS

Mustard-Molasses Glazed Ham

PREP TIME: 10 MINUTES
GRILLING TIME: 3 TO 3½ HOURS

GLAZE
- ½ cup stone ground mustard
- ¼ cup unsulphured dark molasses
- ¼ cup fresh orange juice
- 1 teaspoon ground ginger
- ¼ teaspoon ground cloves

- 1 bone-in, partially cooked, smoked ham [butt end], about 10 pounds

1. To make the glaze: In a small saucepan, combine the glaze ingredients. Bring the glaze to a simmer over medium-high heat, stirring occasionally. Simmer for 1 minute, and then remove the pan from the heat.
2. Allow the ham to stand at room temperature for 30 minutes before grilling. Score the ham by making crosshatches about 1 inch apart and ½ inch deep over the entire surface, except on the flat side. Place the ham, flat side down, in a disposable aluminum pan. Grill over *Indirect Medium* heat for 1 hour. Brush the glaze over the entire surface of the ham, except on the flat side. Continue to grill until the internal temperature reaches 160°F, 2 to 2½ hours more.
3. Transfer the ham to a cutting board and loosely cover with foil. Let rest for about 15 minutes. Slice and serve warm or at room temperature.

MAKES 10 TO 12 SERVINGS

Tequila-Marinated Ham Steaks

PREP TIME: 10 MINUTES
MARINATING TIME: 4 TO 6 HOURS
GRILLING TIME: 12 MINUTES

MARINADE
½ cup tequila
2 tablespoons fresh lime juice
1 cup fresh orange juice
3 tablespoons light brown sugar, divided
2 teaspoons ground cumin
1 jalapeño chile pepper, cut into ⅛-inch slices

2 bone-in ham steaks, about 1 pound each

1. To make the marinade: In a small bowl, combine the tequila, lime juice, orange juice, 2 tablespoons of the brown sugar, cumin, and jalapeño. Stir until the sugar is dissolved.
2. Place the ham steaks in a large, resealable plastic bag and pour in the marinade. Press the air out of the bag and seal tightly. Turn the bag to distribute the marinade and place in a baking dish, making sure the jalapeños are evenly distributed over both steaks. Refrigerate for 4 to 6 hours, turning the steaks once. Allow the steaks to stand at room temperature for 20 to 30 minutes before grilling.
3. Remove the steaks and the jalapeños from the marinade and reserve the marinade. Pour the marinade and a few of the jalapeño slices into a small saucepan. Bring to a boil and boil for 1 full minute. Set aside ½ cup of the liquid for basting the ham. To the remaining liquid, add the remaining 1 tablespoon brown sugar. Reduce the heat to medium and cook the liquid until it has reduced to about ⅓ cup, about 5 minutes.
4. Nick the edges of the ham steaks, making small cuts through the fat every 2 to 3 inches around the perimeter. Grill over *Direct Medium* heat until the ham is nicely marked and crispy on the edges, about 12 minutes, turning once. Brush with some of the reserved marinade after turning.
5. Transfer the ham to a cutting board and cut into serving-size pieces. Drizzle the reduced marinade over the top and garnish with jalapeños. Serve warm.

MAKES 4 TO 6 SERVINGS

Pork Tenderloin and Bacon
with Stewed White Beans

PREP TIME: 30 MINUTES
GRILLING TIME: ABOUT 20 MINUTES

2 teaspoons fennel seed
1/2 teaspoon kosher salt
1/2 teaspoon freshly ground black pepper
2 pork tenderloins, about 1 pound each
12 slices thinly sliced bacon, about 3/4 pound

BEANS

4 ripe plum tomatoes, about 1 pound, cored
2 tablespoons extra virgin olive oil
1/2 cup finely diced yellow onion
1 tablespoon minced garlic
1/4 teaspoon red pepper flakes [optional]
2 cans [15 ounces each] cannellini beans, rinsed

1/4 cup lightly packed torn fresh basil leaves

1. In a small skillet over low heat, toast the fennel seed until the aroma is apparent, 3 to 5 minutes, shaking the skillet occasionally. Crush the fennel seed in a spice grinder or on a cutting board by grinding the seeds under a heavy pan. In a small bowl, combine the fennel with the salt and pepper.

2. Trim any excess fat and silver skin from the tenderloins [see page 126]. Cut the tenderloins into pieces about 1 1/2 inches long. Season them with the fennel mixture. Gently press down on each piece to form a disc the same thickness as the width of the bacon. Wrap a piece of bacon around each piece of pork and secure with a toothpick. The bacon should overlap at the ends by no more than 1 inch. Allow to stand at room temperature for 10 to 15 minutes before grilling.

3. To prepare the beans: Grill the tomatoes over *Direct Medium* heat until the skins are loosened, 6 to 8 minutes, turning occasionally. Cut the tomatoes into 1-inch chunks. In a medium saucepan over medium heat, warm the oil, then cook the onion, garlic, and pepper flakes until softened, about 3 minutes, stirring occasionally. Add the tomatoes and beans, stir to combine, and season to taste with salt and pepper. When the beans come to a boil, reduce the heat and simmer for 15 minutes.

4. Grill the pork over *Direct Medium* heat until the pork is barely pink in the center and the bacon is fully cooked, 12 to 15 minutes, turning once [if flare-ups occur, move the pork temporarily to *Indirect Medium* heat]. Add the basil to the beans. Serve the pork warm with the beans.

MAKES 4 TO 6 SERVINGS

The fattiness of bacon has a tendency to flare-up, so use just enough to wrap around each piece of tenderloin once, overlapping the ends by one inch or less. I like the bacon crisp, so after searing the tenderloin on the cut sides, I roll the bacon directly on the grate.

Pork and Mushroom Skewers
with Basil Sauce

PREP TIME: 15 MINUTES
GRILLING TIME: 5 TO 6 MINUTES

2 pork tenderloins, about 1 pound each
24 small cremini mushrooms, each 1 to 1½ inches across
¼ cup extra virgin olive oil
1 teaspoon kosher salt
1 teaspoon dried thyme
1 teaspoon celery salt
¼ teaspoon freshly ground black pepper

SAUCE
¼ cup finely chopped green onions
¼ cup finely chopped fresh basil
3 tablespoons extra virgin olive oil
1 tablespoon white wine vinegar
½ teaspoon minced garlic
¼ teaspoon kosher salt
⅛ teaspoon freshly ground black pepper

1. Trim any excess fat and silver skin from the tenderloins [see page 126]. Cut each tenderloin in half lengthwise, then cut each half into pieces about 1½ inches long. Trim the stem end from each mushroom. In a large bowl, whisk the oil, salt, thyme, celery salt, and pepper. Add the pork and mushrooms and toss to evenly coat them. Thread the pork and mushrooms onto skewers, alternating them and being careful to push the skewers slowly through the sides of the mushrooms to they don't split apart. Allow to stand at room temperature for 10 to 15 minutes before grilling.

2. Meanwhile, make the sauce: In a small bowl, whisk the sauce ingredients.

3. Grill the skewers over *Direct High* heat until the pork is barely pink in the center and the mushrooms are tender, 5 to 6 minutes, turning once. Spoon some sauce over the skewers. Serve warm.

MAKES 4 TO 6 SERVINGS

Pork Tenderloin
with East-West Barbecue Sauce

PREP TIME: 15 MINUTES
GRILLING TIME: 20 TO 25 MINUTES

SAUCE
  1 tablespoon dark sesame oil
  1/2 cup finely chopped yellow onion
  1/2 cup cola
  1/2 cup ketchup
  2 tablespoons soy sauce
  2 tablespoons fresh lemon juice
  1 teaspoon granulated garlic
  1 teaspoon dried oregano
  1/2 teaspoon dry mustard
  1/2 teaspoon Tabasco® sauce

  2 pork tenderloins, about 1 pound each
  2 tablespoons dark sesame oil
    Kosher salt
    Freshly ground black pepper

1. To make the sauce: In a medium saucepan over medium heat, warm the oil. Add the onion and cook until the onion begins to brown, 4 to 5 minutes, stirring occasionally. Add the remaining sauce ingredients and simmer for 5 to 10 minutes. Remove from the heat.

2. Allow the tenderloins to stand at room temperature for 20 to 30 minutes before grilling. Trim any excess fat and silver skin from the tenderloins [see page 126] and coat them evenly with the sesame oil. Season generously with salt and pepper. Grill over *Direct Medium* heat until well marked on two sides, about 5 minutes, turning once. Using a brush, cover the tenderloins with a thin coating of the sauce and continue to grill until the pork is barely pink in the center, 10 to 15 minutes, turning and basting with the remaining sauce every 5 minutes. Let rest for 3 to 5 minutes before slicing on the bias. Serve warm.

MAKES 4 SERVINGS

Jerk Pork Tenderloin
with Glazed Sweet Potatoes

PREP TIME: 15 MINUTES
MARINATING TIME: 2 TO 4 HOURS
GRILLING TIME: 15 TO 20 MINUTES

PASTE

- 8 green onions, white and light green parts only, coarsely chopped
- 1/4 cup canola oil
- 2 tablespoons roughly chopped fresh ginger
- 2 tablespoons fresh lime juice
- 2 large garlic cloves, crushed
- 1/2 small habañero chile pepper, stemmed and seeded
- 1 tablespoon ground allspice
- 1 teaspoon kosher salt
- 1/2 teaspoon dried thyme
- 1/4 teaspoon ground cinnamon
- 1/4 teaspoon freshly ground black pepper

- 2 pork tenderloins, about 1 pound each
  Grated zest of 2 limes
- 1/4 cup fresh lime juice
- 1/4 cup canola oil
- 2 tablespoons honey
- 1/2 teaspoon kosher salt
- 1/4 teaspoon freshly ground black pepper
- 2 large sweet potatoes, about 1 pound each

1. To make the paste: In a blender, combine the paste ingredients and process on high until smooth, about 2 minutes.

2. Trim any excess fat and silver skin from the tenderloins [see page 126]. Brush the paste over the meat; cover and refrigerate for 2 to 4 hours. Allow the tenderloins to stand at room temperature for 20 to 30 minutes before grilling.

3. In a small bowl, whisk the lime zest, lime juice, canola oil, honey, salt, and pepper. Peel the sweet potatoes, trim the ends and cut each potato into 1/2-inch slices. Brush the potatoes on both sides with the oil mixture.

4. Grill the tenderloins and potatoes over *Direct Medium* heat until the pork is barely pink in the center and the potatoes are easily pierced with a knife, 15 to 20 minutes, turning both and brushing them with the oil mixture about every 5 minutes. Let the pork rest for 3 to 5 minutes before slicing on the bias. Serve warm with the potatoes.

MAKES 4 TO 6 SERVINGS

▲▲▲▲▲▲▲▲▲▲▲▲▲▲▲▲▲▲▲▲▲▲▲▲▲▲▲▲▲▲▲▲▲▲▲▲▲▲

Jerk has nothing to do with the annoying guy at work. It refers to a seasoning blend made popular by cooks in Jamaica. Typically it includes chiles, thyme, garlic, onions, and allspice. If pork is seasoned or marinated with this potent blend and then grilled, it is called "jerk pork."

▼▼▼▼▼▼▼▼▼▼▼▼▼▼▼▼▼▼▼▼▼▼▼▼▼▼▼▼▼▼▼▼▼▼▼▼▼▼

Dry-Rubbed Pork Tenderloin
with Fire-Roasted Tomato Sauce

PREP TIME: 20 MINUTES
GRILLING TIME: 15 TO 20 MINUTES

SAUCE

  8 ripe plum tomatoes, stems removed
  1 jalapeño chile pepper, stem and seeds removed
1/2 cup tightly packed fresh basil leaves
1/3 cup roughly chopped red onion
1/4 cup tightly packed fresh cilantro leaves
  1 tablespoon fresh lime juice
  2 teaspoons minced garlic
    Kosher salt
    Freshly ground black pepper

RUB

  1 teaspoon paprika
  1 teaspoon dark brown sugar
  1 teaspoon kosher salt
1/2 teaspoon pure chile powder
1/2 teaspoon freshly ground black pepper
1/4 teaspoon ground allspice

  2 pork tenderloins, about 1 pound each
    Extra virgin olive oil

1. To make the sauce: Grill the tomatoes and jalapeño over *Direct High* heat until blackened and blistered in spots, turning as needed. The tomatoes will take 4 to 6 minutes and the jalapeño will take 2 to 3 minutes. Put the tomatoes and jalapeño in a food processor along with the remaining sauce ingredients, including salt and pepper to taste, and process until smooth. Transfer the sauce to a medium saucepan and bring to a boil. Reduce to a simmer and allow to cook until the sauce has thickened slightly, 5 to 10 minutes, stirring occasionally.
2. To make the rub: In a small bowl, mix the rub ingredients with your fingertips.
3. Trim any excess fat and silver skin from the tenderloins [see page 126]. Allow to stand at room temperature for 20 to 30 minutes before grilling. Lightly brush or spray with oil and spread the rub all over, pressing the spices into the meat.
4. Grill over *Direct Medium* heat until the pork is barely pink in the center, 15 to 20 minutes, turning every 5 minutes. Remove from the grill and let rest for 3 to 5 minutes before slicing. Serve warm with the sauce.

MAKES 4 SERVINGS

Orange-Glazed Rib Roast of Pork

PREP TIME: 30 MINUTES
MARINATING TIME: 8 TO 12 HOURS
GRILLING TIME: 1¹/₂ TO 1³/₄ HOURS

BRINE
1¹/₄ cups kosher salt
   6 tablespoons granulated sugar
      Grated zest from 1 orange
   4 bay leaves, crushed
   6 whole cloves
 ¹/₄ teaspoon crushed red pepper flakes

   1 eight-bone, center-cut rib roast of pork, about
      6 pounds, chine bone cracked, trimmed of
      excess fat

GLAZE
   3 cups orange juice
   1 tablespoon fresh rosemary leaves
   6 whole cloves
 ¹/₄ teaspoon crushed red pepper flakes
   1 teaspoon Worcestershire sauce

1. To make the brine: In a 6-quart pot, combine the brine ingredients with 3 quarts of water. Bring to a simmer over high heat, stirring to dissolve the salt and sugar. Remove from the heat and let cool to room temperature. Refrigerate the brine in the pot. When the brine is cold, put the roast in the pot. Cover and refrigerate for 8 to 12 hours, turning once or twice if the roast is not completely submerged.

2. To make the glaze: In a small saucepan, bring the orange juice, rosemary, cloves, and red pepper flakes to a boil and then simmer until about ³/₄ cup remains, 45 to 60 minutes. Strain into a bowl then add the Worcestershire sauce. The glaze can be made up to 2 days in advance.

3. Remove the roast from the pot and discard the brine. Allow to stand at room temperature for 1 hour before grilling. Sear the roast, fat side down first, over *Direct Medium* heat until golden brown, 15 to 20 minutes, turning once [watch for flare-ups]. Continue grilling over *Indirect Medium* heat, fat side up, until cooked to desired doneness, 1¹/₄ to 1¹/₂ hours longer for medium, basting the pork with the glaze occasionally. Transfer the roast to a cutting board, loosely cover with foil, and let rest 10 to 15 minutes before carving. Slice between each bone. Serve warm.

MAKES 8 SERVINGS

Pork Loin
with Roasted Garlic and Uptown Slaw

PREP TIME: 35 MINUTES
GRILLING TIME: 45 TO 60 MINUTES

DRESSING
 ½ cup garlic cloves
 ½ cup extra virgin olive oil
 2 tablespoons red wine vinegar
 2 tablespoons fresh thyme leaves
 1 teaspoon honey
 1 teaspoon kosher salt
 ½ teaspoon finely ground black pepper

SLAW
 2 cups thinly sliced green cabbage
 2 cups roughly chopped watercress sprigs
 2 cups thinly sliced radicchio

 1 boneless center-cut pork loin roast, about
   2 pounds
 1 teaspoon kosher salt
 ½ teaspoon ground fennel
 ½ teaspoon freshly ground black pepper

1. To make the dressing: In a medium saucepan, combine the garlic and oil. Bring to a simmer over medium heat, and then reduce the heat to low to maintain a slow sizzle. Cook the garlic until golden brown, about 15 minutes. With a slotted spoon, transfer the garlic to a food processor. Remove the pan from the heat to allow the oil to cool.

2. Meanwhile, make the slaw: In a medium bowl, mix the slaw ingredients.

3. Pour the cooled oil into the food processor and add the remaining dressing ingredients. Process until smooth. Pour enough of the dressing [about ¼ cup] over the slaw to lightly coat the ingredients. Mix well.

4. Allow the roast to stand at room temperature for 20 to 30 minutes before grilling. Season the roast all over with the salt, fennel, and pepper and then lightly brush all over with some of the remaining dressing.

5. Sear over *Direct Medium* heat until nicely browned, 16 to 20 minutes, turning occasionally [watch for flare-ups]. Move the roast over *Indirect Medium* heat and continue grilling until the internal temperature reaches 155°F, 30 to 40 minutes. Transfer to a cutting board and let rest for 5 to 10 minutes before carving. Serve warm with the slaw.

MAKES 4 TO 6 SERVINGS

▲▲

If radicchio is one of those vegetables you avoid because of its bitterness, I have a solution for you. After slicing it thin, soak it in ice water for twenty to thirty minutes. That will remove the bitterness and leave you with crisp, dramatically red leaves for coleslaw.

▼▼

Cuban Pork Sandwiches

PREP TIME: 20 MINUTES
MARINATING TIME: 4 TO 6 HOURS
GRILLING TIME: 45 TO 55 MINUTES

MARINADE
½ cup fresh orange juice
½ cup fresh lemonade
½ cup finely chopped yellow onion
¼ cup extra virgin olive oil
2 tablespoons minced garlic
2 tablespoons dried oregano
2 tablespoons fresh lime juice

1 boneless pork loin roast, about 2 pounds,
   trimmed of excess fat
½ teaspoon kosher salt
½ teaspoon freshly ground black pepper
8 French rolls
8 tablespoons unsalted butter, softened
8 slices Swiss cheese
8 slices deli ham
24 dill pickle slices

1. To make the marinade: In a medium bowl, whisk the marinade ingredients.

2. Place the roast in a large, resealable plastic bag and pour in the marinade. Press the air out of the bag and seal tightly. Turn the bag to distribute the marinade, place in a bowl, and refrigerate for 4 to 6 hours, turning occasionally.

3. Remove the roast from the bag and discard the marinade. Pat dry with paper towels and allow to stand at room temperature for 20 to 30 minutes before grilling. Season with the salt and pepper. Sear over *Direct Medium* heat until well marked, about 10 minutes, turning once. Continue grilling over *Indirect Medium* heat until the internal temperature reaches 155°F, 35 to 45 minutes. Transfer to a carving board and loosely cover with foil. Let rest for about 10 minutes. Slice crosswise as thinly as possible.

4. Just before serving, split the rolls, spread the inside of each roll with 1 tablespoon butter, and grill them, cut side down, over *Direct Medium* heat until toasted, about 30 seconds. Layer each roll with Swiss cheese, ham, pickle slices, and sliced pork loin.

5. Flatten the sandwiches on a cutting board with the palm of your hand and then grill them over *Direct Medium* heat for 30 seconds. Turn the sandwiches and press down firmly with a spatula [you can even place a cast-iron skillet on top of the sandwiches] and grill for 30 seconds more. Serve warm or at room temperature.

MAKES 8 SERVINGS

Lightly Cured Pork Loin
with Orange-Mustard Glaze

PREP TIME: 10 MINUTES
MARINATING TIME: 45 MINUTES TO 1 HOUR
GRILLING TIME: 40 TO 45 MINUTES

SALT CURE

- 3 tablespoons kosher salt
- 2 teaspoons prepared chili powder
- 1 teaspoon granulated garlic
- 1 teaspoon freshly ground black pepper

- 1 boneless pork loin roast, about 2½ pounds, trimmed of excess fat

GLAZE

- 2 tablespoons extra virgin olive oil
- 1 tablespoon orange marmalade
- 1 tablespoon soy sauce
- 1 tablespoon fresh lemon juice
- 1 tablespoon Dijon mustard
- ⅛ teaspoon freshly ground black pepper

1. To make the salt cure: In a small bowl, mix the salt cure ingredients and rub it all over the roast. Cover and refrigerate for 45 minutes to 1 hour.
2. To make the glaze: In a small saucepan, stir the glaze ingredients. Bring to a boil, reduce the heat, and cook until the marmalade melts.
3. Rinse the roast under cold water, washing away all the salt and spices, and pat dry with paper towels. Allow to stand at room temperature for 20 to 30 minutes before grilling. Brush the glaze all over the roast. Grill over *Direct Medium* heat until evenly caramelized on all sides, barely pink in the center, and to an internal temperature of 155°F, 40 to 45 minutes, turning every 5 to 10 minutes. Remove from the grill and let rest for 5 minutes before cutting into ⅓-inch slices. Serve warm.

MAKES 4 TO 6 SERVINGS

Basic Baby Back Ribs

PREP TIME: 10 MINUTES
MARINATING TIME: 1 TO 3 HOURS
GRILLING TIME: 1½ TO 2 HOURS

RUB
½ cup light brown sugar
2 tablespoons kosher salt
1 tablespoon prepared chili powder
1 tablespoon freshly ground black pepper

2 racks baby back ribs, 1½ to 2 pounds each

1. To make the rub: In a small bowl, mix the rub ingredients.
2. Remove the thin membrane from the back of each rack of ribs [see page 126]. Season the ribs all over with the rub, pressing the spices into the meat. Wrap the ribs in plastic wrap and refrigerate for 1 to 3 hours.
3. Allow the ribs to stand at room temperature for 20 to 30 minutes before grilling. Grill over *Indirect Low* heat [grill temperature should be about 300°F] until the meat is very tender and has shrunk back from the ends of the bones, 1½ to 2 hours.
4. Transfer the ribs to a baking sheet and tightly cover with aluminum foil. Let rest for 30 minutes before serving. Serve warm.

MAKES 4 SERVINGS

Spice-Rubbed Ribs
with Tomato-Tequila Sauce

PREP TIME: 20 MINUTES
GRILLING TIME: 1¹/₂ TO 2 HOURS

RUB

   2 teaspoons light brown sugar
   2 teaspoons kosher salt
   2 teaspoons pure chile powder
   2 teaspoons paprika
   2 teaspoons dried oregano

   2 racks baby back ribs, 1¹/₂ to 2 pounds each

SAUCE

   1 tablespoon extra virgin olive oil
   1 tablespoon minced garlic
 ¹/₄ cup tequila
 ¹/₂ cup tomato sauce
 ¹/₄ cup fresh orange juice
   2 tablespoons fresh lime juice
   2 teaspoons soy sauce

1. To make the rub: In a small bowl, mix the rub ingredients with your fingertips.
2. Remove the thin membrane from the back of each rack of ribs [see page 126]. Allow to stand at room temperature for 20 to 30 minutes before grilling. Use about half of the rub to season the ribs on both sides. Grill, meat side down, over *Indirect Low* heat [grill temperature should be about 300°F] for 30 minutes.
3. Meanwhile make the sauce: In a small saucepan over medium-high heat, warm the oil. Add the garlic and cook until it begins to brown, about 30 seconds, stirring occasionally. Add the tequila and stand back [it might flame up!]. Add the remaining sauce ingredients and the remaining rub. Stir the mixture, and then simmer until it reaches a thin sauce consistency, 8 to 10 minutes.
4. After the ribs have cooked for 30 minutes, turn them over. Continue to grill for another 30 minutes, and then start basting with the sauce every 15 minutes for the last 30 to 60 minutes of grilling. Grill until the meat is very tender and has shrunk back from the ends of the bones. The total cooking time will be 1¹/₂ to 2 hours. Transfer the ribs to a baking sheet and tightly cover with aluminum foil. Let rest for 30 minutes before slicing into individual ribs. Serve warm.

MAKES 4 SERVINGS

Smoked Baby Back Ribs
with Cola Barbecue Sauce

PREP TIME: 20 MINUTES
GRILLING TIME: 1½ TO 2 HOURS

SAUCE

 1 tablespoon extra virgin olive oil
 ½ teaspoon granulated garlic
 ½ teaspoon pure chile powder
 ½ teaspoon ground cumin
 ⅔ cup ketchup
 ⅓ cup cola
 2 tablespoons soy sauce
 2 tablespoons cider vinegar
 ¼ teaspoon freshly ground black pepper
 ⅛ teaspoon mesquite liquid smoke

 2 racks baby back ribs, 1½ to 2 pounds each

RUB

 2 teaspoons kosher salt
 1 teaspoon granulated garlic
 1 teaspoon pure chile powder
 1 teaspoon freshly ground black pepper

 About 2 cups mesquite chips, soaked in water
 for at least 1 hour

1. To make the sauce: In a medium saucepan over medium heat, warm the oil. Add the garlic, chile powder, and cumin. Cook for 30 seconds, stirring occasionally. Add the remaining sauce ingredients, whisk them together, and allow the sauce to simmer for about 5 minutes.

2. Remove the thin membrane from the back of each rack of ribs [see page 126]. Allow the ribs to stand at room temperature for 20 to 30 minutes before grilling.

3. To make the rub: In a small bowl, mix the rub ingredients. Season the ribs all over with the rub, pressing the spices into the meat.

4. Drain the mesquite chips and toss them onto the burning coals or into the smoking box of a gas grill. Grill the ribs over *Indirect Low* heat [grill temperature should be about 300°F] until the meat is very tender and has shrunk back from the ends of the bones, 1½ to 2 hours. About 15 minutes before the ribs are done, start brushing occasionally with the sauce on both sides.

5. Transfer the ribs to a baking sheet and tightly cover with aluminum foil. Let rest for 30 minutes before serving. Serve warm.

MAKES 4 SERVINGS

As a judge of national and international barbecue competitions, I've seen a lot of prize-winning teams wrap their fully cooked ribs in foil and let them "rest" for about thirty minutes. This technique not only keeps the ribs warm; the moist heat trapped inside makes them unbelievably tender.

P

Barbecued Spareribs
with Apple Cider Mop

PREP TIME: 20 MINUTES
GRILLING TIME: 2½ TO 3 HOURS

RUB

- 1 tablespoon kosher salt
- 2 teaspoons pure chile powder
- 2 teaspoons granulated garlic
- 2 teaspoons paprika
- 1 teaspoon dried oregano
- ½ teaspoon freshly ground black pepper

- 2 racks pork spareribs, 3 to 4 pounds each

MOP

- 1 cup apple cider
- ¼ cup cider vinegar
- ¼ cup Dijon mustard
- 2 tablespoons soy sauce
- 2 tablespoons Worcestershire sauce
- 1 teaspoon kosher salt
- 1 teaspoon Tabasco® sauce

1. To make the rub: In a small bowl, mix the rub ingredients with your fingertips.

2. Put the spareribs, meaty side up, on a cutting board. Follow the line of fat that separates the meaty ribs from the much tougher tips at the base of each rack, and cut off the tips. Turn each rack over. Cut off the flap of meat attached in the center of each rack. Also cut off the flap of meat that hangs below the shorter end of ribs. [The flaps and tips may be grilled separately, but they will not be as tender as the ribs.] Remove the thin membrane from the back of each rack of ribs [see page 126]. If using a rib rack, cut the racks in half crosswise. Allow the ribs to stand at room temperature for 20 to 30 minutes before grilling. Season the ribs all over with the rub.

3. Place the ribs in the rib rack and grill over *Indirect Low* heat for 1 hour [the grill temperature should be about 300°F].

4. Meanwhile, make the mop: In a medium saucepan over high heat, whisk the mop ingredients and bring to a boil. Remove the pan from the heat. After the spareribs have been grilling for 1 hour, baste them with the mop and continue to baste every 30 minutes until the meat has shrunk back from the rib bones about ½ inch and the meat is tender enough to tear with your fingers. The total grilling time will be 2½ to 3 hours.

5. Transfer the ribs to a baking sheet, lightly brush with some remaining mop, and tightly cover with aluminum foil. Let the ribs rest for 30 minutes before serving.

MAKES 4 SERVINGS

Caribbean Spareribs

PREP TIME: 20 MINUTES
GRILLING TIME: 2½ TO 3 HOURS

RUB
- 2 teaspoons paprika
- 2 teaspoons granulated garlic
- 2 teaspoons dried thyme
- 2 teaspoons kosher salt
- 1 teaspoon freshly ground black pepper
- 1 teaspoon ground allspice

MOP
- 1 cup beer
- ½ cup cider vinegar
- ¼ cup yellow mustard
- 1 teaspoon kosher salt

2 racks pork spareribs, 4 to 5 pounds each

1. To make the rub: In a small bowl, mix the rub ingredients with your fingertips.

2. To make the mop: In a medium bowl, whisk the mop ingredients.

3. Put the spareribs, meaty side up, on a cutting board. Follow the line of fat that separates the meaty ribs from the much tougher tips at the base of each rack, and cut off the tips. Turn each rack over. Cut off the flap of meat attached in the center of each rack. Also cut off the flap of meat that hangs below the shorter end of ribs. [The flaps and tips may be grilled separately, but they will not be as tender as the ribs.] Remove the thin membrane from the back of each rack of ribs [see page 126]. If using a rib rack, cut the racks in half crosswise. Allow the ribs to stand at room temperature for 20 to 30 minutes before grilling. Season the ribs all over with the rub.

4. Grill over *Indirect Low* heat for 1 hour [the grill temperature should be about 300°F]. After 1 hour, baste the ribs with the mop and continue to baste every 30 minutes or so until the meat has shrunk back from the rib bones about ½ inch and the meat is tender enough to tear with your fingers. The total grilling time will be 2½ to 3 hours. Transfer the ribs to a baking sheet and tightly cover with foil. Let rest for 30 minutes before serving.

MAKES 4 TO 6 SERVINGS

Country-Style Pork Ribs
with Ancho Barbecue Sauce

PREP TIME: 15 MINUTES
GRILLING TIME: 1 HOUR, 10 MINUTES

SAUCE

- ⅓ cup slivered almonds
- 2 medium dried ancho chile peppers, about ½ ounce total
- 6 tablespoons fresh orange juice
- ⅓ cup roughly chopped roasted red bell peppers from a jar
- 3 tablespoons ketchup
- 2 tablespoons extra virgin olive oil
- 1 tablespoon red wine vinegar
- ½ teaspoon granulated garlic
- ¼ teaspoon kosher salt
- ¼ teaspoon freshly ground black pepper

- 3 pounds bone-in country-style pork ribs, each about 1 inch thick
  Extra virgin olive oil
- 1 teaspoon kosher salt
- ½ teaspoon freshly ground black pepper

1. To make the sauce: In a medium skillet over medium heat, toast the almonds until golden brown, 3 to 5 minutes, stirring occasionally. Transfer the almonds to a food processor. Remove the stems from the chiles, make a slit down the side of each one with scissors, and remove the veins and seeds. Flatten the chiles and place them in the skillet over medium heat. With a spatula hold the chiles flat for 5 seconds, turn over and repeat for another 5 seconds. Transfer the chiles to a medium bowl and soak in hot water for 15 minutes. Remove the chiles, squeeze out the excess water, and then roughly chop [you should have about ¼ cup]. Place the chiles and the remaining sauce ingredients in the food processor with the almonds. Process to create a coarse purée.

2. Trim any excess fat from the ribs. Allow to stand at room temperature for 20 to 30 minutes before grilling. Lightly brush or spray with oil and season with the salt and pepper. Sear the ribs over *Direct Medium* heat until well marked, about 10 minutes [watch for flare-ups], turning once. Move the ribs over *Indirect Low* heat and cook until barely pink in the center, about 1 hour. After about 45 minutes over *Indirect Low* heat, lightly brush the ribs with some of the sauce. Continue to grill for another 15 minutes, turning once and brushing with more of the sauce. If the thinner ribs are getting too brown, remove them from the grill earlier. Let the ribs rest for about 10 minutes before serving. Cut each rib in half and serve with the remaining sauce on the side.

MAKES 4 TO 6 SERVINGS

Country-Style Pork Tacos
with Tomato Salsa

PREP TIME: 20 MINUTES
MARINATING TIME: 2 TO 8 HOURS
GRILLING TIME: 12 TO 15 MINUTES

PASTE
- 1 tablespoon kosher salt
- 1½ teaspoons dried oregano
- 1½ teaspoons granulated garlic
- 1½ teaspoons pure chile powder
- 1½ teaspoons light brown sugar
- ½ teaspoon ground cumin
- ½ teaspoon freshly ground black pepper
- 3 tablespoons extra virgin olive oil

1½ to 2 pounds boneless country-style pork ribs, each about 1-inch thick

SALSA
- 1½ cups roughly chopped ripe tomatoes
- 1 large ripe avocado, finely diced
- 4 to 5 green onions, white part only, finely chopped
- ¼ cup finely chopped fresh cilantro
- 2 tablespoons fresh lime juice
- 1 to 2 tablespoons minced jalapeño chile peppers [without seeds]
- Kosher salt
- Freshly ground black pepper
- Tabasco® sauce

12 soft flour tortillas [8 inches]

1. To make the paste: In a small bowl, mix the paste ingredients.
2. Trim any excess fat from the pork and then rub the paste all over. Cover the pork and refrigerate for 2 hours or as long 8 hours.
3. To make the salsa: In a medium bowl, combine the salsa ingredients, including salt, pepper, and Tabasco sauce to taste. Transfer to a serving bowl.
4. Allow the pork to stand at room temperature for 20 to 30 minutes before grilling. Grill over *Direct Medium* heat until barely pink in the center, 12 to 15 minutes, turning once. While the pork is cooking, divide the tortillas and wrap 6 each in 2 foil packages. Grill over *Direct Medium* heat for 2 to 4 minutes to warm them. Cut the pork crosswise into very thin slices. Serve the sliced pork wrapped in warm tortillas with the salsa.

MAKES 4 TO 6 SERVINGS

Pepperoni Pizzas

PREP TIME: 30 MINUTES
GRILLING TIME: 6 TO 8 MINUTES

DOUGH
    1   envelope active dry yeast
    ½   teaspoon granulated sugar
    2½ cups all-purpose flour, plus more for
         rolling dough
         Extra virgin olive oil
    1   teaspoon kosher salt

    12 ounces low-fat mozzarella cheese,
         coarsely grated
    8   ounces pepperoni, cut into ¼-inch slices
    1   cup thinly sliced roasted red pepper
    1   cup good-quality tomato sauce
    1   teaspoon dried oregano

1. To prepare the dough: In a medium bowl, combine
the yeast and sugar with ¾ cup warm water [105°F
to 115°F]. Stir once and let stand until foamy, 5 to
10 minutes. Add 2½ cups of the flour, 3 tablespoons
of olive oil, and the salt. Stir until the dough holds
together. Transfer to a lightly floured work surface
and knead until smooth, 4 to 6 minutes. Shape into
a ball and place in a lightly oiled bowl. Turn the ball
to cover the surface with oil. Cover the bowl with a
kitchen towel and set aside in a warm place until the
dough doubles in size, 1 to 1½ hours.

2. Punch down the dough in the bowl. Transfer to a
lightly floured surface and cut into 4 equal pieces.
Cut parchment paper into 9-inch squares and lightly
oil each sheet of paper on one side [see page 41].
Roll or press the dough flat on the oiled side of
the paper into circles about 8 inches in diameter.
Lightly oil the top side of the dough. Lay the dough
on the grate, with the paper side facing up. Grab one
corner of the paper with tongs and peel it off.
3. Grill over *Direct Medium* heat until they are
marked on the underside, 2 to 3 minutes, rotating
the crusts occasionally for even cooking. Transfer
the crusts from the cooking grate to the back of a
baking sheet, with the grilled sides facing up.
4. Arrange one quarter of the cheese on each
crust, leaving a ½-inch border around the edges.
Arrange the pepperoni and red peppers over the
cheese. Spoon the tomato sauce here and there,
being careful not to wet the dough with too much
watery sauce. Sprinkle the oregano over the pizzas. Transfer the pizzas from the baking sheets to
the grate. Grill until the crusts are crisp and the
cheese is melted, 4 to 5 minutes, rotating the crusts
occasionally. Transfer to a cutting board. Cut into
wedges. Serve warm.

MAKES 4 SMALL PIZZAS

Pork Burger "Sliders"
with Roasted Onion Relish

PREP TIME: 30 MINUTES
GRILLING TIME: ABOUT 1¼ HOURS

RELISH

- 3 medium yellow onions, unpeeled
- 2 teaspoons extra virgin olive oil
- 1 teaspoon kosher salt, divided
- ¼ teaspoon freshly ground black pepper
- ⅓ cup ketchup
- ⅓ cup dry white wine
- 1 teaspoon cider vinegar
- ⅛ teaspoon Tabasco® sauce
- 2 tablespoons finely chopped fresh Italian parsley

BURGERS

- 2 pounds lean ground pork
- 2 tablespoons ketchup
- 1½ teaspoons kosher salt
- ½ teaspoon ground allspice
- ½ teaspoon dry mustard
- ½ teaspoon freshly ground black pepper
- ¼ teaspoon Tabasco sauce

  Extra virgin olive oil
- 8 small dinner rolls, cut in half

1. To make the relish: In a medium bowl, coat the onions with the olive oil. Season with ½ teaspoon of the salt and the pepper. Loosely wrap each onion in aluminum foil and grill them over *Indirect Medium* heat until soft, about 1 hour. When cool enough to handle, peel the onions. Cut off and discard the stem and root ends. Cut the onions in half lengthwise, and then chop into ½-inch pieces or smaller.

2. In a medium saucepan over medium-high heat, combine the onions, the remaining ½ teaspoon of salt, the ketchup, wine, vinegar, and Tabasco sauce. Stir to combine and bring the mixture to a boil. Reduce the heat and simmer until almost all of the liquid has evaporated, 10 to 15 minutes. Remove the pan from the heat. Add the parsley and mix well. [The relish may be made 1 day in advance and refrigerated. Bring to room temperature before serving.]

3. To prepare the burgers: In a large bowl, combine the burger ingredients, gently mixing by hand. Shape into 8 patties, each about ½ inch thick. Lightly brush or spray each burger with oil. Grill over *Direct Medium* heat until fully cooked, 10 to 12 minutes, turning once. Grill the cut side of the rolls over *Direct Medium* heat until toasted, about 30 seconds. Serve burgers warm on the toasted rolls topped with relish.

MAKES 4 TO 6 SERVINGS

Smoked Pulled Pork

in Hot Chile Sauce

PREP TIME: 30 MINUTES
GRILLING TIME: 5 TO 6 HOURS

RUB

- 1 tablespoon light brown sugar
- 1 tablespoon prepared chili powder
- 1 tablespoon kosher salt

- 1 bone-in pork shoulder roast [Boston butt],
  5 to 6 pounds
- 2 handfuls hickory/mesquite chips, soaked in
  water for at least 30 minutes

SAUCE

- 1 cup cider vinegar
- 1 cup ketchup
- 3 tablespoons granulated sugar
- 1 teaspoon Worcestershire sauce
- 1 teaspoon kosher salt
- 1/2 teaspoon dry mustard
- 1/2 teaspoon ground cayenne pepper
- 1/4 teaspoon freshly ground black pepper

- 12 hamburger buns, lightly toasted
  Mayonnaise

1. To make the rub: In a small bowl, mix the rub ingredients with your fingertips. Allow the roast to stand at room temperature for 20 to 30 minutes before grilling. Massage the rub mixture all over the roast.

2. Grill over *Indirect Medium* heat until the meat is very tender but still juicy [the internal temperature next to, but not touching, the bone should be 180°F to 190°F], 5 to 6 hours, turning every hour or so. Add the soaked wood chips to the smoker box or coals about halfway through grilling time. When done, remove the pork shoulder from the grill, lightly cover with a piece of aluminum foil, and let rest for 30 minutes.

3. Meanwhile, make the sauce: In a medium saucepan, combine the sauce ingredients with 1 cup of water and bring to a boil over high heat, stirring occasionally. Reduce the heat to low and simmer for 10 minutes. Keep warm.

4. Pull the pork into shreds with two forks or your fingers, or chop it with a knife. Discard any outer sections that may have burned or any large bits of fat inside. In a large bowl, moisten the shredded meat with the sauce [you may not need all of it] and mix well. Serve warm on toasted buns brushed with mayonnaise.

MAKES 12 SANDWICHES

▲▲

This is where patience has its rewards. When you barbecue pork shoulder slowly, until the internal temperature climbs near 190°F, the meat tears into shreds of pure satisfaction. If the outside gets dark, that's even better. Barbecue aficionados call that the "bark," and its crispy texture is fabulous in combination with the rest of the meat.

▼▼

Rotisserie Pork
with Bourbon Barbecue Mop

PREP TIME: 30 MINUTES
MARINATING TIME: 12 TO 24 HOURS
GRILLING TIME: $3^1/_2$ TO 4 HOURS

RUB

2 teaspoons whole black peppercorns
2 teaspoons mustard seed
2 tablespoons light brown sugar
1 teaspoon granulated garlic
1 teaspoon granulated onion
1 teaspoon paprika

1 boneless pork shoulder [Boston butt],
   5 to 6 pounds, rolled and tied
1 tablespoon kosher salt

MOP

1 cup bourbon
1 small onion, about 5 ounces, puréed
$^1/_2$ cup light brown sugar
$^1/_4$ cup dark corn syrup
$^1/_4$ cup ketchup
2 tablespoons coarse brown mustard

1. To make the rub: Using a spice/coffee grinder or a mortar and pestle, pulverize the peppercorns with the mustard seed. Place in a small bowl and combine with the remaining rub ingredients.
2. Season the pork with the rub. Wrap in plastic wrap and place on a plate. Refrigerate for 12 to 24 hours. Allow the pork to stand at room temperature for 45 minutes before grilling. Season with the salt.
3. Meanwhile, make the mop: In a medium bowl, whisk the mop ingredients.
4. Follow the grill's instructions for using the rotisserie. Center the pork on the spit and secure it in place. Rotate over *Direct Low* heat until the internal temperature reaches 175°F, $3^1/_2$ to 4 hours, or 30 minutes per pound. After the first hour, if the pork starts looking too brown, finish grilling over *Indirect Low* heat. After the first hour, baste the pork generously with the mop every 20 minutes. Remove from the rotisserie, loosely cover with foil and let rest for about 20 minutes before slicing [the internal temperature of the pork will rise 5 to 10 degrees during this time]. Serve warm.

MAKES 12 SERVINGS

Grilled Pork Shoulder Stew

PREP TIME: 30 MINUTES
GRILLING TIME: ABOUT 3 HOURS

- 1 boneless pork shoulder [Boston butt], about 4 pounds
- 1 teaspoon ground cumin
- 1 teaspoon pure chile powder
- 1 teaspoon kosher salt
- 1/2 teaspoon freshly ground black pepper
- 1/4 cup extra virgin olive oil
- 1 large yellow onion, cut into 1/2-inch dice
- 1 tablespoon minced garlic
- 1/4 cup all-purpose flour
- 1/2 cup dry red wine
- 2 to 3 cups reduced-sodium beef stock
- 1 can [28 ounces] whole tomatoes
- 1 1/2 pounds Yukon Gold potatoes, cut into 1-inch chunks
- 3 tablespoons finely chopped fresh Italian parsley

1. Trim any excess fat from the pork and cut the meat into 1 1/2-inch chunks [you should have about 3 pounds of chunks]. Put the chunks in a large bowl. Season with the cumin, chile powder, salt, and pepper, stirring the pork to coat evenly.

2. Sear the pork over *Direct Medium* heat until dark brown, 8 to 10 minutes, turning once. Return the pork to a clean bowl.

3. In an ovenproof 10-inch saucepan or Dutch oven over high heat, heat the oil. Before it begins to smoke, add the diced onions and cook until they begin to brown, about 5 minutes, stirring occasionally. Add the pork and the garlic to the pan. Sprinkle the flour over the top, and then stir to evenly coat the pork. Cook for 1 to 2 minutes. Add the wine and cook until it has evaporated, scraping any brown bits off the bottom of the pan. Add 2 cups of the beef stock and the tomatoes, crushing the tomatoes with a fork. Bring to a simmer, and then set the pan over *Indirect Medium* heat. Cover the pan and cook for 1 hour, occasionally stirring all the way to the bottom [the liquid should simmer slowly]. Uncover the pan and cook for another hour, stirring occasionally. Add the potatoes and continue to cook, uncovered, until the pork and potatoes are fork tender, 45 to 60 minutes longer. If the sauce is getting too thick, add a little more beef stock. Add the parsley. Mix well. Season with more salt and pepper to taste. Serve warm.

MAKES 6 SERVINGS

POULTRY

Turn, Turn, Burn

Have you been to *that* party? You know the one where the host—let's call him Innocent Ed—takes a stab at making barbecued chicken. Innocent Ed is a great guy but he is not much of a cook and he sees no use for cookbooks. He figures all guys can grill. It's part of our genetic code. So Innocent Ed trots off to the market to buy bone-in chicken pieces and some barbecue sauce. Back home, he fires up the coals, taking great delight in the blazing heat. He scatters the raw chicken pieces on the grate and begins a male ritual that has survived countless generations. He flips his food. He figures he is not really grilling unless he is poking the food and turning it over regularly. Trouble is, the chicken is sticking. Every time he picks up a piece, he leaves a little skin behind on the grate. The fat in the skin melts and drips into the grill. With the lid open, the fat begins to flare-up. Innocent Ed has created the ideal environment for burning: lots of heat, lots of fat, and lots of air. Ed notices that the chicken pieces are looking dark, so he tries to cover up the blackened spots with some barbecue sauce. He brushes the sauce on liberally and continues the ritual. Turn, turn, turn. Burn, burn, burn. Eventually the sauce has burned so much that he figures the chicken must be cooked, so he pulls it off the grill and serves it. Guess what? It is still raw at the bone.

Once the chicken pieces have a nice golden brown color on all sides, move them over indirect heat.

I've seen Innocent Ed in backyards and patios from coast to coast. You have probably seen him, too. Please do us all a favor and ask him to sear bone-in chicken pieces over direct medium heat, waiting patiently for them to release from the grate before trying to turn them. Tell him that once the chicken pieces have a nice golden brown color on all sides, move them over indirect heat, where they will roast evenly. And explain to him that by keeping the lid closed as much as possible, he will prevent flare-ups, he will speed up the cooking time, and he will capture the smokiness that gives grilled food its unique appeal. In short, Innocent Ed will be Excellent Ed, a true grilling guru and a much better host.

What to Look For in Chicken

Chicken is chicken, right? Not exactly. Most supermarkets carry big national brands, or sometimes supermarkets put their own brands on these mass-produced birds raised in cages. They are low in fat, they cook quickly, and they are pretty tender, however their flavor is pretty darn bland. Fortunately the grill provides just what they need. With a little oil, some seasonings, and maybe a sauce, they are very good on the grill.

Today we are seeing more and more premium chickens available, and usually they are worth their higher price, though not always. Typically, these chickens are from old-fashioned breeds known more for their flavor than their plump breasts and perfectly even shape. Often called "free-range" chickens, they have access to the outdoors, or at least the freedom to wander indoors. The exercise contributes to firmer, more flavorful meat. Check them out. Any chickens you buy should have skins that fit their bodies well, not spotty or shriveled or too far overlapping. The color of the skin says little about quality, but the smell of a chicken will tell everything you need to know about freshness. If it smells funny, don't buy it.

REAL GRILLING 101 — Cutting Up a Whole Chicken

When a chicken is fully cooked, allow it to rest at room temperature for 5 to 10 minutes, during which time the internal temperature will rise about 5°F. Then carve the chicken into serving pieces. Here's how.

1. Cut the twine and remove it. With the breast side facing up, cut through the skin between the first leg and the breast.

2. Once you have cut through the skin, pull the leg away from the breast and bend it behind the chicken. The joint that holds the leg to the chicken will pop up.

3. Cut through the joint to remove the leg. Repeat the process with the second leg.

4. Lift each wing to expose the joint that connects it to the chicken. Cut through each joint to remove the wings.

5. Cut along either side of the breastbone. Work the knife over the top of the rib cage on either side of the breastbone, and push the meat away from the bones.

6. Cut through the joint between each thigh and drumstick.

POULTRY

Poultry: When Is It Done?

The USDA recommends cooking chicken and turkey until the internal temperature of the breast meat is 170°F and the thigh meat has reached 180°F for optimal safety. But most chefs today cook the breast meat to 165°F and the thigh meat to 175°F for juicier results. Keep in mind that the internal temperature will rise 5 to 10 degrees during resting. Whatever temperature you choose is entirely up to you.

Check the thigh meat by inserting the probe of a thermometer in the thickest part [but not touching the bone]. If you don't have a thermometer, insert a thin knife between the thigh and drumstick. The juices should run clear and the meat should no longer be pink at the bone.

Grilling Guide for Poultry

Type	Weight	Approximate Grilling Time
Chicken breast, boneless, skinless	6 ounces	**8 to 12 minutes** Direct Medium
Chicken thigh, boneless, skinless	4 ounces	**8 to 10 minutes** Direct High
Chicken pieces, bone-in breast/wing		**30 to 40 minutes** Indirect Medium
Chicken pieces, bone-in leg/thigh		**40 to 50 minutes** Indirect Medium
Chicken, whole	3½ to 5 pounds	**1 to 1½ hours** Indirect Medium
Cornish game hen	1½ to 2 pounds	**30 to 45 minutes** Indirect Medium
Turkey breast, boneless	2½ pounds	**1 to 1¼ hours** Indirect Medium
Turkey, whole, unstuffed	10 to 11 pounds	**1¾ to 2½ hours** Indirect Medium
	12 to 14 pounds	**2¼ to 3 hours** Indirect Medium
	15 to 17 pounds	**2¾ to 3¾ hours** Indirect Medium
	18 to 22 pounds	**3½ to 4 hours** Indirect Medium
Duck breast, boneless	7 to 8 ounces	**12 to 15 minutes** Direct Low
Duck, whole	5½ to 6 pounds	**40 minutes** Indirect High

Cilantro Pesto Chicken Tenders

PREP TIME: 10 MINUTES
MARINATING TIME: 2 HOURS
GRILLING TIME: 6 TO 8 MINUTES

MARINADE
2 tablespoons coarsely chopped walnuts
2 medium garlic cloves
1½ cups loosely packed fresh cilantro leaves
and tender stems
½ cup loosely packed fresh Italian parsley
leaves and tender stems
½ teaspoon kosher salt
¼ teaspoon freshly ground black pepper
¼ cup extra virgin olive oil

2 pounds chicken breast tenders
1 lime, cut into wedges

1. To make the marinade: In a food processor, finely chop the walnuts and garlic. Scrape down the sides of the bowl. Add the cilantro, parsley, salt, and pepper and process until finely chopped. With the motor running, slowly add the oil to create a smooth purée.

2. Place the chicken in a large, resealable plastic bag and add the marinade. Press the air out of the bag and seal tightly. Turn the bag to distribute the marinade, place in a bowl, and refrigerate for 2 hours.

3. Remove the chicken from the bag and thread onto skewers. Grill over *Direct High* heat until the meat is firm and the juices run clear, 6 to 8 minutes, turning once. Serve warm with the lime wedges.

MAKES 4 TO 6 SERVINGS

To me, pesto is more of a technique than a recipe. Literally, it means "pounded" in Italian. To most people, it means a sauce made with garlic, pine nuts, Parmesan cheese, olive oil, and lots of fresh basil. But why not use other herbs instead, like cilantro and parsley? In this recipe they are "pounded" in a food processor.

Tandoori-Style Chicken Kabobs

PREP TIME: 20 MINUTES
MARINATING TIME: 2 TO 4 HOURS
GRILLING TIME: 8 TO 10 MINUTES

MARINADE
- 1 cup plain yogurt
- 1 tablespoon grated fresh ginger
- 1 tablespoon paprika
- 1 tablespoon vegetable oil
- 2 teaspoons minced garlic
- 2 teaspoons kosher salt
- 1½ teaspoons ground cumin
- 1 teaspoon ground turmeric
- ½ teaspoon ground cayenne pepper

- 3 boneless, skinless chicken breast halves, about 6 ounces each
- 1 pint grape or cherry tomatoes, stemmed
- 1 medium green bell pepper, seeded and cut into 1½-inch squares
- ½ medium red or yellow onion, cut into 8 wedges and separated into layers
  Vegetable oil

1. To make the marinade: In a blender or food processor, combine the marinade ingredients and process until smooth.

2. Cut each chicken breast in half lengthwise and then cut each half into 4 equal-sized pieces, about 1½ inches each. Place the chicken in a large, resealable plastic bag and pour in the marinade. Press the air out of the bag and seal tightly. Turn the bag to distribute the marinade and place in a bowl. Refrigerate for 2 to 4 hours.

3. Remove the chicken from the bag and discard the marinade. Thread chicken pieces with tomatoes, bell pepper, and onion onto skewers, alternating chicken and vegetables. Lightly brush or spray with oil. Grill the skewers over *Direct Medium* heat until the chicken is cooked through, 8 to 10 minutes, turning once.

MAKES 4 SERVINGS

Sweet Chili-Mustard Chicken Salad
with Toasted Almonds

PREP TIME: 15 MINUTES
GRILLING TIME: 8 TO 12 MINUTES

DRESSING
3/4 cup pineapple juice
  2 tablespoons mild chili sauce
  2 tablespoons white wine vinegar
  1 tablespoon soy sauce
  1 tablespoon Dijon mustard
  1 teaspoon dark sesame oil

1/2 cup sliced almonds

  4 boneless, skinless chicken breast halves,
     about 6 ounces each
     Canola oil
1/2 teaspoon finely chopped fresh marjoram
     Kosher salt
     Freshly ground black pepper
  4 cups mixed baby greens
  1 four-inch section cucumber, halved lengthwise
     and thinly sliced

1. To make the dressing: In a medium saucepan, whisk together the pineapple juice, chili sauce, vinegar, and soy sauce. Bring the mixture to a boil, reduce the heat, and simmer until 1/2 cup remains, 15 to 20 minutes. Transfer to a medium bowl. Whisk in the mustard and sesame oil and allow to cool to room temperature.

2. In a medium skillet over medium heat, cook the almonds until lightly toasted, about 5 minutes, stirring occasionally.

3. Lightly brush or spray both sides of the chicken with oil. Season with the marjoram and salt and pepper to taste. Grill over *Direct Medium* heat until the meat is firm to the touch and no longer pink in the center, 8 to 12 minutes, turning once. Cut into bite-size pieces.

4. In a large bowl, combine the greens, chicken, almonds, and cucumbers. Drizzle the dressing over the top [you may not need all of it] and toss to evenly coat the leaves. Serve immediately.

MAKES 4 TO 6 SERVINGS

Shredded Barbecue Chicken Sandwiches

PREP TIME: 10 MINUTES
GRILLING TIME: 8 TO 12 MINUTES

SAUCE

 2 tablespoons unsalted butter
 ¹/₂ cup minced yellow onion
 1 cup ketchup
 2 tablespoons soy sauce
 2 tablespoons fresh lemon juice
 ¹/₂ teaspoon Tabasco® sauce

 4 boneless, skinless chicken breast halves, about 6 ounces each
  Vegetable oil
  Kosher salt
  Freshly ground black pepper
 4 large sandwich rolls

1. To make the sauce: In a medium saucepan over medium heat, melt the butter. Add the onion and cook until soft, 3 to 4 minutes, stirring occasionally. Add the remaining sauce ingredients. Stir and cook for about 3 minutes.
2. Lightly brush or spray the chicken on both sides with oil and season with salt and pepper to taste. Grill over *Direct Medium* heat until the meat is firm to the touch and no longer pink in the center, 8 to 12 minutes, turning once. Remove from the grill and let rest for 3 to 5 minutes. Shred the chicken, add to the sauce, and heat through over medium heat.
3. Grill the rolls over *Direct Medium* heat until lightly toasted, 30 to 60 seconds. Build each sandwich with a roll and some shredded chicken.

MAKES 4 SERVINGS

Hurry Up I'm Hungry Chicken Breasts

PREP TIME: 5 MINUTES
GRILLING TIME: 8 TO 12 MINUTES

RUB

 1 teaspoon granulated onion
 1 teaspoon granulated garlic
 ³/₄ teaspoon kosher salt
 ¹/₂ teaspoon prepared chili powder
 ¹/₂ teaspoon freshly ground black pepper

 4 boneless, skinless chicken breast halves, about 6 ounces each
  Extra virgin olive oil

1. To make the rub: In a small bowl, mix the rub ingredients.
2. Lightly brush or spray the chicken with oil and season with the rub, pressing the spices into the meat. Grill the chicken over *Direct Medium* heat until the meat is firm to the touch and no longer pink in the center, 8 to 12 minutes, turning once. Serve warm.

MAKES 4 SERVINGS

Lemon Miso-Marinated Chicken Breasts

PREP TIME: 5 MINUTES
MARINATING TIME: 1 TO 2 HOURS
GRILLING TIME: 8 TO 12 MINUTES

PASTE

  2 tablespoons red miso
  2 tablespoons fresh lemon juice
  1 tablespoon dark sesame oil
  1 tablespoon canola oil
  1/2 teaspoon Tabasco® sauce
  1/2 teaspoon granulated garlic
  1/4 teaspoon freshly ground black pepper

  4 boneless, skinless chicken breast halves, about 6 ounces each

1. To make the paste: In a small bowl, whisk the paste ingredients.
2. Spread the paste evenly over both sides of the chicken. Cover and refrigerate for 1 to 2 hours.
3. Grill the chicken over *Direct Medium* heat until the meat is firm to the touch and no longer pink in the center, 8 to 12 minutes, turning once. Serve warm.

MAKES 4 SERVINGS

Thin-Crusted Pizzas
with Yesterday's Grilled Chicken

PREP TIME: 20 MINUTES
GRILLING TIME: 6 TO 8 MINUTES

  1 four-inch ball ready-made pizza dough
    Extra virgin olive oil
  2 cups good-quality tomato sauce
  4 grilled chicken breasts, thinly sliced
  1 1/2 to 2 cups thinly sliced grilled bell peppers
  1/2 cup sliced black olives
  1/2 cup tightly packed fresh basil leaves, torn into small pieces

1. Cut the dough into 4 equal pieces. Cut parchment paper into 9-inch squares and lightly oil each sheet of paper on one side. Roll or press the dough flat on the oiled side of the paper into circles about 8 inches in diameter, leaving the dough a little thicker at the edge than in the middle. Then lightly oil the top side of the dough. Lay the dough on the grate, with the paper side facing up. Grab one corner of the paper with tongs and peel it off. Grill over *Direct Medium* heat until they are marked on the underside, 2 to 3 minutes, rotating the crusts occasionally for even cooking. Transfer the crusts from the cooking grate to the back of a baking sheet, with the grilled sides facing up.
2. Spread about 1/2 cup of the sauce over each crust, leaving a 1/2-inch border around the edges. Arrange the chicken, peppers, olives, and basil over the sauce. Transfer the pizzas from the baking sheet to the cooking grate. Grill until the crusts are crisp and the cheese is melted, 4 to 5 minutes, rotating the crusts occasionally for even cooking. Transfer to a cutting board. Cut into wedges. Serve warm.

MAKES 4 SMALL PIZZAS

Barbecued Chicken Pizzas

with Smoked Gouda and Chives

PREP TIME: 45 MINUTES
GRILLING TIME: 15 TO 20 MINUTES

DOUGH
1 envelope active dry yeast
½ teaspoon granulated sugar
2½ cups all-purpose flour, plus more for rolling dough
Extra virgin olive oil
1 teaspoon kosher salt

SAUCE
2 tablespoons unsalted butter
¼ cup finely chopped yellow onion
2 teaspoons minced garlic
¾ cup ketchup
¼ cup dry red wine
¼ cup Dijon mustard
2 tablespoons fresh lemon juice
1 tablespoon Worcestershire sauce
½ teaspoon prepared chili powder
½ teaspoon dried oregano
¼ teaspoon freshly ground black pepper

4 boneless, skinless chicken breast halves, 5 to 6 ounces each
Extra virgin olive oil
Kosher salt
Freshly ground black pepper
2 cups grated smoked Gouda cheese
¼ cup finely chopped fresh chives

1. To prepare the dough: In a medium bowl, combine the yeast and sugar with ¾ cup warm water [105°F to 115°F]. Stir once and let stand until foamy, 5 to 10 minutes. Add 2½ cups of the flour, 3 tablespoons of olive oil, and the salt. Stir until the dough holds together. Transfer to a lightly floured work surface and knead until smooth, 4 to 6 minutes. Shape into a ball and place in a lightly oiled bowl. Turn the ball to cover the surface with oil. Cover the bowl with a kitchen towel and set aside in a warm place until the dough doubles in size, 1 to 1½ hours.

2. Punch down the dough in the bowl. Transfer to a lightly floured surface and cut into 4 equal pieces. Cut parchment paper into 9-inch squares and lightly oil each sheet of paper on one side. Roll or press the dough flat on the oiled side of the paper into circles about 8 inches in diameter, leaving the dough a little thicker at the edge than in the middle. Then lightly oil the top side of the dough.

3. To make the sauce: In a medium saucepan over medium-high heat, melt the butter. Add the onion and cook until soft, about 5 minutes, stirring occasionally. Add the garlic and cook until light brown, about 1 minute, stirring occasionally. Add the remaining sauce ingredients. Whisk to combine. Bring the sauce to a boil, then lower heat to a simmer. Cook for 5 to 10 minutes. Pour about half the sauce into a small bowl, reserving the other half in the saucepan.

4. Lightly brush or spray the chicken on both sides with oil and season with salt and pepper to taste. Lightly coat the chicken on both sides with the sauce in the small bowl. Grill the chicken over *Direct Medium* heat until the meat is firm to the touch and no longer pink in the center, 8 to 12 minutes, turning once. Finely chop or shred the chicken and moisten with some reserved sauce in the saucepan [you may not need all of it].

5. Lay the dough on the grate, with the paper side facing up. Grab one corner of the paper with tongs and peel it off. Grill over *Direct Medium* heat until they are marked on the underside, 2 to 3 minutes, rotating the crusts occasionally for even cooking. Don't worry if the crusts bubble; they will deflate when turned over. Transfer the crusts from the cooking grate to the back of a baking sheet, with the grilled sides facing up.

6. Sprinkle ½ cup of the cheese over each pizza, leaving a ½-inch border around the edges. Arrange the chicken and chives over the cheese. Transfer the pizzas from the baking sheets to the cooking grate. Grill until the crusts are crisp and the cheese is melted, 4 to 5 minutes, rotating the pizzas occasionally for even cooking. Transfer to a cutting board. Cut into wedges. Serve warm.

MAKES 4 SMALL PIZZAS

Blue Cheese Caesar Salad
with Grilled Chicken

PREP TIME: 20 MINUTES
GRILLING TIME: 9 TO 15 MINUTES

DRESSING

- 2 large garlic cloves
- 3 anchovy fillets
- 2 teaspoons Dijon mustard
- 1 large pasteurized egg yolk
- 1/2 cup extra virgin olive oil
- 1/4 cup crumbled blue cheese
- 1 tablespoon fresh lemon juice
- 1/4 teaspoon Worcestershire sauce
- 1/4 teaspoon freshly ground black pepper

PASTE

- 2 teaspoons extra virgin olive oil
- 2 teaspoons Dijon mustard
- 1/2 teaspoon prepared chili powder
  Kosher salt
  Freshly ground black pepper

- 2 boneless, skinless chicken breast halves, about 6 ounces each

- 15 to 20 thin slices of a baguette [about 1/2 baguette]
- 2 large hearts of romaine lettuce, cut into 1-inch pieces
- 1/2 small red onion, thinly sliced

1. To make the dressing: In a food processor, mince the garlic. Add the anchovies, mustard, and egg yolk and process until smooth. With the processor running, very slowly add the oil in a thin stream to emulsify the ingredients. Add the remaining dressing ingredients and pulse to combine. Refrigerate dressing until ready to use.

2. To make the paste: In a small bowl, mix the paste ingredients, including salt and pepper to taste, and spread it all over the chicken. Grill the chicken over *Direct Medium* heat until the meat is firm to the touch and no longer pink in the center, 8 to 12 minutes, turning once [if flare-ups occur, move the chicken temporarily over *Indirect Medium* heat]. Cut into bite-size pieces.

3. Grill the baguette slices over *Direct Medium* heat until toasted, 1 to 2 minutes, turning once.

4. In a large bowl, combine the lettuce, onion, and chicken. Add enough of the dressing to lightly coat the leaves [you may not need all of it] and toss. Add the toasted baguette slices. Season with pepper to taste. Toss again. Serve immediately.

MAKES 4 SERVINGS

Honey-Mustard Chicken
with Lemon and Curry

PREP TIME: 10 MINUTES
MARINATING TIME: 3 TO 4 HOURS
GRILLING TIME: 35 TO 40 MINUTES

MARINADE
- $\frac{1}{2}$ cup Dijon mustard
- $\frac{1}{4}$ cup honey
- 2 tablespoons extra virgin olive oil
- 1 teaspoon freshly grated lemon zest
- 2 tablespoons fresh lemon juice
- 2 teaspoons curry powder
- $\frac{1}{2}$ teaspoon granulated garlic
- $\frac{1}{2}$ teaspoon kosher salt
- $\frac{1}{4}$ teaspoon ground cayenne pepper
- $\frac{1}{4}$ teaspoon freshly ground black pepper

- 4 chicken breast halves [with bone and skin], 10 to 12 ounces each

1. To make the marinade: In a medium bowl, whisk the marinade ingredients.
2. Place the chicken in a large, resealable plastic bag and pour in about $\frac{2}{3}$ of the marinade, reserving the other $\frac{1}{3}$. Press the air out of the bag and seal tightly. Turn the bag several times to distribute the marinade and refrigerate for 3 to 4 hours.
3. Remove the chicken from the bag and discard the marinade in the bag. Grill, skin side down, over *Direct Medium* heat until nicely marked, about 5 minutes. Turn the chicken over, move over *Indirect Medium* heat, and cook until the meat is no longer pink at the bone, 30 to 35 minutes more, brushing occasionally with the reserved marinade during the last 15 minutes of grilling. Serve warm.

MAKES 4 SERVINGS

Mojo Marinated Chicken

PREP TIME: 10 MINUTES
MARINATING TIME: 6 TO 8 HOURS
GRILLING TIME: 30 TO 40 MINUTES

MARINADE
½ cup fresh orange juice
2 tablespoons fresh lime juice
2 tablespoons soy sauce
2 tablespoons extra virgin olive oil
1 tablespoon minced garlic
½ teaspoon Tabasco® sauce
½ teaspoon ground cumin
¼ teaspoon kosher salt
¼ teaspoon freshly ground black pepper

4 chicken breast halves [with bone and skin],
10 to 12 ounces each

1. To make the marinade: In a medium bowl, whisk the marinade ingredients.
2. Place the chicken in a large, plastic resealable bag and pour in the marinade. Press the air out of the bag and seal tightly. Turn the bag to distribute the marinade, place in a bowl, and refrigerate for 6 to 8 hours, turning occasionally.
3. Remove the chicken from the bag and reserve the marinade. Pour the marinade into a small saucepan, bring to a boil over high heat, and boil for 1 minute.
4. Grill, bone side down, over *Indirect Medium* heat until the juices run clear and the meat is no longer pink at the bone, 30 to 40 minutes. Baste once or twice with the boiled marinade. For crispier skin, grill the chicken, skin side down, over *Direct Medium* heat during the last 5 minutes of grilling time. Brush with a little of the marinade just before serving.

MAKES 4 SERVINGS

Jamaican Jerk Chicken

PREP TIME: 15 MINUTES
MARINATING TIME: 3 HOURS
GRILLING TIME: 8 TO 12 MINUTES

PASTE
    2   scotch bonnet or jalapeño chile peppers, stems
        removed, roughly chopped
    4   scallions, white and light green parts only,
        roughly chopped
  1/4   cup vegetable oil
    1   tablespoon red wine vinegar
    1   tablespoon finely chopped fresh thyme
    1   tablespoon soy sauce
    1   tablespoon light brown sugar
    1   teaspoon kosher salt
  1/2   teaspoon freshly ground black pepper
  1/2   teaspoon ground allspice
  1/4   teaspoon ground nutmeg
  1/4   teaspoon ground cinnamon
  1/8   teaspoon ground cloves

    4   boneless chicken breast halves [with skin],
        about 6 ounces each

1. To make the paste: In a food processor, combine the paste ingredients and process until smooth.
2. Using a sharp knife, make parallel cuts, about 1 inch apart and 1/4 inch deep, into both sides of each chicken breast. Make similar cuts perpendicular to the first cuts to create crosshatch designs. Using a spoon [to protect your skin from the hot chiles], spread the paste all over the chicken, pushing it inside the cuts. Cover and refrigerate for 3 hours.
3. Grill the chicken, skin side down first, over *Direct Medium* heat until the meat is firm to the touch and no longer pink in the center, 8 to 12 minutes, turning once. Serve warm.

MAKES 4 SERVINGS

Spanish Chicken Breasts
Marinated in Citrus and Tarragon

PREP TIME: 15 MINUTES
MARINATING TIME: 3 TO 4 HOURS
GRILLING TIME: 8 TO 12 MINUTES

MARINADE
¼ cup extra virgin olive oil
¼ cup roughly chopped fresh tarragon
2 tablespoons sherry vinegar
Zest and juice of 1 orange
Zest and juice of 1 lemon
2 teaspoons kosher salt
1 teaspoon minced garlic
1 teaspoon grated ginger
½ teaspoon prepared chili powder
½ teaspoon freshly ground black pepper

4 boneless chicken breast halves [with skin],
about 6 ounces each

1. To make the marinade: In a medium bowl, whisk the marinade ingredients.
2. Place the chicken in a large, resealable plastic bag, and pour in the marinade. Press the air out of the bag and seal tightly. Turn the bag several times to distribute the marinade, place the bag in a bowl, and refrigerate for 3 to 4 hours.
3. Remove the chicken from the bag and reserve the marinade. Pour the marinade into a small saucepan, bring to a boil, and boil for 1 full minute.
4. Grill the chicken, skin side down first, over *Direct Medium* heat until the meat is firm to the touch and no longer pink in the center, 8 to 12 minutes, turning and basting with the boiled marinade once. Serve warm.

MAKES 4 SERVINGS

Chicken Breasts
with Soy and Mustard Marinade

PREP TIME: 5 MINUTES
MARINATING TIME: 2 TO 3 HOURS
GRILLING TIME: 8 TO 12 MINUTES

MARINADE
- ½ cup dry white wine
- 2 tablespoons soy sauce
- 2 tablespoons Dijon mustard
- 1 tablespoon fresh lemon juice
- 2 teaspoons hot chili oil
- 2 teaspoons dark sesame oil

- 4 boneless chicken breast halves [with skin], about 6 ounces each

1. To make the marinade: In a medium bowl, whisk the marinade ingredients.
2. Place the chicken in a large, resealable plastic bag and pour in the marinade. Press out the air and seal the bag tightly. Turn the bag to distribute the marinade, place the bag in a bowl, and refrigerate for 2 to 3 hours.
3. Remove the chicken from the bag and discard the marinade. Grill over *Direct Medium* heat, skin side down first, until the meat is firm to the touch and no longer pink in the center, 8 to 12 minutes, turning once. Serve warm.

MAKES 4 SERVINGS

Chicken Wings
with a Garlicky Glaze

PREP TIME: 15 MINUTES
MARINATING TIME: 4 TO 6 HOURS
GRILLING TIME: 16 TO 18 MINUTES

MARINADE
- 1 large yellow onion, roughly chopped
- ½ cup Dijon mustard
- ½ cup rice vinegar
- ½ cup soy sauce
- 6 large garlic cloves
- 2 tablespoons dark sesame oil
- 2 tablespoons light brown sugar
- 2 teaspoons lemon zest
- 2 tablespoons fresh lemon juice
- ½ teaspoon freshly ground black pepper

- 20 chicken wings, wing tips removed

1. To make the marinade: In a blender or food processor, combine the marinade ingredients and process until smooth.
2. Place the wings in a large, resealable plastic bag and pour in the marinade. Press the air out of the bag and seal tightly. Turn the bag to distribute the marinade, place in a bowl, and refrigerate for 4 to 6 hours, turning the bag occasionally.
3. Remove the wings from the bag and discard the marinade. Grill over *Direct Medium* heat, skin side down first, until the meat is no longer pink at the bone, 16 to 18 minutes, turning occasionally. Serve warm.

MAKES 4 TO 6 SERVINGS

Chile-Marinated Chicken Wings

PREP TIME: 20 MINUTES
MARINATING TIME: 2 HOURS
GRILLING TIME: 16 TO 18 MINUTES

MARINADE
- 4 dried pasilla chile peppers, about ¾ ounce total
- 2 tablespoons canola oil
- ½ cup ketchup
- 3 tablespoons soy sauce
- 2 tablespoons balsamic vinegar
- 3 medium garlic cloves, crushed
- 1 teaspoon ground cumin
- ½ teaspoon dried oregano
- ¼ teaspoon kosher salt
- ¼ teaspoon freshly ground black pepper

16 chicken wings, about 2½ pounds, wing tips removed

1. To make the marinade: Remove the stems and cut the chiles crosswise into sections about 2 inches long. Remove most of the seeds. In a medium skillet over high heat, warm the oil. Add the chiles and toast them until they puff up and begin to turn color, 2 to 3 minutes, turning once. Transfer the chiles and oil to a small bowl. Cover with 1 cup of hot water and soak the chiles for 30 minutes. Pour the chiles, along with the oil and water, into a blender or food processor. Add the remaining marinade ingredients and process until very smooth.

2. Place the wings in a large, resealable plastic bag and pour in the marinade. Press the air out of the bag and seal tightly. Turn the bag to distribute the marinade, place in a bowl, and refrigerate for about 2 hours, turning the bag occasionally.

3. Remove the wings from the bag and discard the marinade. Grill over *Direct Medium* heat until the meat is no longer pink at the bone, 16 to 18 minutes, turning occasionally. Serve warm.

MAKES 4 SERVINGS

Greek Chicken Salad Sandwiches

PREP TIME: 15 MINUTES
MARINATING TIME: 2 TO 3 HOURS
GRILLING TIME: 8 TO 10 MINUTES

MARINADE

    Zest and juice of 1 lemon
  2 tablespoons extra virgin olive oil
  2 tablespoons finely chopped fresh oregano
  2 tablespoons finely chopped fresh dill
  1/2 teaspoon granulated garlic
  1/4 teaspoon dry mustard
  1/4 teaspoon ground cumin
  1/4 teaspoon ground coriander
  1/4 teaspoon kosher salt
  1/4 teaspoon ground cayenne pepper

  8 boneless, skinless chicken thighs,
    about 4 ounces each

 3/4 cup creamy cucumber or blue cheese dressing

  4 pita pockets
  8 small green lettuce leaves
  8 thin slices ripe tomato

1. To make the marinade: In a small bowl, whisk the marinade ingredients.
2. Place the thighs in a large, resealable plastic bag and pour in the marinade. Press the air out of the bag and seal tightly. Turn the bag several times to distribute the marinade. Refrigerate for 2 to 3 hours.
3. Remove the thighs from the bag and discard the marinade. Grill over *Direct High* heat until the meat is firm and the juices run clear, 8 to 10 minutes, turning once or twice. Remove from the grill and let rest for a few minutes until cool enough to handle. Chop the chicken into 1/4-inch pieces and place in a bowl. Add enough of the dressing to coat the chicken well. Mix well.
4. Cut each pita pocket into 2 half moons. Open the 8 pockets and slide a lettuce leaf and tomato slice into each one. Fill with the chicken salad. Serve at room temperature.

MAKES 4 SERVINGS

Ginger Chicken Satay
with Peanut Sauce

PREP TIME: 20 MINUTES
MARINATING TIME: 1 HOUR
GRILLING TIME: 5 TO 7 MINUTES

PASTE
- ¼ cup thinly sliced ginger
- ¼ cup thinly sliced shallots
- 4 large garlic cloves, crushed
- 1 serrano chile pepper, stem removed, thinly sliced
- 2 teaspoons red miso [optional]
- ⅓ cup canola oil

- 12 boneless, skinless chicken thighs, about 4 ounces each
- ½ teaspoon kosher salt
- ¼ teaspoon ground cayenne pepper
- 1¼ cups coconut milk
- ½ cup smooth peanut butter
- 2 tablespoons fresh lime juice
- 1 tablespoon fish sauce
- ¼ teaspoon freshly ground black pepper

1. To make the paste: In a blender, or using a large mortar and pestle, process the ginger, shallots, garlic, chile, and red miso, adding the oil slowly to create a paste. Put half of the paste in a large, resealable plastic bag and half in a medium saucepan. Cut the chicken into ½-inch-thick strips and add to the plastic bag, along with the salt and cayenne. Press the air out of the bag and seal tightly. Turn the bag to distribute the paste and refrigerate for 1 hour.

2. Meanwhile, set the saucepan with the paste over medium-high heat and cook until deep golden brown, 3 to 4 minutes, stirring often to prevent burning. Add the remaining ingredients, whisk until smooth, and simmer until it reaches a creamy sauce consistency, 2 to 3 minutes.

3. Remove the chicken strips from the bag and thread them onto skewers so they lie as flat as possible. Grill over *Direct High* heat until fully cooked but not dry, 5 to 7 minutes, turning once. Serve warm with the reheated sauce.

MAKES 4 TO 6 SERVINGS

Sweet and Sour Chicken Thighs
with Wilted Baby Spinach

PREP TIME: **15** MINUTES
MARINATING TIME: **1** TO **2** HOURS
GRILLING TIME: **8** TO **10** MINUTES

MARINADE
1/4 cup rice vinegar
2 tablespoons canola oil
2 tablespoons granulated sugar
1 tablespoon soy sauce
1 to 2 teaspoons hot chili-garlic sauce, such as sambal oelek

6 boneless, skinless chicken thighs, about 4 ounces each
1 plum tomato, seeded and chopped
4 large handfuls baby spinach leaves, about 12 ounces total

1. To make the marinade: In a small bowl, whisk the marinade ingredients.
2. Place the thighs in a large, plastic resealable bag and pour in the marinade. Press the air out of the bag and seal tightly. Turn the bag to distribute the marinade, place the bag in a bowl, and refrigerate for 1 to 2 hours, turning the bag occasionally.
3. Remove the thighs from the bag, reserving the marinade. Pour the marinade into a very large skillet and set it aside. Grill the thighs over *Direct High* heat until the meat is firm and the juices run clear, 8 to 10 minutes, turning once or twice.
4. Meanwhile, bring the marinade to a boil over high heat and allow to boil for 1 full minute. Add the tomato and spinach leaves and cook until the spinach is just wilted, 2 to 3 minutes, turning occasionally. Serve the warm spinach mixture under the chicken.

MAKES 4 SERVINGS

Beer-Marinated Chicken Tacos

PREP TIME: 20 MINUTES
MARINATING TIME: 2 TO 4 HOURS
GRILLING TIME: 8 TO 10 MINUTES

MARINADE
1 cup dark Mexican beer, such as
   Negra Modelo
2 tablespoons dark sesame oil
1 tablespoon finely chopped garlic
1 teaspoon dried oregano
1 teaspoon kosher salt
1/2 teaspoon freshly ground black pepper
1/4 teaspoon ground cayenne pepper

6 boneless, skinless chicken thighs,
   about 4 ounces each

GUACAMOLE
2 ripe Hass avocados
1 tablespoon fresh lime juice
1/4 teaspoon kosher salt

6 flour or corn tortillas [6 to 7 inches]

1. To make the marinade: In a small bowl, whisk the marinade ingredients. Place the thighs in a large, plastic resealable bag and pour in the marinade. Press the air out of the bag and seal tightly. Turn the bag to distribute the marinade, place the bag in a bowl, and refrigerate for 2 to 4 hours, turning the bag occasionally.

2. To make the guacamole: Scoop the avocado flesh into a medium bowl. Add the lime juice and salt. Using a fork, mash the ingredients together. Cover with plastic wrap, placing it directly on the surface to prevent browning, and refrigerate until about 1 hour before serving.

3. Remove the thighs from the bag and discard the marinade. Grill over *Direct High* heat until the meat is firm and the juices run clear, 8 to 10 minutes, turning once or twice. Cut the chicken into thin strips.

4. Warm the tortillas over *Direct Medium* heat for about 1 minute, turning once. Pile the sliced chicken inside the tortillas. Top each with a spoonful of guacamole. Serve warm.

MAKES 4 TO 6 SERVINGS

My friend Marsha was in the Upper Michigan Peninsula. She wanted to make this recipe but couldn't find dark beer or sesame oil. So she called me. I told her to use any beer around and olive oil and to cover her tracks with a little extra Tabasco. Was it perfect? No. Was it still good? Yes. The moral of the story: when in doubt, improvise.

Southwest Chicken and Poblano Burritos

PREP TIME: 25 MINUTES
GRILLING TIME: 14 TO 18 MINUTES

RUB
½ teaspoon pure chile powder
½ teaspoon granulated garlic
½ teaspoon paprika
½ teaspoon kosher salt
¼ teaspoon ground coriander
¼ teaspoon ground cumin
¼ teaspoon freshly ground black pepper

6 boneless, skinless chicken thighs,
 about 4 ounces each
 Extra virgin olive oil
4 medium poblano chile peppers
1 can [16 ounces] refried beans
4 flour tortillas [10 inches]
4 plum tomatoes, cut into ½-inch chunks
2 cups thinly sliced Romaine lettuce
⅓ cup sour cream
1 teaspoon grated lime zest [optional]
1 teaspoon fresh lime juice [optional]

1. To make the rub: In a small bowl, mix the rub ingredients with your fingertips. Lightly brush or spray the thighs with oil. Season with the rub.
2. Grill the chiles over *Direct High* heat until evenly charred on all sides, 6 to 8 minutes, turning as needed. Remove from the grill and allow to cool. Peel away and discard the charred skins and stems. Cut into ¼-inch pieces.
3. In a medium saucepan over low heat, warm the beans for about 10 minutes, stirring occasionally.
4. Grill the thighs over *Direct High* heat until the meat is firm and the juices run clear, 8 to 10 minutes, turning once or twice. Cut into ½-inch chunks. Grill the tortillas over *Direct High* heat until lightly marked and warm, about 20 seconds per side.
5. Lay the tortillas on a work surface. Spoon the refried beans in the center of each tortilla, spreading them to within 1 inch of the edge. Evenly divide the chiles, chicken, tomatoes, and lettuce over the beans. Spoon some sour cream on top [you can spice up the sour cream by blending it with the lime zest and lime juice]. Roll up the burritos and serve warm.

MAKES 4 SERVINGS

Bottle o' Beer Chicken Thighs

PREP TIME: 15 MINUTES
MARINATING TIME: 6 TO 8 HOURS
GRILLING TIME: 20 MINUTES

MARINADE
  1   bottle [12 ounces] beer, preferably lager
  ¼   cup Dijon mustard
  3   tablespoons extra virgin olive oil
  6   scallions, white and light green parts only,
       thinly sliced
  2   large garlic cloves, thinly sliced
  1   tablespoon Worcestershire sauce
  1   teaspoon kosher salt
  ½   teaspoon freshly ground black pepper
  ¼   teaspoon Tabasco® sauce

  8   chicken thighs [with bone and skin],
       5 to 6 ounces each

1. To make the marinade: In a medium bowl, whisk the marinade ingredients.

2. Trim the thighs of any excess skin and fat. Place in a large, resealable plastic bag and pour in the marinade. Press the air out of the bag and seal tightly. Turn the bag to distribute the marinade, place in a bowl, and refrigerate for 6 to 8 hours, turning occasionally.

3. Remove the thighs from the bag and discard the marinade. Pat dry with paper towels and grill over *Direct Medium* heat, skin side down first, until the meat next to the bone is opaque, about 20 minutes, turning every 5 minutes. Serve warm.

MAKES 4 SERVINGS

Mexican Chicken Thighs

PREP TIME: 20 MINUTES
MARINATING TIME: 4 TO 6 HOURS
GRILLING TIME: 35 TO 45 MINUTES

MARINADE
  2 tablespoons extra virgin olive oil
  6 medium garlic cloves, peeled
  1/3 cup finely chopped red onion
  2 dried pasilla chile peppers, stemmed, seeded, and cut into strips
  1 cup diced canned tomatoes with juice
  1 cup amber Mexican beer
  1 tablespoon cider vinegar
  1 teaspoon kosher salt
  1/2 teaspoon dried oregano
  1/4 teaspoon freshly ground black pepper

  12 chicken thighs [with bone and skin], 5 to 6 ounces each

1. To make the marinade: In a small, heavy saucepan over medium heat, warm the oil and cook the garlic until lightly browned, 4 to 5 minutes, turning occasionally. Add the onion and chiles. Cook for about 3 minutes, stirring occasionally. Add the remaining marinade ingredients, bring to a boil, then simmer for 15 minutes. Remove the saucepan from the heat and let the mixture stand for 15 minutes to soften the chiles and blend the flavors. Purée the marinade in a blender.

2. Place the thighs in a large, resealable plastic bag and pour in the marinade [if the bag is not big enough to hold all of them easily, use 2 bags]. Press the air out of the bag[s] and seal tightly. Turn the bag[s] several times to distribute the marinade, place the bag[s] in a bowl, and refrigerate for 4 to 6 hours, turning the bag[s] occasionally.

3. Remove the thighs from the bag[s] and wipe off and discard most of the marinade. Sear the thighs, skin side down first, over *Direct Medium* heat for about 5 minutes, turning once. Continue grilling over *Indirect Medium* heat until the juices run clear and the meat is no longer pink at the bone, 30 to 40 minutes more. Serve warm.

MAKES 4 TO 6 SERVINGS

Chicken in Red Wine Marinade

PREP TIME: 20 MINUTES
MARINATING TIME: 24 HOURS
GRILLING TIME: 40 TO 50 MINUTES

MARINADE
  1 large yellow onion, quartered
  6 large cloves garlic
  1 can [2 ounces] anchovy filets, drained
    Extra virgin olive oil
  ½ cup fresh Italian parsley leaves and
    tender stems
  ¼ cup fresh rosemary leaves
    Kosher salt
    Freshly ground black pepper
  1 bottle [750 ml] dry red wine

  2 whole chickens, about 3 pounds each,
    excess fat removed

1. To make the marinade: In a food processor,
combine the onion, garlic, anchovies, ½ cup of
olive oil, the parsley, rosemary, 1 teaspoon salt,
and 1 teaspoon pepper. Process until the onion is
finely chopped.

2. Place each chicken, breast side down, on a cutting board. Using poultry shears, cut along each
side of the backbone and remove it. Open each
chicken like a book. Split each chicken in half by
cutting right along one side of the breastbone.
Remove and discard the wing tips. Put the chicken
halves in a large, resealable plastic bag [if one bag
isn't large enough, use 2]. Pour the marinade into
the bag[s] and add the wine. Press the air out of the
bag[s] and seal tightly. Turn the bag[s] to distribute the marinade, place in a bowl, and refrigerate
for 24 hours, turning occasionally [the meat and
skin will be red in places from the wine].
3. Remove the chickens from the bag and discard
the marinade. Pat dry with paper towels, brush all
over with olive oil, and season with ½ teaspoon
salt and ¼ teaspoon pepper. Grill, skin side up,
over *Indirect Medium* heat for 40 to 50 minutes.
For crispier skin, turn and move over *Direct
Medium* heat for the last 5 to 10 minutes [watch
for flare-ups]. Remove from the grill and let rest
for about 5 minutes before cutting into pieces.
Serve warm.

MAKES 4 SERVINGS

Honey-Shallot Roasted Chicken

PREP TIME: 20 MINUTES
MARINATING TIME: 4 TO 6 HOURS
GRILLING TIME: 45 TO 55 MINUTES

BRINE
2   lemons, thinly sliced
1½ cups honey
¾   cup kosher salt
½   cup thinly sliced shallots
2   tablespoons lemon-pepper seasoning
1   tablespoon roughly chopped fresh rosemary
1   teaspoon crushed red chile flakes

2   whole chickens, 3 to 4 pounds each

PASTE
¼   cup extra virgin olive oil
2   tablespoons lemon-pepper seasoning
1   tablespoon finely chopped shallots
1   tablespoon finely chopped fresh rosemary
    Zest and juice of 1 lemon
¼   teaspoon ground cayenne pepper

1. To make brine: In a large pot, mix the brine ingredients with 4 cups of water. Bring the brine to a boil and cook for 5 minutes. Remove from the heat, add 8 cups of ice cubes, and allow to cool.
2. Place one of the chickens, breast side down, on a cutting board. Using poultry shears, cut along each side of the backbone and remove it. Open the chicken like a book, and then cut the chicken in half lengthwise. Repeat the process with the other chicken. Submerge the chicken halves in the brine and refrigerate for 4 to 6 hours.
3. To make the paste: In a small bowl, mix the paste ingredients.
4. Remove the chicken halves from the brine and pat dry with paper towels. Rub the paste evenly over the chicken halves.
5. Grill the chicken, skin side down, over *Direct Medium* heat until the skin is golden brown, 5 to 10 minutes. Move the chicken over *Indirect Medium* heat, skin side up, and grill until the juices run clear and the internal temperature reaches 170°F in the breast and 180°F in the thickest part of the thigh, 40 to 45 minutes. Remove from the grill and let rest for 5 minutes before carving and serving.

MAKES 4 TO 6 SERVINGS

Bangkok Barbecued Chicken

PREP TIME: 20 MINUTES
MARINATING TIME: 4 TO 6 HOURS, OR
AS LONG AS 12 HOURS
GRILLING TIME: 30 TO 40 MINUTES

MARINADE

- 4 large garlic cloves
- 1 large shallot, roughly chopped
- 1 one-inch piece of fresh ginger, roughly chopped
- 1 medium jalapeño chile pepper, stem removed and roughly chopped
- 1 cup lightly packed fresh basil leaves
- ½ cup coconut milk
- 2 tablespoons fresh lime juice
- 1 tablespoon brown sugar
- 1 tablespoon fish sauce
- 1 tablespoon soy sauce
- ½ teaspoon ground cumin

- 1 whole chicken, 4 to 5 pounds

1. To make the marinade: In a food processor with the motor running, drop the garlic, shallot, ginger, and jalapeño through the feed tube and process until they are finely minced. Add the basil and process until finely chopped. Add the remaining marinade ingredients and process until well combined.
2. Cut the chicken into 6 pieces: 2 breast pieces, 2 legs with thighs, and 2 wings [remove and discard the wing tips]. Cut 3 or 4 slashes, about ½ inch deep, into the meatier side of the breast and leg-thigh pieces. Place the chicken pieces in a large, plastic resealable bag, and pour in the marinade. Press the air out of the bag and seal tightly. Turn the bag to distribute the marinade, place the bag in a bowl, and refrigerate for 4 to 6 hours, or as long as 12 hours, turning the bag occasionally.
3. Remove the chicken pieces from the bag and discard the marinade. Grill, skin side down, over *Indirect Medium* heat until fully cooked. The breast and wing pieces will take about 30 minutes. The leg-thigh pieces will take about 40 minutes. During the last 10 minutes of grilling time, move the chicken over *Direct Medium* heat until well browned all over, turning once. Serve warm.

MAKES 4 SERVINGS

Barcelona Chicken

PREP TIME: 15 MINUTES
MARINATING TIME: 4 TO 6 HOURS, OR
AS LONG AS 12 HOURS
GRILLING TIME: 30 TO 40 MINUTES

MARINADE
    5 scallions, cut into 1-inch pieces
    1 cup lightly packed fresh basil leaves
    3 large garlic cloves
    2 serrano chile peppers, roughly chopped
  1/4 cup extra virgin olive oil
    2 tablespoons sherry vinegar
    1 teaspoon kosher salt
  1/2 teaspoon freshly ground black pepper

    1 whole chicken, 4 to 5 pounds

1. To make the marinade: In a food processor or blender, combine the marinade ingredients and process to a smooth paste, 1 to 2 minutes.

2. Cut the chicken into 6 pieces: 2 breast pieces, 2 legs with thighs, and 2 wings [remove and discard the wing tips]. Then cut the legs through the joint between the drumsticks and thighs. Cut each half-breast in half crosswise. Place the chicken pieces in a large, plastic resealable bag and pour in the marinade. Press the air out of the bag and seal it tightly. Turn the bag several times to distribute the marinade, place the bag in a bowl, and refrigerate for 4 to 6 hours, or as long as 12 hours, turning the bag occasionally.

3. Remove the chicken pieces from the bag and discard the marinade. Grill, skin side down, over *Indirect Medium* heat until fully cooked. The breast and wing pieces will take about 30 minutes. The leg-thigh pieces will take about 40 minutes. During the last 10 minutes of grilling time, move the chicken over *Direct Medium* heat until well browned all over, turning once. Serve warm.

MAKES 4 SERVINGS

Beer Can Chicken
with Rosemary and Thyme

PREP TIME: 15 MINUTES
GRILLING TIME: 1¼ TO 1½ HOURS

RUB
  1 teaspoon kosher salt
  1 teaspoon paprika
  1 teaspoon finely chopped fresh rosemary
  1 teaspoon dried thyme
  ½ teaspoon lemon zest
  ½ teaspoon freshly ground black pepper

  1 whole chicken, about 4 pounds
  2 teaspoons extra virgin olive oil
  1 can [12 ounces] beer, at room temperature
  2 sprigs fresh rosemary
  1 clove garlic, crushed
    Juice of 1 lemon
  1 teaspoon dried thyme
  ½ teaspoon crushed red pepper flakes

▲▲▲▲▲▲▲▲▲▲▲▲▲▲▲▲▲▲▲▲▲▲▲▲▲▲▲▲▲▲▲▲▲▲▲▲

If you don't like the idea of setting your chicken on a can that's been who-knows-where, you can buy a device that does the same thing.

▼▼▼▼▼▼▼▼▼▼▼▼▼▼▼▼▼▼▼▼▼▼▼▼▼▼▼▼▼▼▼▼▼▼▼▼

1. To make the rub: In a small bowl, mix the rub ingredients.
2. Remove and discard the neck and giblets and any excess fat from the chicken. Lightly rub the chicken all over with the oil. Season the chicken inside and out with the rub. Tuck the tips of the wings behind the chicken's back.
3. Open the beer can and pour out about half the beer. Put the rosemary, garlic, lemon juice, thyme, and red pepper flakes into the beer can [so they will flavor the steam]. Using a can opener, make 2 more holes in the top of the can. Place the beer can on a solid surface. Plunk the chicken cavity over the beer can.
4. Transfer the bird-on-a-can to the grill, balancing the bird on its two legs and the can, like a tripod. Grill over *Indirect Medium* heat until the juices run clear and the internal temperature registers 170°F in the breast and 180°F in the thickest part of the thigh, 1¼ to 1½ hours. Carefully remove the chicken and can from the grill [do not spill contents of beer can, as it will be very hot]. Let the chicken rest for about 10 minutes before lifting from the beer can and cutting into serving pieces. Serve warm.

MAKES 4 SERVINGS

Chicken Under Bricks
with Barbecue Dipping Sauce

RUB
- 1 teaspoon kosher salt
- 1 teaspoon granulated garlic
- ½ teaspoon granulated onion
- ¼ teaspoon freshly ground black pepper

- 1 whole chicken, about 5 pounds, excess fat removed
  Vegetable oil
- 1 cup your favorite barbecue sauce

1. To make the rub: In a small bowl, mix the rub ingredients.
2. Place chicken, breast side down, on a cutting board. Using poultry shears, cut along each side of the backbone and remove it. Open the chicken like a book. Using a sharp knife, make a ½-inch-deep incision between the breasts and flatten the chicken as much as possible. For even cooking, make a ½-inch-deep incision in each joint between the drumsticks and thighs. Remove and discard the wing tips.
3. Season the chicken all over with the rub.
4. Place the chicken, skin side down, over *Indirect High* heat. Lightly coat the bottom of a baking sheet with oil. Place the baking sheet on top of the chicken and weight it down with bricks wrapped in foil [or a cast-iron pan]. Grill until golden brown on the edges, 30 to 35 minutes.
5. Using pot holders, carefully remove the hot bricks and the baking sheet. Using a wide spatula carefully release the chicken from the grate, being careful not to tear the skin. Move the chicken over *Direct Medium* heat and grill until the skin is golden brown all over, 5 to 10 minutes [watch for flare-ups]. Transfer the chicken to a cutting board and let rest for 5 minutes before serving. Cut the chicken into serving pieces. Serve warm with the barbecue sauce for dipping.

MAKES 4 SERVINGS

▲▲

Grilling a flattened chicken under bricks is much more than a gimmick. The weight of the bricks cooks the chicken evenly and presses almost all the skin onto the grate, developing a crispy surface. Be sure to wrap the bricks in foil first, or just use a heavy cast-iron skillet as the weight.

▼▼

Rotisserie Five-Spice Chicken

PREP TIME: 20 MINUTES
MARINATING TIME: 4 TO 6 HOURS
GRILLING TIME: 1 TO 1¼ HOURS

MARINADE
¼ cup orange juice concentrate, defrosted
¼ cup soy sauce
¼ cup fresh lime juice
¼ cup finely chopped fresh cilantro
1 tablespoon dark sesame oil
1 tablespoon minced garlic
1 teaspoon Chinese five-spice powder
½ teaspoon freshly ground black pepper

1 whole chicken, about 4 pounds

1. To make the marinade: In a medium bowl, whisk the marinade ingredients.

2. Remove and discard the wing tips, giblets and excess fat from the chicken. Place the chicken in a large, resealable plastic bag, and pour in the marinade. Press the air out of the bag and seal it tightly. Turn the bag several times to coat the chicken evenly with the marinade. Place the bag in a bowl and refrigerate for 4 to 6 hours, turning the bag occasionally.

3. Remove the chicken from the bag and discard the marinade. Truss the chicken with twine. Following the grill's instructions, secure the chicken in the middle of the rotisserie's spit, put the spit in place, and turn the rotisserie on. Let the chicken rotate over *Indirect High* heat until the juices run clear and the internal temperature reaches 170°F in the breast and 180°F in the thickest part of the thigh, 1 to 1¼ hours. Check the chicken after 30 minutes; if the skin is browning too quickly, reduce the heat to *Indirect Medium*.

4. When the chicken is fully cooked, turn off the rotisserie and, using thick pot holders, remove the spit from the grill. Slide the chicken from the spit onto a cutting board, being careful not to splatter yourself with the hot juices. Let the chicken rest for about 10 minutes before carving into serving pieces. Serve warm.

MAKES 4 SERVINGS

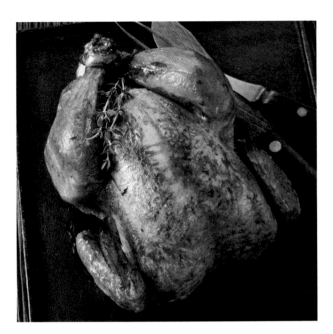

Brined Whole Chicken
with Lemon and Thyme

PREP TIME: 20 MINUTES
MARINATING TIME: 3 TO 4 HOURS
GRILLING TIME: 1¼ TO 1½ HOURS

BRINE
- 1 cup granulated sugar
- 1 cup kosher salt
- 1 tablespoon dried thyme
- 2 lemons

- 1 whole chicken, 3½ to 4 pounds
  Extra virgin olive oil
- 1 teaspoon freshly ground black pepper
- 4 garlic cloves, crushed
- 6 to 8 whole sprigs fresh thyme

1. To make the brine: In a large pot, combine the sugar, salt, and dried thyme. Squeeze the lemon juice into the pot and add the juiced lemon halves. Add 1 gallon of cold water and stir the mixture to dissolve the sugar and salt.
2. Remove and discard the neck, giblets, wing tips, and any excess fat from the chicken. Submerge the chicken in the brine, breast side down, and cover and refrigerate for 3 to 4 hours.
3. Remove the chicken from the pot and discard the brine. Pat the chicken dry with paper towels. Lightly brush the outside of the chicken with oil. Season with the pepper inside and out. Place the garlic and fresh thyme in the cavity of the chicken. Tie the legs together. Grill, breast side up, over *Indirect Medium* heat until the juices run clear and the internal temperature reaches 170°F in the breast and 180°F in the thickest part of the thigh, 1¼ to 1½ hours. Transfer the chicken to a cutting board and let rest for about 10 minutes before carving. Serve warm.

MAKES 4 SERVINGS

Cornish Game Hens
with Garlic-Mint Butter

PREP TIME: 20 MINUTES
GRILLING TIME: 45 TO 55 MINUTES

BUTTER
- 1 stick [½ cup] unsalted butter, softened
- 1 tablespoon minced garlic
- 1 teaspoon kosher salt
- 1 tablespoon finely chopped fresh mint
- ½ teaspoon grated lime zest
- 2 teaspoons fresh lime juice
- ½ teaspoon prepared chili powder
- ¼ teaspoon freshly ground black pepper

- 4 Cornish game hens, 1¼ to 1½ pounds each, wing tips removed

1. To prepare the butter: Place the softened butter in a small bowl. Roughly chop the garlic, and then sprinkle the salt on top. Using both the sharp edge and the flat side of the knife blade, crush the garlic and salt together to create a paste. Add the paste to the bowl along with the remaining butter ingredients and mix well.
2. Remove the giblets from the hens and discard. Working from the cavity end of each hen, run your fingers between the skin and flesh of the breasts and legs to loosen the skin without tearing. Push half of the butter mixture under the skin and massage from the outside to spread the butter mixture evenly over the breasts and legs. Spread the remaining butter over the entire surface of the hens.
3. Truss the hens with twine. Grill over *Indirect High* heat until the juices run clear and the meat is no longer pink at the bone, 45 to 55 minutes. Remove from the grill and let rest for about 5 minutes. Serve warm.

MAKES 4 SERVINGS

Turkey Burgers
with Creamy Cucumber Relish

PREP TIME: 20 MINUTES
GRILLING TIME: 5 TO 7 MINUTES

BURGERS
1¼ pounds ground turkey [or chicken]
 ½ cup bread crumbs
  4 green onions, white and light green parts
     only, minced
  2 tablespoons finely chopped fresh basil
  2 tablespoons fresh lime juice
  1 tablespoon soy sauce
  2 teaspoons minced garlic
 ¼ teaspoon pure chile powder
 ¼ teaspoon kosher salt
 ¼ teaspoon freshly ground black pepper

RELISH
1½ cups coarsely grated seedless cucumber
  2 tablespoons sour cream
  1 tablespoon finely chopped fresh dill
  1 teaspoon minced jalapeño chile
 ½ teaspoon minced garlic
 ¼ teaspoon kosher salt
 ⅛ teaspoon freshly ground black pepper

     Extra virgin olive oil

1. To prepare the burgers: In a large bowl, mix the burger ingredients. Lightly wet your hands and shape the mixture into 8 equal-sized balls. Place them on a baking sheet; press down gently to create burgers about ¾ inch thick. Cover with plastic wrap and refrigerate until ready to grill.
2. To make the relish: Put the cucumber in a fine sieve and squeeze out the excess moisture. In a medium bowl, mix the cucumber with the remaining relish ingredients. Cover with plastic wrap and refrigerate until ready to serve.
3. Generously brush or spray the burgers with oil on both sides. Grill over *Direct Medium* heat until just cooked through [cut one burger open to check], 5 to 7 minutes, turning once. Serve burgers warm with the relish spooned over the top.

MAKES 4 SERVINGS

Turkey Burgers
with Sweet and Sour Pepper Relish

PREP TIME: 30 MINUTES
GRILLING TIME: 26 TO 28 MINUTES

RELISH

- 1 small yellow onion, cut crosswise into ½-inch-thick slices
  Extra virgin olive oil
- 3 red/yellow bell peppers
- 1½ tablespoons cider vinegar
- 2 tablespoons honey
- ½ teaspoon kosher salt
- ¼ teaspoon freshly ground black pepper
- ⅛ teaspoon ground cayenne pepper

BURGERS

- 2 pounds ground turkey
- ¼ cup plain bread crumbs
- 1½ teaspoons kosher salt
- 1 teaspoon dried sage
- ½ teaspoon freshly ground black pepper
- ¼ teaspoon ground nutmeg
- ¼ teaspoon ground ginger
- 2 to 4 tablespoons milk

- 6 hamburger buns or other round rolls
- ⅓ cup stone ground mustard

1. To make the relish: Brush both sides of the onions with oil. Grill the onions and peppers over *Direct Medium* heat until the onions are tender and the peppers are blackened and blistered all over, turning occasionally. The onions will take 8 to 12 minutes and the peppers will take 12 to 15 minutes. Cut the onions into ¼-inch pieces. Divide the onions, reserving half for the relish and half for the burgers. Place the peppers in a bowl and cover with plastic wrap. Let stand for 10 minutes, then peel away the charred skins. Cut each pepper into ¼-inch pieces.

2. In a small saucepan over medium heat, combine the vinegar and honey with 2 tablespoons of water. Stir until the honey dissolves and then simmer for 3 minutes. Add the salt, pepper, and cayenne. In a medium bowl combine the peppers and half of the reserved onions, and pour the warm vinegar mixture over the vegetables. Mix well.

3. To prepare the burgers: In a large bowl, gently mix the reserved onions and all the burger ingredients except the milk. Add as much of the milk as the mixture will absorb. Form into 6 burgers, each about 4 inches in diameter and 1 inch thick. Brush the burgers with oil and grill over *Direct Medium* heat until fully cooked, but still juicy, about 15 minutes, turning once.

4. Grill the buns over *Direct Medium* heat until toasted, about 1 minute. Spread mustard inside each bun, add a burger, and top with the relish. Serve warm.

MAKES 6 SERVINGS

Whole Roasted Turkey Breast
with Sage and Prosciutto

PREP TIME: 20 MINUTES
GRILLING TIME: 1 TO 1¼ HOURS

RUB
  1 tablespoon minced fresh sage
  2 teaspoons kosher salt
  1 teaspoon minced garlic
  1 teaspoon freshly grated lemon zest
  ¼ teaspoon freshly ground black pepper

  1 boneless turkey breast [with skin], about
    2½ pounds
  6 thin slices prosciutto, about 3 ounces
  1 tablespoon extra virgin olive oil

1. To make the rub: In a small bowl, mix the rub ingredients.

2. Gently slide your fingertips under the skin of the turkey breast on one side so that it pulls away from the meat, but leave the skin attached to the meat on all other sides. Spread some of the rub under the skin and pull the skin back in place. Coat the rest of the breast with the remaining rub, pressing it into the meat.

3. On a work surface, arrange four to six 18-inch pieces of twine each 3 to 4 inches apart and perpendicular to the edge of the work surface. Lay 3 of the prosciutto slices vertically, side by side, over the twine. Place the turkey breast, skin side down, on the prosciutto and bring up the ends of the prosciutto around the turkey breast. Place the remaining 3 prosciutto slices over the turkey breast to enclose the rest of the exposed meat. Tie the roast securely with the pieces of twine. Rub the breast with the olive oil.

4. Sear the breast over *Direct Medium* heat until well marked on all sides, 15 minutes, turning 3 times. Move to *Indirect Medium* heat and grill until the internal temperature reaches 165°F, 45 to 60 minutes, turning 2 or 3 times. Remove from the grill and let rest for about 15 minutes before carving [the internal temperature will rise 5 to 10 degrees during this time]. Remove the twine and slice into ¼-inch slices.

MAKES 4 SERVINGS

Anytime you have grilled a big piece of meat like a turkey breast, let it "rest" at room temperature for at least fifteen minutes. The heat of the grill pushes juices toward the center of the meat. The resting period allows juices to ease back into all areas of the meat.

Buttermilk Barbecued Turkey Legs

PREP TIME: 10 MINUTES
MARINATING TIME: 3 TO 4 HOURS
GRILLING TIME: 1½ TO 2 HOURS

MARINADE
   2 cups buttermilk
   2 tablespoons Dijon mustard
   2 tablespoons honey
   2 tablespoons finely chopped fresh rosemary
   2 teaspoons kosher salt
   1 teaspoon dried thyme
   1 teaspoon dried sage
   1 teaspoon dried marjoram
   1 teaspoon freshly ground black pepper

   4 turkey drumsticks, 14 to 16 ounces each
      Canola oil
  ½ cup barbecue sauce

1. To make the marinade: In a medium bowl, whisk the marinade ingredients. Place the drumsticks in a large, resealable plastic bag and pour in the marinade. Press the air out of the bag and seal it tightly. Turn the bag several times to distribute the marinade, and refrigerate for 3 to 4 hours.

2. Remove the drumsticks from the bag, wipe off the excess marinade, and discard the marinade. Lightly brush or spray the drumsticks with oil. Grill over *Indirect Medium* heat until the juices run clear and the internal temperature reaches 180°F, 1½ to 2 hours, turning about every 30 minutes. During the last 15 to 20 minutes, brush occasionally with the barbecue sauce. Serve warm.

MAKES 4 SERVINGS

Smoked Barbecued Turkey

PREP TIME: 15 MINUTES
GRILLING TIME: 2¼ TO 3 HOURS

1 turkey, 11 to 13 pounds, fresh or defrosted
  Extra virgin olive oil
  Kosher salt
  Freshly ground black pepper
3 cups chicken stock
1 stick unsalted butter, cut into 8 pieces
1 tablespoon dried marjoram
1 teaspoon dried thyme
1 teaspoon granulated garlic

3 handfuls hickory chips, soaked in water for
  at least 30 minutes

1. Remove the neck and giblets from the turkey cavity and reserve for another use. If your turkey has a metal or plastic trussing clamp, leave it in place. Lightly brush or spray the turkey all over with oil. Season generously with salt and pepper inside and out.

2. In a medium saucepan over medium-high heat, cook the chicken stock, butter, marjoram, thyme, garlic, and ½ teaspoon of pepper until the butter has melted. Pour 1 cup of the chicken stock mixture into a small bowl. Draw the mixture in the bowl into a kitchen syringe. Inject the syringe into the drumsticks, thighs, and breast of the turkey, refilling the syringe each time. Pour the remaining 2 cups of the chicken stock mixture inside a heavy-duty roasting pan. Place the turkey, breast side up, on a roasting rack, and set inside the pan.

3. Follow the grill's instructions for using wood chips. Grill the turkey over *Indirect Medium* heat, using wood chips for the first 30 minutes. Check the turkey after the first hour. If any parts are getting too dark, wrap them tightly with aluminum foil. Check again after another hour and cover any dark areas with foil. The turkey is done when the internal temperature reaches 165°F in the breast and 175°F in the thickest part of the thigh, 2¼ to 3 hours. Transfer the turkey to a cutting board and let rest for 20 to 30 minutes before carving [the internal temperatures will rise 5°F to 10°F during resting]. Serve warm or at room temperature.

MAKES 11 TO 13 SERVINGS

Barbecued Turkey
with White Wine Gravy

PREP TIME: 30 MINUTES
GRILLING TIME: 2¼ TO 3 HOURS

8 to 10 medium garlic cloves, finely chopped
2 cups lightly packed Italian parsley leaves,
  finely chopped
  Kosher salt
  Freshly ground black pepper
2 teaspoons prepared chili powder
  Zest of 2 oranges
1 stick unsalted butter, softened
1 turkey, 11 to 13 pounds, fresh or defrosted
2 to 4 cups reduced-sodium chicken stock
1 large onion, roughly chopped
1 large carrot, roughly chopped

GRAVY [MAKES ABOUT 3 CUPS]
6 tablespoons collected fat [use melted
  butter if necessary]
6 tablespoons all-purpose flour
4 cups reduced-sodium chicken stock and
  pan juices
½ cup dry white wine
2 tablespoons finely chopped fresh parsley

1. In a small bowl, combine the garlic, parsley, 1 tablespoon of kosher salt, 2 teaspoons of pepper, the chili powder, orange zest [reserve the oranges], and butter. Remove the neck and giblets from the turkey cavity and reserve for another use. If your turkey has a metal or plastic trussing clamp, leave it in place. Starting from the neck end of the turkey, carefully separate the skin from the breast meat with your fingers. Push about half of the butter mixture onto the breast meat under the skin and spread it out evenly. Use the other half of the butter mixture to evenly cover the top and sides of the turkey. Generously season with salt and pepper. Quarter the oranges and place the sections into the cavity of the turkey.

2. Put 2 cups of the chicken stock, the onion, and carrot inside a heavy-duty roasting pan. Place the turkey, breast side up, on a roasting rack, and set inside the pan. Grill over *Indirect Medium* heat, about 350°F. Check the turkey after the first hour. If any parts are getting too dark, wrap them tightly with aluminum foil. If the pan looks dry, add the remaining 2 cups of chicken stock so the pan drippings don't burn. Check the turkey again after another hour. Cover any dark areas with foil. The turkey is done when the internal temperature reaches 165°F in the breast and 175°F in the thickest part of the thigh, 2¼ to 3 hours. Transfer the turkey to a cutting board and let rest for 20 to 30 minutes before carving [the internal temperatures will rise 5°F to 10°F during resting]. It will remain warm for 45 minutes.

3. Meanwhile make the gravy: Pour the juices from the roasting pan into a heatproof glass bowl or measuring cup, leaving any browned bits in the bottom of the roasting pan. Let stand for 3 to 5 minutes while the clear yellow fat rises to the top of the juices. Skim off the fat and put it in a small bowl. If necessary, add enough melted butter to total 6 tablespoons of fat. Place the roasting pan on a side burner or two stovetop burners over medium heat. Add the fat to the pan, sprinkle the flour into the pan, and cook, stirring occasionally with a wooden spoon, until it turns dark brown, 1 to 2 minutes. Whisk in the stock and reserved juices [4 cups total] plus the wine, scraping the browned bits from the bottom of the pan. Simmer for about 5 minutes, whisking occasionally. If the gravy seems to thin, simmer it longer until it is as thick as you like. If it seems too thick, add more stock. Season with salt and pepper to taste. Strain the gravy. Add the parsley. Carve the turkey and serve warm with the gravy.

MAKES 11 TO 13 SERVINGS

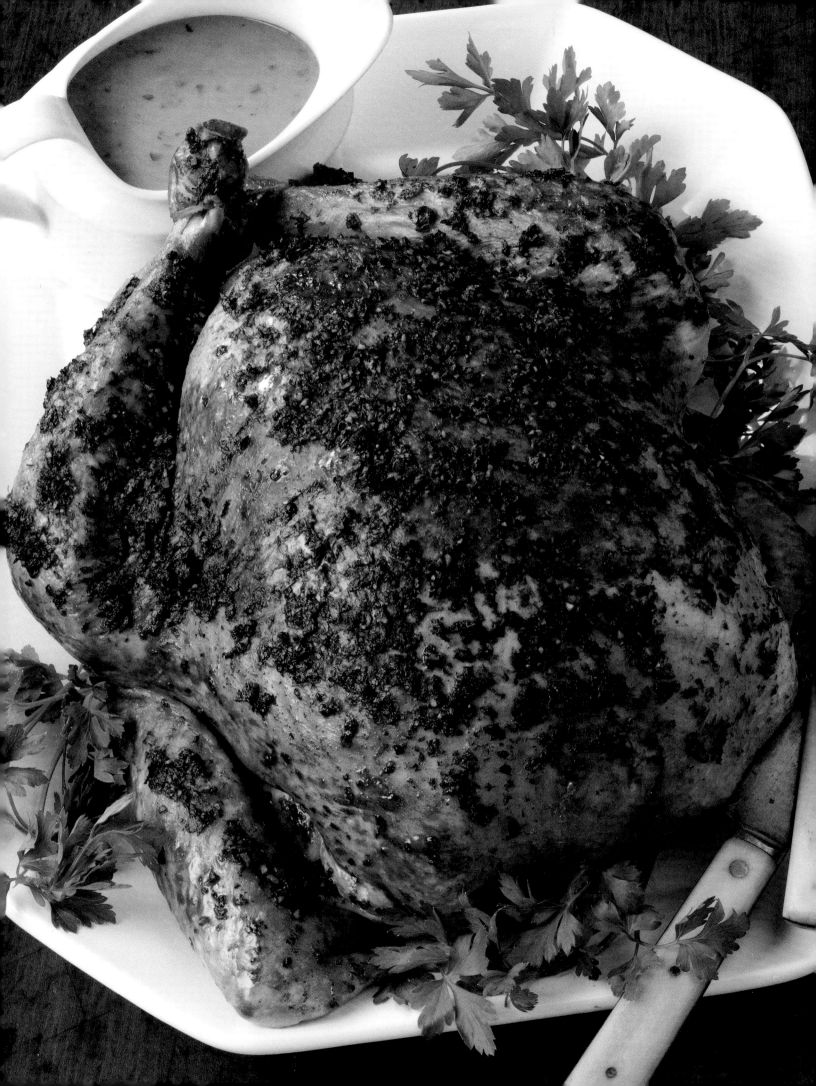

Crispy Duck
with Orange-Ginger Glaze

PREP TIME: 15 MINUTES
MARINATING TIME: 1 TO 2 HOURS
GRILLING TIME: 12 TO 15 MINUTES

MARINADE
- 1/4 cup orange juice concentrate, thawed
- 1/4 cup hoisin sauce
- 1 tablespoon cider vinegar
- 1 tablespoon grated ginger
- 2 teaspoons dark sesame oil
- 1 teaspoon minced garlic
- 1/2 teaspoon kosher salt
- 1/2 teaspoon freshly ground black pepper
- 1/4 teaspoon Tabasco® sauce

- 4 boneless duck breast halves, 6 to 8 ounces each and about 1/2 inch thick

1. To prepare the marinade: In a large bowl, whisk the marinade ingredients.
2. Trim the duck breasts of any skin or fat that hangs over the edges. Score the skin in a diamond pattern with cross hatches at 1/2-inch intervals, but do not cut into the flesh. Place the duck in a large, resealable plastic bag and pour in the marinade. Press the air out of the bag and seal tightly. Turn the bag to distribute the marinade, place in a bowl, and refrigerate for 1 to 2 hours.
3. Remove the duck from the bag and discard the marinade. Grill, skin side down first, over *Direct Low* heat until the internal temperature reaches 160°F, 12 to 15 minutes, turning once. The juices should be slightly pink; the skin, golden brown and crisp. Let the duck rest for 3 to 5 minutes. Serve warm.

MAKES 4 SERVINGS

Hoisin Barbecued Duck

PREP TIME: 10 MINUTES
GRILLING TIME: 40 MINUTES

- 1 whole duck, 5 1/2 to 6 pounds
- 1 teaspoon kosher salt
- 1/4 teaspoon freshly ground black pepper
- 3/4 cup hoisin sauce, divided

1. Remove and discard the neck, giblets, and any excess fat from either end of the duck. Prick the duck skin all over with a small knife, especially along the sides under the breasts, to allow fat to escape during cooking. Fill a large pot with enough water to cover the duck and bring it to a boil. Carefully lower the duck into the water. Place a heavy lid or plate on the duck to keep it submerged [ducks float]. After the water comes back to a boil, lower the heat to a simmer and cook the duck for 15 minutes. Place a long handled spoon or closed tongs into the duck cavity, and carefully remove the duck from the water, allowing the liquid from the cavity to drain back into the pot. Place the duck on a rimmed baking sheet lined with paper towels and pat dry, inside and out.
2. Season the duck with the salt and pepper inside and out. Bend back the wings and tie the legs together with twine. Grill over *Indirect High* heat for 30 minutes. Brush the duck all over with 2 tablespoons of the hoisin sauce. Continue to grill until the skin is dark brown, about 10 minutes more [turn if necessary to prevent sauce from burning on bottom]. Remove from the grill and let rest for 10 to 15 minutes before carving. Serve warm with the remaining hoisin sauce.

MAKES 4 SERVINGS

Penne Pasta with Grilled Duck,
Tomatoes, and Mushrooms

PREP TIME: 30 MINUTES
GRILLING TIME: 10 TO 12 MINUTES

   2 boneless duck breast halves, 4 to 6 ounces each
     Extra virgin olive oil
     Kosher salt
     Freshly ground black pepper
   4 portabello mushrooms, each 4 to 5 inches across
   1 small yellow onion, finely chopped
   2 teaspoons minced garlic
 1/2 teaspoon red pepper flakes
   2 tablespoons red wine vinegar
   1 cup chicken stock
   1 can [14 1/2 ounces] diced tomatoes with juice
 1/2 teaspoon dried oregano
 3/4 pound penne pasta
   1 tablespoon finely chopped fresh thyme
   1 tablespoon unsalted butter
     Freshly grated Parmigiano-Reggino cheese [optional]

1. Trim the duck breasts of any skin or fat that hangs over the edges. Lightly brush the meat side of the duck with oil and season both sides with salt and pepper. Prepare the mushrooms by removing the stems and scraping out the black gills with a teaspoon. Generously brush or spray both sides of the mushrooms with oil and season with salt and pepper. Grill the duck and mushrooms over *Indirect High* heat for 10 to 12 minutes, turning once [the duck will be rare at this point, but it will be cooked further in the sauce]. Set the duck and mushrooms aside to cool. When cool enough to handle, cut the duck and mushrooms into bite-size pieces. Remove the skin from the duck, if desired.

2. In a large skillet over medium-high heat, warm 2 tablespoons of olive oil and cook the onions until they begin to brown, about 5 minutes, stirring occasionally. Add the garlic and red pepper flakes and cook for 1 minute, stirring constantly. Add the red wine vinegar and cook until almost all of the liquid has evaporated. Add the chicken stock, tomatoes with juice, oregano, and salt and pepper to taste. Bring to a boil and then simmer for about 5 minutes.

3. While the sauce is simmering, cook the pasta in large pot of boiling salted water until al dente. Drain. Add the duck, mushrooms, and pasta to the skillet. Cook for 2 to 3 minutes, stirring to combine the pasta with the sauce. Remove from the heat. Add the thyme and butter, stirring to melt the butter. Mix well. Serve warm with the cheese, if desired.

MAKES 4 SERVINGS

FISH

Life is a Beach

I have had some of my best meals at the beach, and I don't mean in posh dining rooms with ocean views. I mean literally *on the beach* ...sitting at a plastic table under an awning while a couple cooks worked nearby on a hot grill. I've found these places, more like stalls than restaurants, along the coast of Mexico, Indonesia, and California; though I'm sure they are all over the tropics. The menu is usually scribbled on a chalkboard, and it doesn't get much more complicated than whatever the local fishermen have brought in that day. The cooks grill the fish quickly, retaining juicy textures and ocean flavors while they turn out regional specialties like fish tacos with fresh salsa, seafood skewers with an herb sauce, and plump fillets with a squeeze of lemon.

Back home I made attempts to recreate these meals and, to be honest, I wasn't always successful. To grill the fish just right, so it is full of flavor and it doesn't stick or break apart on the grate, requires a little finesse. The secrets to success aren't difficult, but they make a huge difference. For example, it seems so obvious to me now, but it took a griller in Baja to teach me about cutting slashes in a whole fish to help the marinade penetrate the flesh. The following pages outline much more of what I've learned through the years. If you follow along, I can't necessarily promise you the sound of

It took a griller in Baja to teach me about cutting slashes in a whole fish to help the marinade penetrate the flesh.

waves lapping on the shore or the feel of tropical breezes over your skin, but your fish will taste great and you will be well on your way to a little culinary vacation in your own backyard.

Types of Fish for the Grill

Firm fillets and steaks	Medium-firm fillets and steaks	Tender fillets	Whole Fish	Shellfish
Swordfish	Monkfish	Striped Bass	Red Snapper	Shrimp
Tuna	Halibut	Bluefish	Striped Bass	Scallops
Salmon	Mahi-mahi	Trout	Grouper	Lobster
Grouper	Mackerel		Bluefish	Oysters
Squid	Chilean Sea Bass		Mackerel	Mussels
	Red Snapper			Clams

Choosing the Perfect Fish

The first thing to know is that firm fish and seafood are the easiest to grill. The meatier they are, the better they hold together as they cook and as you turn them over. Many tender fish work nicely, too, though they require a little more care.

The chart above features many of the delicious, widely available choices from the sea.

Feel free to substitute within the categories above. If you find two fish with similar textures cut into similar portions, you can replace one for the other in almost any grilling recipe.

Another consideration for the grill is the amount of natural oils in fish...the more the better, as in salmon, bluefish, and mackerel. Not only are the oils healthy, but they keep fish moist as it cooks, basting it from within. With leaner fish like halibut and mahi-mahi there is a slightly smaller window of time when the fish go from just right to overcooked [see page 227 for tips on doneness].

Several whole fish lend themselves to grilling, and every professional chef knows a larger piece of fish is more likely to retain its juiciness, though the really big ones are a little cumbersome to turn, so I recommend looking for those that are smaller than two pounds.

You can grill almost any kind of shellfish. Shrimp and scallops top the list in popularity, but one day you must try grilled lobster tails bathed in butter. And if oysters are your thing, buy the largest ones you can. They will be the most succulent hot off the grill.

Freshness

It has been said again and again, but freshness really is the key to the flavor and texture of fish. Buy from a market where the inventory turns over every three days or even faster. The flesh should look bright and glistening. It should be firm and elastic to the touch, and it should smell like fresh seawater, not like fish. Whole fish should have red, moist gills and reflective skin. Oysters, clams, and mussels must be alive when you buy them. Their shells should be tightly closed. Live mussels sometimes gape open ever so slightly, but they should close right away when you tap on them.

Refrigerate fish and seafood as soon as you can. In a world where you have time and energy to spare, you would take the fillets and steaks out of their packaging, sit them on top of some crushed ice in a bowl, cover them with plastic wrap to prevent them absorbing other aromas in the refrigerator, and replace the ice before it melts. But realistically, if you store them in their packaging in the coldest part of your refrigerator for no more than a couple days, they will be fine...except for mollusks like oysters, clams, and mussels, which need to breathe, so take them out of their bags and grill them the same day.

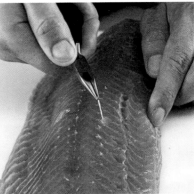

1. If any part of a fish is much thinner than the rest, such as the belly of this salmon, cut it off. Either grill the thinner part separately or discard it if it is just trim.

2. Some fillets look completely boneless, but if you run a fingertip over their surface you might feel the ends of tiny bones [called pin bones], which must be removed.

3. Use needle-nose pliers or a similar tool, like tweezers, to grab the end of each bone and carefully pull it out at an angle [towards the head of the fish] without tearing the flesh.

Five Keys to Prevent Sticking

1. High Heat. Preheat the grill on high for ten minutes to get it hot, really hot. Fish comes off the grate after a delicate crust of caramelization develops between the flesh and grate. That requires heat, usually high heat.

2. A Clean Grate. Use a brass-bristle brush to get the grate really clean.

3. A Little Oil. Coat the fish on all sides with a thin layer of oil, but don't oil the grate.

4. A Lot of Patience. Leave the fish alone. Caramelization happens faster when the fish stays in place on the hot grate. Keep the lid down as much as possible and turn the fish only once.

5. Good Timing. Grill the first side a little longer than the second. The first side down on the grates will be the side that eventually faces you on the plate. By grilling it a few minutes longer than the second, it will release more easily and will look fabulous on the plate, with picture-perfect grill marks.

1. Shellfish like shrimp and scallops do best over direct high heat, and so do fillets up to 1¼ inches thick. For thicker fillets, use direct medium heat.

2. Turn fish fillets when dark grill marks have developed on the first side, indicating that the surface has caramelized to a point where it releases naturally from the grate.

3. Once a fillet is cooked, you can remove the skin by sliding a long spatula between the skin and flesh. The skin will stay on the grate, and the fillet goes to the plate.

Peeling and Deveining Shrimp

1. Grab the shell where it meets the legs and peel it back.

2. Remove the shell and the legs. If you like, leave one section of the shell attached near the tail. The shrimp looks better this way.

3. With a small, sharp knife, cut a very shallow slit along the back of the shrimp, exposing the thin black vein.

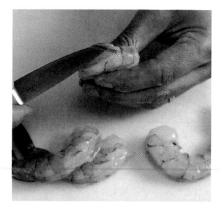

4. Use the tip of the knife or your fingers to lift the vein out. A little running water helps, too.

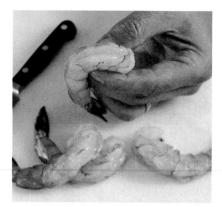

5. The shrimp should be deveined with the shallowest cut possible, to keep the meat plump.

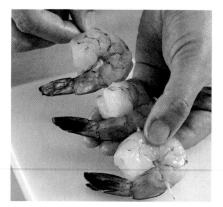

6. Thread each one through both its head and tail. Leaving a little room between them ensures even grilling.

The Perfect Scallop

Scallops are at the top of my list of grilled seafood. Of course, they need to be big enough that they don't fall through the grate, so look for bay scallops or sea scallops that are at least 1 inch wide [never the tiny, rubbery calico scallops]. I am not a fan of skewering scallops, because the skewers have a tendency to rip the buttery flesh when you turn them.

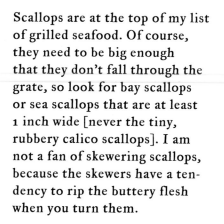

Scallops should be cream colored or slightly pink. The bright white ones have been soaked in tripoly-phosphate and water. As soon as they get hot, the water runs out and prevents browning.

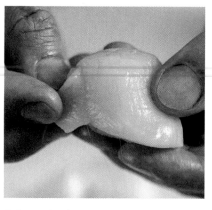

Often the large abductor muscle, which was once attached to the scallop's shell, is left on. Peel it off and discard it. It's chewy.

Donenness

Overcooking fish is a crime. With almost every kind of fish, you should get it off the grill before it flakes by itself. You are looking for an internal temperature of 125°F to 130°F, but that's tough to measure with fillets or steaks, so rely on the knife poke test, as well as the times given in the recipes and in the chart below.

Shellfish don't flake, but they turn an opaque, pearly white color at the center when they are cooked. The only way to know for sure how the center looks is to cut into it, so plan on sacrificing one or two shellfish [a nice little snack for the chef, if they are done].

If the flesh just begins to flake [in other words, to separate into layers] when you poke it with the tip of a sharp knife, that's perfect.

In this photo, the shrimp on the left is underdone, the shrimp on the right is overdone, and the shrimp in the middle is just right.

Grilling Guide for Fish and Seafood

Type	Thickness/Weight	Approximate Grilling Time
Fish, fillet or steak*	¼ to ½ inch thick	**3 to 5 minutes** Direct High
	½ to 1 inch thick	**5 to 10 minutes** Direct High
	1 to 1¼ inches thick	**10 to 12 minutes** Direct High
Fish, whole	1 pound	**15 to 20 minutes** Indirect Medium
	2 to 2½ pounds	**20 to 30 minutes** Indirect Medium
	3 pounds	**30 to 45 minutes** Indirect Medium
Shrimp		**2 to 4 minutes** Direct High
Scallop		**3 to 6 minutes** Direct High
Mussel (discard any that do not open)		**5 to 6 minutes** Direct High
Clam (discard any that do not open)		**8 to 10 minutes** Direct High
Oyster		**3 to 5 minutes** Direct High
Lobster tail		**7 to 11 minutes** Direct Medium

*includes halibut, red snapper, salmon, sea bass, swordfish, and tuna

Note: General rule for grilling fish: 4 to 5 minutes per ½ inch thickness; 8 to 10 minutes per 1 inch thickness.

Marinated Scallop Brochettes
with Roasted Tomatillo Salsa

PREP TIME: 30 MINUTES
MARINATING TIME: 1 HOUR
GRILLING TIME: 10 TO 12 MINUTES

MARINADE

- 3 tablespoons extra virgin olive oil
- 1 teaspoon freshly grated lime zest
- 1 tablespoon fresh lime juice
- 1 tablespoon minced garlic
- ½ teaspoon crushed red pepper flakes
- ½ teaspoon kosher salt
- ¼ teaspoon freshly ground black pepper

24 large sea scallops, about 1½ ounces each

SALSA

- 1 small yellow onion, cut crosswise into ½-inch slices
  Extra virgin olive oil
- 8 medium tomatillos, about ½ pound total, husked and rinsed
- 1 medium poblano chile
- ¼ cup lightly packed fresh cilantro leaves and tender stems
- 1 medium garlic clove, crushed
- ½ teaspoon dark brown sugar
- ½ teaspoon kosher salt

1. To make the marinade: In a medium bowl, whisk the marinade ingredients.

2. Rinse the scallops under cold water. Remove and discard the small, tough side muscle from each scallop that has one. Place the scallops in the bowl with the marinade and toss to evenly coat them. Cover the bowl and refrigerate for 1 hour.

3. To make the salsa: Lightly brush or spray the onion slices on both sides with oil. Grill the onions, tomatillos, and chile over *Direct High* heat until lightly charred all over, 6 to 8 minutes, turning once or twice. Transfer the onions and tomatillos to a blender or food processor and place the chile on a work surface. When the chile is cool enough to handle, remove and discard the skin, stem, and seeds. Add the chile to the onions and tomatillos, along with the remaining salsa ingredients. Process until fairly smooth. Taste and adjust the seasonings if necessary.

4. Remove the scallops from the bowl and discard the marinade. Thread the scallops through their sides onto skewers so the scallops lie flat. Grill over *Direct High* heat until just opaque in the center, 4 to 6 minutes, turning once. Serve warm with the salsa.

MAKES 4 SERVINGS

▲▲▲

I love this salsa because it is delicious as it is written here but also because it adapts so well to ingredients I usually have in the kitchen: tomatoes, cucumbers, avocados, jalapeños, and scallions. Just be sure to grill the tomatillos long enough to develop some sweetness. Otherwise they are too tangy for my taste.

▼▼▼

Seared Sea Scallops
with Sweet and Spicy Dipping Sauce

PREP TIME: 10 MINUTES
GRILLING TIME: 4 TO 6 MINUTES

SAUCE
- 4 large garlic cloves, thinly sliced
- 2 tablespoons soy sauce
- 2 tablespoons rice vinegar
- 1 tablespoon fish sauce
- 1 tablespoon granulated sugar
- ½ teaspoon crushed red pepper flakes
- 1 tablespoon fresh lemon juice
- 10 fresh cilantro leaves

- 20 large sea scallops, about 1½ ounces each
  Vegetable oil
  Kosher salt
  Freshly ground black pepper

1. To make the sauce: In a small saucepan, combine the garlic, soy sauce, vinegar, fish sauce, sugar, and red pepper flakes. Bring the mixture barely to a simmer over medium heat, but do not boil it. Remove the pan from the heat. Add the lemon juice. Set the sauce aside until ready to serve. Add cilantro leaves just before serving.

2. Rinse the scallops under cold water and pat dry. Remove and discard the small, tough side muscle from each scallop that has one. Brush or spray the scallops on all sides with oil and season with salt and pepper to taste. Thread the scallops through their sides onto skewers so the scallops lie flat. Grill over *Direct High* heat until just opaque in the center, 4 to 6 minutes, turning once. Serve warm with the dipping sauce.

MAKES 4 SERVINGS

Grilled Shrimp
with Smooth Mango-Lime Vinaigrette

PREP TIME: 20 MINUTES
MARINATING TIME: 1 HOUR
GRILLING TIME: 2 TO 4 MINUTES

MARINADE
- ¼ cup canola oil
- 1 teaspoon kosher salt
- 1 teaspoon granulated garlic
- ½ teaspoon freshly ground black pepper
- ½ teaspoon ground cayenne pepper

- 32 large shrimp, about 1½ pounds, peeled and deveined

VINAIGRETTE
- ½ cup roughly chopped ripe mango [about ½ mango]
- ¼ cup canola oil
- ¼ cup fresh cilantro leaves
- 1 whole scallion, root end trimmed
- 1 tablespoon fresh lime juice
- 1 tablespoon rice vinegar
- 1 half-inch section fresh ginger, peeled and chopped
- ½ teaspoon kosher salt
- ¼ teaspoon freshly ground black pepper

1. To make the marinade: In a large bowl, mix the marinade ingredients. Add the shrimp and toss to coat thoroughly. Cover and refrigerate for up to 1 hour.

2. To make the vinaigrette: In a blender or food processor, combine the vinaigrette ingredients. Process for about 1 minute or until the texture is smooth and emulsified.

3. Remove the shrimp from the bowl and discard the marinade. Grill over *Direct High* heat until the shrimp are firm to the touch and just turning opaque in the center, 2 to 4 minutes, turning once. Serve the shrimp warm with the vinaigrette.

MAKES 4 TO 6 SERVINGS

Shrimp and Andouille
Skewers with Roasted Tomatoes

PREP TIME: 15 MINUTES
MARINATING TIME: 30 MINUTES
GRILLING TIME: 2 TO 4 MINUTES

MARINADE
    Juice of 1 lemon
  2 teaspoons extra virgin olive oil
$1/4$ teaspoon granulated garlic
$1/4$ teaspoon paprika
$1/4$ teaspoon kosher salt
$1/4$ teaspoon freshly ground black pepper

32 large shrimp, about $1^{1}/_{2}$ pounds, peeled and deveined, tails removed

12 cherry tomatoes
 6 ounces andouille sausage
 2 tablespoons finely chopped fresh Italian parsley

1. To make the marinade: In a medium bowl, whisk the marinade ingredients. Add the shrimp and toss to coat evenly. Cover and refrigerate up to 30 minutes.
2. Cut each of the tomatoes in half through its stem. Cut the sausage crosswise into slices about $1/3$ inch thick. Alternating the shrimp, tomato halves, and sausage, thread the ingredients onto skewers [be sure to skewer each shrimp through both its head and tail so it doesn't spin around]. Grill over *Direct High* heat until the shrimp are firm to the touch and just turning opaque in the center, 2 to 4 minutes, turning once. Transfer the skewers to a platter and scatter the parsley over the top. Serve warm.

MAKES 4 TO 6 SERVINGS

Shrimp
with "Ooo-Wee" Rémoulade

PREP TIME: 15 MINUTES
GRILLING TIME: 2 TO 4 MINUTES

SAUCE
$1/2$ cup mayonnaise
 1 tablespoon capers, drained and minced
 1 tablespoon sweet pickle relish
 1 tablespoon finely chopped fresh tarragon
 2 teaspoons minced shallot
 1 teaspoon tarragon vinegar
 1 teaspoon minced garlic
$1/2$ teaspoon Dijon mustard
$1/4$ teaspoon paprika
$1/8$ teaspoon kosher salt

40 large shrimp, about 2 pounds, peeled and deveined
    Extra virgin olive oil
    Kosher salt
    Freshly ground black pepper

1. To make the sauce: In a medium bowl, whisk the sauce ingredients. If not using right away, cover and refrigerate for as long as 24 hours.
2. Thread the shrimp onto skewers through both the heads and tails. Lightly brush or spray the shrimp all over with oil and season with salt and pepper to taste. Grill over *Direct High* heat until the shrimp are firm to the touch and just turning opaque in the center, 2 to 4 minutes, turning once. Serve warm with the sauce.

MAKES 4 TO 6 SERVINGS

Grilled Shrimp
with Mexican Salsa

PREP TIME: 20 MINUTES
GRILLING TIME: 6 TO 10 MINUTES

SALSA
- 12 tomatillos, husked and rinsed
- 1 ripe Hass avocado, cut into $1/4$-inch dice
- 1 medium ripe tomato, cut into $1/4$-inch dice
- $1/4$ cup finely chopped white onion
- 2 tablespoons finely chopped fresh cilantro
- 1 teaspoon minced jalapeño chile
- $1/2$ teaspoon minced garlic
- $1/4$ teaspoon kosher salt
- $1/4$ teaspoon freshly ground black pepper

- 16 to 20 jumbo shrimp, $1^1/2$ to 2 pounds, peeled and deveined
  Extra virgin olive oil
  Kosher salt
  Freshly ground black pepper
  Paprika

1. To make the salsa: Grill the tomatillos over *Direct High* heat until they are well marked and beginning to collapse, 4 to 6 minutes, turning occasionally. Put the tomatillos in a food processor and process until smooth. Pour the tomatillos into a medium bowl. Add the remaining salsa ingredients and mix well.
2. Lightly brush or spray the shrimp with oil and season to taste with salt, pepper, and paprika. Grill over *Direct High* heat until the shrimp are firm to the touch and just turning opaque in the center, 2 to 4 minutes, turning once. Serve warm with the salsa.

MAKES 4 SERVINGS

Jerk Shrimp

PREP TIME: 15 MINUTES
MARINATING TIME: 30 TO 45 MINUTES
GRILLING TIME 2 TO 4 MINUTES

MARINADE
- $1/2$ cup roughly chopped yellow onion
- 1 jalapeño chile, roughly chopped
- 3 tablespoons white wine vinegar
- 2 tablespoons soy sauce
- 2 tablespoons canola oil
- $1/2$ teaspoon Tabasco® sauce
- $1/2$ teaspoon ground allspice
- $1/4$ teaspoon granulated garlic
- $1/4$ teaspoon ground cinnamon
- $1/4$ teaspoon kosher salt
- $1/4$ teaspoon freshly ground black pepper
- $1/8$ teaspoon ground nutmeg

- 40 large shrimp, about 2 pounds, peeled and deveined
- 1 lime, cut into wedges

1. To make the marinade: In a food processor, combine the marinade ingredients. Process until smooth.
2. Put the shrimp in a large, plastic resealable bag and pour in the marinade. Press out the air and seal the bag tightly. Turn the bag to distribute the marinade and refrigerate for 30 to 45 minutes.
3. Remove the shrimp from the bag and discard the marinade. Thread shrimp onto skewers through both the heads and tails. Grill over *Direct High* heat until the shrimp are firm to the touch and just turning opaque in the center, 2 to 4 minutes, turning once. Place on a serving platter, squeeze a little lime juice over the shrimp, and serve warm.

MAKES 4 TO 6 SERVINGS

Shrimp Tacos
with Poblano-Avocado Salsa

PREP TIME: 20 MINUTES
GRILLING TIME: 13 TO 17 MINUTES

SALSA

 1 ear corn, husked
 6 scallions, white and light green parts only
    Extra virgin olive oil
 1 medium poblano chile
 1 cup cherry tomatoes, cut into ¼-inch dice
 1 Hass avocado, cut into ¼-inch dice
 1 tablespoon finely chopped fresh cilantro
 1 tablespoon fresh lime juice
 1 teaspoon minced garlic
 ½ teaspoon kosher salt, divided
 ½ teaspoon freshly ground black pepper, divided

32 large shrimp, about 1½ pounds, peeled and
    deveined
 8 flour tortillas [8 inches]

1. To make the salsa: Brush or spray the corn and scallions all over with oil. Grill the corn until browned in spots and tender, the scallions until lightly marked, and the chile until blackened and blistered in spots, over *Direct Medium* heat, turning occasionally. The corn and chile will take 10 to 12 minutes and the scallions will take 3 to 4 minutes. Trim the root ends off the scallions; finely chop the remaining parts and put them in a medium bowl. Cut the kernels off the corn and add them to the bowl. When cool enough to handle, peel off the loosened bits of skin from the chile and discard along with the stem; finely chop the remaining parts of the chile and add to the bowl. Add the remaining salsa ingredients, including ¼ teaspoon salt and ¼ teaspoon pepper. Drizzle 1 tablespoon of olive oil into the bowl and mix thoroughly.

2. Brush or spray the shrimp all over with oil and season with the remaining ¼ teaspoon salt and ¼ teaspoon pepper. Grill over *Direct High* heat until the shrimp are firm to the touch and just turning opaque in the center, 2 to 4 minutes, turning once. Grill the tortillas over *Direct Medium* heat until warm, 30 to 60 seconds, turning once. Fill the tortillas with salsa and shrimp. Serve warm.

MAKES 4 SERVINGS [8 TACOS]

Tangerine Lobster Tails

PREP TIME: 10 MINUTES
GRILLING TIME: 7 TO 11 MINUTES

- 1 cup unsalted butter
  Zest and juice of 2 tangerines
- 1/2 teaspoon kosher salt
- 4 lobster tails, 6 to 8 ounces each

1. In a small saucepan over very low heat, melt the butter. After the butter has melted, skim off the foam. Add the tangerine zest, juice, and salt. Pour about 1/2 cup of the butter mixture into a small cup; reserve the rest for the dipping sauce.
2. Using kitchen shears split each tail in half lengthwise. [If desired to prevent the lobster meat from curling during cooking, thread a skewer lengthwise through the center of the meat of each piece.] Lightly brush the exposed meat with the butter in the cup. Grill the lobster tails, meat side down, over *Direct Medium* heat until lightly marked, 2 to 3 minutes [watch for flare-ups]. Turn the tails over and grill until the meat is white and firm but not dry, 5 to 8 minutes longer, brushing occasionally with some of the butter in the cup. Remove from the grill and serve warm with the reserved butter on the side.

MAKES 4 SERVINGS

Halibut á la Tunisia

PREP TIME: 10 MINUTES
MARINATING TIME: 1 HOUR
GRILLING TIME: 6 TO 8 MINUTES

PASTE
- 2 tablespoons fresh lemon juice
- 2 tablespoons extra virgin olive oil
- 2 teaspoons paprika
- 1 teaspoon ground coriander
- 1 teaspoon ground cumin
- 1 teaspoon granulated garlic
- 1 teaspoon kosher salt
- 1/4 teaspoon freshly ground black pepper

- 4 halibut fillets, about 6 ounces each
  and 1 inch thick
  Extra virgin olive oil

1. To make the paste: In a small bowl, thoroughly mix the paste ingredients.
2. Spread the paste evenly on all sides of the halibut. Cover with plastic wrap and refrigerate for about 1 hour.
3. Grill over *Direct High* heat until the halibut just begins to flake when you poke it with the tip of a knife [see page 227], 6 to 8 minutes, turning once. Remove from the grill, drizzle each fillet with about 1/2 teaspoon of olive oil. Serve immediately.

MAKES 4 SERVINGS

Soft Tacos with Halibut,
Guacamole, and South American Slaw

PREP TIME: 30 MINUTES
GRILLING TIME: 7 TO 9 MINUTES

SLAW

  8 ounces jicama, peeled and coarsely shredded
  1 medium carrot, coarsely shredded
  1 small red bell pepper, stem and seeds removed, thinly sliced
  1 small red onion, halved lengthwise and thinly sliced crosswise
  2 tablespoons extra virgin olive oil
  2 tablespoons fresh lime juice
  1/2 teaspoon granulated sugar
  1/4 teaspoon ground cumin
  1/4 teaspoon kosher salt
  1/4 teaspoon freshly ground black pepper

GUACAMOLE

  2 large ripe Hass avocados, mashed
  1 tablespoon finely chopped fresh cilantro
  2 teaspoons fresh lime juice
  2 teaspoons minced garlic
  1/2 teaspoon kosher salt
  1/4 teaspoon freshly ground black pepper

  4 halibut fillets, about 8 ounces each and 3/4 inch thick
    Extra virgin olive oil
  1 teaspoon pure chile powder
  1/2 teaspoon kosher salt
  1/4 teaspoon freshly ground black pepper

  8 flour tortillas [8 inches]

1. To make the slaw: In a medium bowl, toss to combine the slaw ingredients.

2. To make the guacamole: In a medium bowl, combine the guacamole ingredients and stir with a fork until thoroughly blended. Cover the surface with plastic wrap to prevent browning.

3. Lightly brush or spray the halibut all over with oil; season with the chile powder, salt, and pepper. Grill over *Direct High* heat until the halibut just begins to flake when you poke it with the tip of a knife [see page 227], 6 to 8 minutes, turning once. Remove from the grill and break into 1-inch pieces with a fork.

4. Heat the tortillas over *Direct High* heat for about 20 seconds per side. Wrap in a kitchen towel to keep warm. For each taco, layer a warm tortilla with fish, slaw, and guacamole. Roll up loosely. Serve warm.

MAKES 8 TACOS

If the halibut sticks a little to the grate and falls apart when you turn it, don't worry. This recipe calls for breaking the fish into pieces anyway. The main thing is that the fish isn't overcooked.

Halibut
with Grill-Roasted Lemon and Caper Dressing

PREP TIME: 15 MINUTES
GRILLING TIME: 10 TO 14 MINUTES

DRESSING
2 medium lemons
4 tablespoons extra virgin olive oil, divided
1 tablespoon capers, drained
1 tablespoon finely chopped fresh chives
¼ teaspoon kosher salt
¼ teaspoon freshly ground black pepper

RUB
1 teaspoon granulated onion
1 teaspoon finely chopped fresh dill
½ teaspoon kosher salt
¼ teaspoon freshly ground black pepper

4 halibut fillets, 6 to 8 ounces each
and about 1 inch thick
Extra virgin olive oil

1. To make the dressing: Cut a ½-inch slice off both ends of each lemon. Cut each lemon in half lengthwise. Lightly brush or spray the cut sides of the lemons with 1 tablespoon of the oil. Grill the lemons over *Direct High* heat until nicely browned, 4 to 6 minutes, turning once. Remove the lemons from the grill and allow to cool. Squeeze the lemons through a sieve into a small bowl. Discard the rinds and seeds. You should have about 1 tablespoon of lemon juice. Add the capers, then whisk in the remaining 3 tablespoons oil to form a dressing. Whisk in the rest of the dressing ingredients, and adjust the seasonings if necessary.
2. To make the rub: In a small bowl, mix the rub ingredients.
3. Generously brush or spray the halibut on both sides with oil and season with the rub. Grill over *Direct High* heat until the halibut just begins to flake when you poke it with the tip of a knife [see page 227], 6 to 8 minutes, turning once. Whisk the dressing one last time. Serve the fish warm with the dressing poured over the top.

MAKES 4 SERVINGS

Jamaican Halibut
with Tropical Salsa

PREP TIME: 30 MINUTES
MARINATING TIME: 1 HOUR
GRILLING TIME: 6 TO 8 MINUTES

MARINADE
1 cup fresh orange juice
½ cup Jamaican dark rum
¼ cup soy sauce
2 tablespoons fresh lime juice
1 tablespoon freshly grated ginger
1 tablespoon dried thyme
1 teaspoon kosher salt
½ teaspoon ground allspice
½ teaspoon ground cayenne pepper

4 halibut fillets, about 6 ounces each
and 1 inch thick

SALSA
1 cup finely diced ripe pineapple
½ cup finely diced ripe banana
½ cup finely diced cucumber
1½ tablespoons fresh lime juice
1 tablespoon minced red bell pepper
4 green onions, thinly sliced
½ teaspoon dark sesame oil
½ teaspoon kosher salt
½ teaspoon Tabasco® sauce
¼ teaspoon freshly ground black pepper

Vegetable oil

1. To make the marinade: In a medium bowl, whisk the marinade ingredients. Add the fillets and turn to coat them evenly. Cover with plastic wrap and refrigerate for 1 hour, turning once or twice.
2. To make the salsa: In a medium bowl, combine the salsa ingredients.
3. Remove the halibut from the bowl, pat dry with paper towels, and discard the marinade. Brush or spray both sides with oil. Grill over *Direct High* heat until the halibut just begins to flake when you poke it with the tip of a knife [see page 227], 6 to 8 minutes, turning once. Serve warm with the salsa.

MAKES 4 SERVINGS

FISH

Grilled Salmon
and Smoky Tomato-Chipotle Sauce

PREP TIME: 20 MINUTES
GRILLING TIME: 8 TO 11 MINUTES

SAUCE
- 2 tablespoons extra virgin olive oil
- ½ cup finely chopped red onion
- 2 teaspoons minced garlic
- 1 teaspoon dried oregano
- 1 can [28 ounces] whole tomatoes
- 1 canned chipotle chile in adobo sauce
- ½ teaspoon granulated sugar
- ½ teaspoon kosher salt
- ¼ teaspoon finely chopped black pepper

- 4 salmon fillets [with skin], 6 to 8 ounces each and about 1 inch thick
  Extra virgin olive oil
  Kosher salt
  Freshly ground black pepper

1. To make the sauce: In a medium saucepan over medium-high heat, warm the oil. Add the onion and cook until soft, 4 to 5 minutes, stirring occasionally. Add the garlic and oregano and cook until the garlic is light brown, about 1 minute, stirring occasionally. Add the tomatoes with the juice and the chile. Season with the sugar, salt, and pepper. Bring the sauce to a boil, then lower the heat to a simmer. Cook for 30 to 40 minutes, stirring occasionally and crushing the tomatoes with the back of a large spoon as they soften. Carefully pour the sauce into a food processor. Puree and return to the pan. Keep warm over low heat.

2. Generously brush or spray the fillets with oil and season with salt and pepper to taste. Grill, flesh side down, over *Direct High* heat until you can lift the fillets off the grate with tongs without sticking, 6 to 8 minutes. Turn the fillets and cook them to desired doneness, 2 to 3 minutes for medium-rare. Slip a spatula between the skin and flesh, and transfer the fillets to serving plates. Serve warm with the sauce.

MAKES 4 SERVINGS

Grilled Salmon
with Green Goddess Dressing

PREP TIME: 10 MINUTES
GRILLING TIME: 8 TO 11 MINUTES

SAUCE
- 1/3 cup mayonnaise
- 1/4 cup sour cream
- 2 tablespoons finely chopped fresh chives
- 1 tablespoon minced scallions
- 1 tablespoon tarragon vinegar
- 3 anchovy fillets, minced

- 4 salmon fillets [with skin], 6 to 8 ounces each and about 1 inch thick
  Extra virgin olive oil
  Kosher salt
  Freshly ground black pepper

1. To make the sauce: In a medium bowl, whisk the sauce ingredients.
2. Generously brush or spray the fillets with oil and season with salt and pepper to taste. Grill, flesh side down, over *Direct High* heat until you can lift the fillets with tongs off the grate without sticking, 6 to 8 minutes. Turn the fillets and cook them to desired doneness, 2 to 3 minutes for medium-rare. Slide a spatula between the skin and flesh, and transfer the fillets to serving plates. Spoon the sauce over the fillets. Serve immediately.

MAKES 4 SERVINGS

Salmon
with Thai Cucumber Relish

PREP TIME: 15 MINUTES
MARINATING TIME: 15 MINUTES TO 4 HOURS
GRILLING TIME: 6 TO 8 MINUTES

RELISH
- 2 tablespoons fresh lime juice
- 1 tablespoon fish sauce
- 1 tablespoon soy sauce
- 1 tablespoon granulated sugar
- 1 tablespoon finely chopped fresh mint
- 1 tablespoon finely chopped fresh cilantro
- 1 teaspoon minced serrano chile
- 1/2 teaspoon minced garlic
- 1 cup finely chopped or thinly sliced seedless cucumber

- 4 salmon steaks, 5 to 7 ounces each and about 3/4 inch thick
- 3 tablespoons dark sesame oil
  Freshly ground black pepper

1. To make the relish: In a medium bowl, whisk the relish ingredients except the cucumber. Add the cucumber, stir well, and allow to sit at room temperature for 15 minutes or as long as 4 hours.
2. Lightly brush or spray the steaks all over with the oil. Season with pepper to taste. Grill over *Direct High* heat until cooked to desired doneness, 6 to 8 minutes for medium-rare, turning once [make sure you leave the salmon grilling long enough on the first side so that it releases from the grate and is easy to turn]. Serve warm with the relish.

MAKES 4 SERVINGS

Cedar-Planked Salmon
with Honey-Lime Dressing

PREP TIME: 20 MINUTES
GRILLING TIME: 25 TO 35 MINUTES

DRESSING
  2 tablespoons fresh lime juice
  2 tablespoons rice vinegar
  2 tablespoons Dijon mustard
  2 tablespoons honey
  2 tablespoons minced fresh chives
  1 teaspoon kosher salt
  1/2 teaspoon granulated garlic
  1/2 teaspoon freshly ground black pepper
  1/4 teaspoon ground cayenne pepper
  1/4 cup extra virgin olive oil

  1 large salmon fillet [with skin],
    2 1/2 to 3 pounds, about 16 inches long
    and 3/4 inch thick
  1/2 teaspoon kosher salt
  1/4 teaspoon freshly ground black pepper
  1 untreated cedar plank [about 16 inches by
    8 inches and at least 3/4 inch thick],
    submerged in water for at least 1 hour

1. To make the dressing: In a blender, combine the dressing ingredients except the oil. Mix until well blended. With the blender still running, slowly pour in the oil to make a smooth dressing.

2. Place the salmon on a rimmed baking sheet. Using needle nose pliers, remove and discard any pin bones from the salmon. Season the flesh side of the salmon with the salt and pepper. Pour about half of the dressing over the flesh and use a brush to distribute it evenly.

3. Remove the soaked plank from the water and immediately place it over *Direct High* heat until the edges start to smoke and char, 3 to 10 minutes [watch carefully so it doesn't flame]. Move the plank over *Indirect High* heat and place the salmon, skin side down, on the plank. Grill until the salmon is just slightly pink in the center and brown on the edges, 20 to 25 minutes. Remove the plank and salmon to a heatproof surface. Serve warm with the remaining dressing.

MAKES 8 TO 10 SERVINGS

Soft Tacos with Red Snapper
and Tomatillo-Avocado Salsa

PREP TIME: 20 MINUTES
GRILLING TIME: 16 TO 20 MINUTES

SALSA

   1 small green bell pepper
   4 medium tomatillos, husked and rinsed
  1/2 cup loosely packed fresh cilantro leaves and tender stems
  1/2 large ripe Hass avocado
   1 medium garlic clove
   2 teaspoons fresh lime juice
  1/4 teaspoon kosher salt
  1/4 teaspoon freshly ground black pepper
      Tabasco® sauce

   1 Romaine lettuce heart
   4 skinless red snapper fillets, about 6 ounces each
      Vegetable oil
   1 teaspoon pure chile powder
  1/2 teaspoon kosher salt
   8 to 10 flour tortillas [10 inches]

1. To make the salsa: Grill the bell pepper over *Direct High* heat until the skin is blackened and blistered all over, 12 to 15 minutes, turning occasionally. Place the pepper in a small bowl and cover with plastic wrap to trap the steam. Set aside for at least 10 minutes, then peel the skin from the pepper, discarding the stem and seeds.

2. Grill the tomatillos over *Direct High* heat until they are well marked and beginning to collapse, 4 to 6 minutes, turning occasionally. Put the tomatillos and the bell pepper in the bowl of a food processor and process for a few seconds. Add the remaining salsa ingredients, including Tabasco sauce to taste. Process until well combined but still a bit chunky.

3. Clean, core, and cut the lettuce into thin, cross-wise slices and put into a medium bowl. Lightly brush or spray both sides of the fillets with oil and season with the chile powder and salt. Grill over *Direct High* heat just until the fish begins to flake when poked with small, sharp knife, 3 to 4 minutes, turning once. Remove from the grill, separate into large flakes with two forks, and put into a medium bowl.

4. Heat the tortillas over *Direct High* heat for about 20 seconds per side. Wrap in a kitchen towel to keep warm. Pile the lettuce and fish on the warm tortillas and top with the salsa.

MAKES 4 SERVINGS

Red Snapper
Veracruz Style

PREP TIME: 30 MINUTES
GRILLING TIME: 15 TO 16 MINUTES

SAUCE
- 2 tablespoons extra virgin olive oil
- 1 small yellow onion, halved lengthwise and thinly sliced crosswise
- 1 can [14½ ounces] ready-cut tomatoes with juice
- ⅓ cup stuffed green olives, coarsely chopped
- 2 tablespoons capers, rinsed and drained
- 2 teaspoons finely chopped jalapeño chile
- 1 teaspoon minced garlic
- ½ teaspoon dried oregano
- ½ teaspoon dried thyme
- ¼ teaspoon kosher salt
- ⅛ teaspoon freshly ground black pepper

- 2 whole red snappers, about 1½ pounds each, scaled, cleaned, fins removed
- 2 tablespoons fresh lime juice
- ½ teaspoon kosher salt
- 4 large Romaine lettuce leaves
  Extra virgin olive oil

1. To make the sauce: In a large skillet over medium heat, warm the oil and cook the onion until tender, about 10 minutes, stirring occasionally. Add the remaining sauce ingredients and simmer until most of the tomato liquid has evaporated, 12 to 15 minutes, stirring occasionally. Keep warm.
2. Rinse the fish under cold water and pat dry. With a sharp knife, make 2 diagonal slashes almost to the bone on each side of the fish. Rub the lime juice and salt into the slashes. Lightly brush or spray the lettuce leaves on both sides with the oil and place 2 of them on the grill. Place each fish on a lettuce leaf and grill over *Direct Medium* heat for 8 minutes. Place the remaining 2 leaves on the grill, next to the fish, and carefully roll each fish over onto a new leaf. Continue to grill until each fish is opaque at the bone, 7 to 8 minutes more. Transfer each fish with two spatulas to a cutting board. Remove the lettuce leaf and skin, cut off the heads and tails, and lift portions of the fish off the bone and onto serving plates. Spoon some warm sauce alongside the fish.

MAKES 4 SERVINGS

Sea Bass
with Roasted Pepper Vinaigrette

PREP TIME: 20 MINUTES
GRILLING TIME: 17 TO 22 MINUTES

VINAIGRETTE

- 3 bell peppers, preferably red, yellow, and orange
- 3 tablespoons extra virgin olive oil
- 2 tablespoons fresh orange juice
- 2 tablespoons finely chopped Italian parsley
- 1 tablespoon fresh lemon juice
- 1/2 teaspoon minced garlic
- 1/2 teaspoon ground cumin
- 1/4 teaspoon kosher salt
- 1/4 teaspoon freshly ground black pepper
- 1/4 teaspoon Tabasco® sauce

- 4 skinless Chilean sea bass fillets, about 6 ounces each, and 1 inch thick
  Extra virgin olive oil
  Kosher salt
  Freshly ground black pepper

1. To make the vinaigrette: Grill the bell peppers over *Direct High* heat until the skins are blackened and blistered all over, 12 to 15 minutes, turning occasionally. Place the peppers in a small bowl and cover with plastic wrap to trap the steam. Set aside for at least 10 minutes, then remove the peppers from the bowl and peel away the charred skins. Cut off the tops and remove the seeds. Cut the peppers into 1/4-inch strips and set aside. In a medium bowl, whisk the remaining vinaigrette ingredients. Add the peppers and set aside for as long as 1 day.

2. Lightly brush or spray the fillets with oil and season with salt and pepper to taste. Grill over *Direct High* heat until the flesh is opaque in the center, 5 to 7 minutes, carefully turning once. Serve warm with the vinaigrette spooned over the top.

MAKES 4 SERVINGS

Sea bass in one of the best fish for grill. Its slightly oily flesh stays moist even when it is fully cooked and starting to flake. It also releases from the grate easily, as long as the grill is hot enough, the grate is clean enough, and you wait until the fish is beautifully browned on the first side before trying to turn it.

Seared Sea Bass
with Green Pea Sauce

PREP TIME: 15 MINUTES
GRILLING TIME: 5 TO 7 MINUTES

SAUCE
2 tablespoons unsalted butter
¼ cup finely chopped yellow onion
1 cup low-sodium chicken stock
1 cup frozen petite green peas
2 teaspoons finely chopped fresh tarragon
2 tablespoons heavy cream
½ teaspoon kosher salt
⅛ teaspoon freshly ground black pepper

6 skinless Chilean sea bass fillets, about
6 ounces each and 1 inch thick
Extra virgin olive oil
1 tablespoon finely chopped fresh tarragon
¾ teaspoon kosher salt
¼ teaspoon freshly ground black pepper
1½ cups medium-diced cherry tomatoes

1. To make the sauce: In a medium saucepan over medium heat, melt the butter. Add the onions and cook until tender but not brown, 2 to 3 minutes, stirring occasionally. Add the chicken stock. Raise the heat to high and bring to a vigorous boil. Add the peas and cook until just tender, 1 to 2 minutes. Pour into a blender and add the tarragon. With the lid of the blender off, process until very smooth, 1 to 2 minutes. Clean the medium saucepan and return the sauce to it. Add the remaining sauce ingredients, mix well, and simmer until it reaches a sauce consistency, about 5 minutes, stirring occasionally.

2. Lightly brush or spray the fillets with oil. Season with the tarragon, salt, and pepper. Grill over *Direct High* heat until the flesh is opaque in the center, 5 to 7 minutes, carefully turning once.

3. Meanwhile reheat the sauce. Spoon some sauce on each plate, place a fillet in the middle, and scatter the tomatoes over the top. Serve warm.

MAKES 6 SERVINGS

Whole Striped Bass
in Moroccan Marinade

PREP TIME: 15 MINUTES
MARINATING TIME: 2 TO 3 HOURS
GRILLING TIME: 12 TO 15 MINUTES

MARINADE
 3 large garlic cloves
 1 large shallot, roughly chopped
 1 one-inch section fresh ginger, peeled and
   roughly chopped
 ½ cup loosely packed fresh Italian parsley leaves
   and tender stems
 ½ cup loosely packed fresh basil leaves and
   tender stems
 6 tablespoons extra virgin olive oil
 1 teaspoon freshly grated lemon zest
 2 tablespoons fresh lemon juice
 1½ teaspoons kosher salt
 1 teaspoon paprika
 ½ teaspoon ground cumin
 ¼ teaspoon freshly ground black pepper

 2 whole striped bass, 1½ to 2 pounds each,
   scaled, cleaned, fins removed
   Kosher salt
 6 lemon wedges

1. To make the marinade: In a food processor, mince the garlic, shallot, and ginger. Add the parsley and basil, and process until finely chopped. Add the remaining marinade ingredients. Process until smooth.

2. Cut 3 or 4 slashes about ½ inch deep on each side of the fish about 1 inch apart.

3. Spread the marinade over the fish, inside and out, working it well into the cuts. Place the fish on a baking sheet, cover with plastic wrap, and refrigerate for 2 to 3 hours.

4. Grill over *Direct Medium* heat until the flesh is opaque near the bone but still juicy, 12 to 15 minutes, carefully turning once. Transfer to a cutting board and cut off the heads and tails. Cut along the backbone of each fish and use the side of the knife to push the fillets off the bones. Season with salt to taste and serve warm with the lemon wedges.

MAKES 4 TO 6 SERVINGS

Swordfish Steaks
with Gazpacho Salsa

PREP TIME: 20 MINUTES
MARINATING TIME: 30 TO 60 MINUTES
GRILLING TIME: 16 TO 20 MINUTES

DRESSING
   3 tablespoons extra virgin olive oil
   1 tablespoon red wine vinegar
   1 teaspoon Dijon mustard
   1 teaspoon minced garlic
   1 teaspoon kosher salt
   1/4 teaspoon Worcestershire sauce
   1/4 teaspoon freshly ground black pepper

SALSA
   1 three-inch section English cucumber
   2 small tomatoes, halved crosswise
   1 large zucchini
   1 medium yellow onion
   1 tablespoon finely chopped fresh dill

MARINADE
   2 tablespoons extra virgin olive oil
   2 teaspoons red wine vinegar
   1 teaspoon herbes de Provence
   1/2 teaspoon kosher salt
   1/4 teaspoon freshly ground black pepper

   4 swordfish steaks, about 8 ounces each
     and 1 inch thick

1. To make the dressing: In a small bowl, whisk the dressing ingredients.
2. To make the salsa: Cut the cucumber into 1/2-inch dice and drain on paper towels. Gently squeeze the seeds from the tomato halves. Cut the zucchini lengthwise into 4 slices about 1/3 inch thick, and the onion crosswise into 4 slices about 1/3 inch thick. Evenly brush about half the dressing over the tomatoes, zucchini, and onions, and grill over *Direct Medium* heat until well marked, 8 to 10 minutes for each vegetable, turning once or twice. Transfer the grilled vegetables to a work surface. Cut the zucchini and onions into small pieces, each about 1/4 inch, and roughly chop the tomatoes. In a serving bowl, mix the grilled vegetables with the cucumber, dill, and the remaining dressing. Set aside at room temperature.
3. To make the marinade: In a small bowl, whisk the marinade ingredients.
4. Place the swordfish steaks on a large plate and evenly brush the marinade over both sides. Cover the steaks with plastic wrap and refrigerate for 30 to 60 minutes.
5. Grill over *Direct Medium* heat until the steaks are opaque in the center but still juicy, 8 to 10 minutes, turning once. Serve warm with the salsa spooned over the top.

MAKES 4 SERVINGS

Swordfish Steaks
with Watercress Sauce

PREP TIME: 15 MINUTES
GRILLING TIME: 8 TO 10 MINUTES

SAUCE
  1 large garlic clove
  1 cup tightly packed fresh watercress leaves
$^1/_4$ cup tightly packed fresh basil leaves
$^1/_2$ cup sour cream
  2 tablespoons mayonnaise
$^1/_2$ teaspoon grated lemon zest
  1 tablespoon fresh lemon juice
$^1/_2$ teaspoon Worcestershire sauce
$^1/_4$ teaspoon kosher salt
$^1/_8$ teaspoon freshly ground black pepper

  4 swordfish steaks, about 6 ounces each
     and 1 inch thick
     Extra virgin olive oil
  1 teaspoon minced garlic
$^1/_2$ teaspoon paprika
$^1/_4$ teaspoon kosher salt
$^1/_4$ teaspoon freshly ground black pepper

1. To make the sauce: In a food processor mince the garlic. Add the watercress and basil and process until chopped. Add the remaining sauce ingredients and process until smooth. Pour the sauce into a small bowl. If not using right away, cover and refrigerate for as long as 24 hours.

2. Lightly brush or spray the steaks on both sides with oil and then season evenly with the garlic, paprika, salt, and pepper. Grill over *Direct Medium* heat until the steaks are opaque in the center but still juicy, 8 to 10 minutes, turning once. Serve warm with the sauce.

MAKES 4 SERVINGS

Smokehouse Almond-Crusted Ruby Red Trout Fillets

PREP TIME: 15 MINUTES
GRILLING TIME: 5 MINUTES

CRUST
- 1 cup plain bread crumbs
- ½ cup smokehouse almonds
- ¼ cup fresh Italian parsley leaves
- 2 tablespoons finely chopped shallots
- ½ teaspoon kosher salt
- ¼ teaspoon freshly ground black pepper
  Zest and juice of 1 lemon
- 3 tablespoons unsalted butter, melted but not hot

- 6 ruby red trout fillets, 4 to 6 ounces each, trimmed

1. To make the crust: In a food processor, pulse the crust ingredients, except the butter, until the almonds and parsley leaves are finely chopped. Add the butter and pulse just to combine.

2. Place the trout fillets, skin side down, on a work surface. Cover the flesh of each fillet with the crust. Grill, skin side down, over *Indirect High* heat until the fish is opaque in the center, about 5 minutes. Serve warm.

MAKES 4 TO 6 SERVINGS

Provençal Tuna Sandwiches

PREP TIME: 25 MINUTES
GRILLING TIME: 9 TO 11 MINUTES

DRESSING
 ½ cup black olives, pitted and finely chopped
 ⅓ cup extra virgin olive oil
 2 tablespoons finely chopped fresh basil
 2 tablespoons red wine vinegar
 1 tablespoon minced shallots
 2 teaspoons capers, minced
 ½ teaspoon stone ground mustard
    Kosher salt
    Freshly ground black pepper

 1 pound fresh albacore or ahi tuna, about
    1 inch thick
    Extra virgin olive oil
 ¼ teaspoon kosher salt
 ¼ teaspoon freshly ground black pepper
 6 French sandwich rolls
 2 ripe tomatoes, thinly sliced
 3 hard-cooked eggs, thinly sliced
    Arugula or Boston [bibb] lettuce

1. To make the dressing: In a large bowl, whisk the dressing ingredients including salt and pepper to taste.

2. Lightly coat both sides of the tuna with oil and season with the salt and pepper. Grill over *Direct High* heat until just turning opaque throughout, 8 to 10 minutes, turning once. While the tuna is still warm, break into bite-size pieces and add to the bowl with the dressing; toss gently.

3. Cut the rolls open and brush the cut sides with oil. Grill, cut side down, over *Direct High* heat until lightly toasted, about 30 seconds.

4. Spoon some of the tuna mixture on the bottom half of each roll. Top with tomatoes, eggs, and lettuce, and drizzle with a little more olive oil if desired. Serve at room temperature.

MAKES 6 SERVINGS

Citrus Pesto Tuna

with Fennel-Tangerine Salad

PREP TIME: 30 MINUTES
GRILLING TIME: 50 TO 60 MINUTES

MARINADE

- 2 medium heads garlic
- 1/4 cup plus 2 tablespoons extra-virgin olive oil
- 2 tablespoons finely chopped fresh basil
- 1 tablespoon finely chopped oregano leaves
  Zest and juice of 1 tangerine
  Zest and juice of 1 lemon
- 1 teaspoon kosher salt
- 1/2 teaspoon freshly ground black pepper

- 4 sushi-grade [ahi] tuna steaks, about 10 ounces each and 1 1/2 inches thick

SALAD

- 1 cup thinly shaved fennel bulb
- 1/2 cup tangerine segments
- 2 tablespoons finely chopped scallions, green tops only
- 1 tablespoon finely chopped fresh mint
- 1 tablespoon fresh tangerine juice
- 1 tablespoon fresh lemon juice
- 1 tablespoon extra virgin olive oil
- 1/4 teaspoon kosher salt
- 1/8 teaspoon freshly ground black pepper

1. To make the marinade: Remove the loose, papery outer skin from the heads of garlic. Using a sharp knife, cut about 1/2 inch off the top to expose the cloves. Place each garlic head on a large square of heavy-duty aluminum foil and drizzle 1 tablespoon of olive oil over the top of the cloves. Fold up the foil sides and seal to make a packet, leaving a little room for the expansion of steam. Grill over *Indirect Medium* heat until the cloves are soft and golden brown, 45 minutes to 1 hour. When cool enough to handle, squeeze out the garlic cloves into a medium bowl. Add the remaining marinade ingredients, including the remaining 1/4 cup olive oil, and mash the ingredients with the back of a fork. Coat the tuna steaks with the marinade and refrigerate for 20 to 30 minutes before grilling.
2. To make the salad: In a small bowl, gently mix the salad ingredients.
3. Grill the tuna steaks over *Direct High* heat just until the surface is well marked and the center is still red, 3 to 4 minutes, turning once. Remove from the grill and serve warm with the salad.

MAKES 4 SERVINGS

VEGGIES AND SIDES

VEG & SIDES

Grilling with a Diva

Whenever I grill vegetables, I think of one summer evening when I made them with a culinary diva. My friend Don had invited my wife and me for dinner at his home in Santa Barbara, California, to christen his new Weber® gas grill. He decided to have several people over and ask each one to help with a part of the meal. He would provide the raw ingredients and set us loose to grill. It sounded like my kind of fun.

When we arrived, Don handed me a bag of bell peppers, onions, and corn. "See what you can do with these," he said. We had a couple hours before dinner, so when Don asked if anyone wanted to join him in picking up one of the other guests, I volunteered. We wound our way through the hillsides of Santa Barbara and into Montecito, a little town right on the edge of the Pacific Ocean. Don drove through the gates of a retirement community, parked outside a townhouse, and we walked to the front door.

There stood a tall, elegant woman with a big smile. It was the legendary Julia Child. I had read every cookbook she had written and watched her on television for hours and hours. She was my culinary diva. I knew all about her straight-talking style, so I shouldn't have been surprised by it on the way back to Don's house. He mentioned that I would be grilling vegetables that night, and she immediately said, "Oh, I don't like grilled vegetables at all, do you?" I laughed nervously, and she went on. "People grill them into a mish-mash and make them all taste the same. You don't cook fish and chicken the same way for the same meal. I think each vegetable should have its own taste, too."

The pressure was on, to say the least. I figured the best way to improve my chances of serving Julia vegetables that she would enjoy was to recruit her to my team. Fortunately she agreed. We decided to grill-roast the peppers and peel them so they would be sweet and tender. We made a balsamic vinaigrette and used it as a marinade for the onions, to give them a boost of flavor before they went on the grill. And we blended softened butter with parmesan cheese and fresh herbs to slather on the grilled corn. "Yes, definitely butter," Julia said. "People would probably be happier if they ate a bit more butter."

While we grilled, Julia and I talked about organic vegetables [she was not necessarily impressed with them] and the miniature greens so popular at the time [she thought they were pointless] and also politics [she was a staunch Democrat]. Her opinions about food and everything else were direct and unapologetic, but she was never cruel. Her honesty was endearing. I am relieved to say dinner went well and she loved the grilled vegetables, but even more importantly, I am grateful for what she taught me about good cooking. Vegetables and side dishes may not be the main attraction, but if you give each one a bit of its own pizzazz, it's *bon appetit!*

She immediately said, "Oh, I don't like grilled vegetables at all, do you?" I laughed nervously...

Grilling Vegetables: The Five Essentials

1. Grill what's growing at the time. Vegetables in season locally have big advantages over whatever has been shipped from across the world. They are riper, so they taste better. That means you can grill them simply with great results. Plus, they cost less.

2. Expose as much surface area as possible. Cut each vegetable to give you the biggest area to put in direct contact with the grate. The more direct contact the better the flavors will be. For example, rather than cutting a zucchini crosswise into round circles, cut it lengthwise to expose more of the interior.

Look for bell peppers with smooth sides, so you can cut them lengthwise and lay the pieces flat for the most direct contact with the grate.

3. Use the good oil. Vegetables need oil to prevent sticking and burning. Neutral oils like canola oil will do the job fine, but an extra virgin olive oil provides the added benefit of improving the flavor of virtually every vegetable. Brush on just enough to coat each side thoroughly but not so much that the vegetables would drip oil and cause flare-ups. Season the vegetables generously with salt and pepper [some of it will fall off]. For more flavors, marinate the vegetables at room temperature for 20 minutes to an hour in olive oil, vinegar, garlic, herbs, and spices.

4. Baste now and then. Vegetables have a lot of water that evaporates quickly on a hot grill. That's good news for flavor because as the water evaporates the real vegetable flavors get more intense. But some vegetables, especially mushrooms, are prone to shrinking and drying out when they loose water, so if they start to wrinkle, brush them with a little oil.

5. Stay in the zone. Just about everything from asparagus to zucchini tends to cook best over direct medium heat. The temperature on the grill's thermometer should be somewhere between 350° and 450°F. If any parts get a little too dark, turn the vegetables over. Otherwise turn them as few times as possible.

When ears of corn are done, many of the kernels are golden brown and some are much darker. The juices of the sweet corn have caramelized right on the surface. Serve the ears of corn right away or use a sharp knife to cut the kernels off the cobs as seen here. The bowl is helpful for catching the kernels.

When is it done?

Each vegetable has its own character. The right doneness for one type may be quite different than another. And personal preference plays as big a role here as it does with red meat. I like firm vegetables such as onions and fennel to be somewhere between crisp and tender. If you want them softer, grill them a few minutes longer, although watch them carefully for burning. The grill intensifies the sweetness of vegetables quickly and that can lead to burning. Also, cut the vegetables as evenly as you can. A ½ inch thickness is right for most of them. If one edge is much thinner than the other, it tends to burn before the others are done.

Grilling Guide for Vegetables

Type	Thickness/Size	Approximate Grilling Time
Artichoke	whole	Boil 12 to 15 minutes; cut in half and grill **4 to 6 minutes** Direct Medium
Asparagus		**6 to 8 minutes** Direct Medium
Beet		**1 to 1½ hours** Indirect Medium
Bell pepper	whole	**10 to 15 minutes** Direct Medium
Bell/Chile pepper	¼-inch slices	**6 to 8 minutes** Direct Medium
Corn, husked		**10 to 15 minutes** Direct Medium
Corn, in husk		**25 to 30 minutes** Direct Medium
Eggplant	½-inch slices	**8 to 10 minutes** Direct Medium
Fennel	¼-inch slices	**10 to 12 minutes** Direct Medium
Garlic	whole	**45 to 60 minutes** Indirect Medium
Green onion	whole	**3 to 4 minutes** Direct Medium
Leek	halved	Steam 4 to 5 minutes; grill **3 to 5 minutes** Direct Medium
Mushroom, shiitake or button		**8 to 10 minutes** Direct Medium
Mushroom, portabello		**10 to 15 minutes** Direct Medium
Onion	halved	**35 to 40 minutes** Indirect Medium
Onion	½-inch slices	**8 to 12 minutes** Direct Medium
Potato	whole	**45 to 60 minutes** Indirect Medium
Potato	½-inch slices	**14 to 16 minutes** Direct Medium
Potato, new	halved	**15 to 20 minutes** Direct Medium
Pumpkin (3 pounds)	halved	**1½ to 2 hours** Indirect Medium
Squash, acorn (2 pounds)	halved	**45 to 60 minutes** Indirect Medium
Squash, buttercup or butternut (2 pounds)	halved	**50 to 55 minutes** Indirect Medium
Squash, patty pan		**10 to 12 minutes** Direct Medium
Squash, yellow	½-inch slices	**6 to 8 minutes** Direct Medium
Squash, yellow	halved	**6 to 10 minutes** Direct Medium
Sweet potato	whole	**50 to 60 minutes** Indirect Medium
Sweet potato	¼-inch slices	**8 to 10 minutes** Direct Medium
Tomato, garden	½-inch slices	**2 to 4 minutes** Direct Medium
Tomato, garden	halved	**6 to 8 minutes** Direct Medium
Tomato, plum	halved	**6 to 8 minutes** Direct Medium
Tomato, plum	whole	**8 to 10 minutes** Direct Medium
Zucchini	½-inch slices	**6 to 8 minutes** Direct Medium
Zucchini	halved	**6 to 10 minutes** Direct Medium

Basic Grilled Asparagus

PREP TIME: 5 MINUTES
GRILLING TIME: 4 TO 6 MINUTES

  1 pound asparagus
  2 tablespoons extra virgin olive oil
  ½ teaspoon kosher salt

1. Remove and discard the tough bottom of each
asparagus spear by grasping each end and bending it
gently until it snaps at its natural point of tenderness, usually ⅔ of the way down the spear. Using
a vegetable peeler, peel off the outer skin from the
bottom half of each remaining spear.
2. Spread the asparagus on a large plate. Drizzle the
oil over the top and sprinkle the salt evenly. Turn
the spears until they are evenly coated.
3. Grill the asparagus [perpendicular to the grate]
over *Direct Medium* heat until browned in spots
but not charred, 4 to 6 minutes, turning occasionally. Serve warm or at room temperature.

MAKES 4 SERVINGS

▲▲▲▲▲▲▲▲▲▲▲▲▲▲▲▲▲▲▲▲▲▲▲▲▲▲▲▲▲▲▲▲▲▲▲▲▲▲▲

Look for firm asparagus stalks with deep green or
purplish tips. Also check the bottom of the spears.
If they are dried up, chances are they have been sitting around for too long. Thicker spears fare better
on the grill.

▽▽

Asparagus
with Sherry-Bacon Vinaigrette

PREP TIME: 10 MINUTES
GRILLING TIME: 6 TO 8 MINUTES

  ¼ pound bacon [4 to 6 slices]
  1 teaspoon finely chopped fresh thyme
  ½ teaspoon minced garlic
  1 tablespoon sherry vinegar
  ¼ teaspoon kosher salt
  ¼ teaspoon freshly ground black pepper
  1 pound asparagus
  ½ small red onion, thinly sliced crosswise

1. In a medium skillet over medium heat, lay the
bacon in a single layer and cook until crispy, 8 to 10
minutes, turning occasionally. Drain the bacon on
paper towels, reserving the bacon fat in the skillet.
2. Pour off all but 3 tablespoons of the bacon fat
and return the skillet over medium heat. Add the
thyme and garlic to the skillet and let them sizzle
for about 10 seconds. Add the vinegar, salt, and
pepper, and then remove the skillet from the heat.
3. Remove and discard the tough bottom of each
asparagus spear by grasping each end and bending it
gently until it snaps at its natural point of tenderness, usually ⅔ of the way down the spear. Using
a vegetable peeler, peel off the outer skin from the
bottom half of each remaining spear. Put the asparagus on a plate or platter. Pour the vinaigrette over
the asparagus. Turn the asparagus to coat them
evenly. Finely chop the drained bacon.
4. Grill the asparagus over *Direct Medium* heat
until browned in spots but not charred, 6 to 8 minutes, turning them occasionally. Arrange the asparagus on a serving platter. Sprinkle the bacon over
the asparagus. Arrange the onions on top. Serve
warm or at room temperature.

MAKES 4 SERVINGS

Artichokes
with Oregano and Salt

PREP TIME: 20 MINUTES
GRILLING TIME: 4 TO 6 MINUTES

- 4 large artichokes, 10 to 12 ounces each
  Juice of 1 lemon
- 1 tablespoon extra virgin olive oil
- 1/2 teaspoon dried oregano
- 1/4 teaspoon granulated garlic
- 1/4 teaspoon kosher salt
- 1/2 cup [1 stick] unsalted butter, melted

1. Bring a large pot of salted water to a boil.
2. Cut the stem off each artichoke, leaving about 1/2 inch attached. Peel off the dark outer leaves until you expose the light green, yellowish leaves underneath. Lay each artichoke on its side and cut off the top half so you have just the firm base to work with. Cut each base in half lengthwise through the stem and drop each half into a large bowl of water mixed with the lemon juice [to prevent discoloration].
3. One at a time, lift the artichokes from the water and use a teaspoon to scoop out all of the fuzzy choke and purplish leaves. Cook the artichokes in the boiling salted water until you can pierce them easily with a knife, 12 to 15 minutes, but don't overcook them or they will fall apart on the grill. Drain the artichokes in a colander and place in a large bowl. While still warm, add the oil, oregano, granulated garlic, and salt. Toss gently to coat the artichokes. [The artichokes may be made up to this point and refrigerated for up to 4 hours. Bring to room temperature before grilling.]
4. Grill the artichokes over *Direct Medium* heat until well browned and warm, 4 to 6 minutes, turning once. Serve warm with the butter.

MAKES 4 SERVINGS

Corn on the Cob
with Basil-Parmesan Butter

PREP TIME: 10 MINUTES
GRILLING TIME: 10 TO 15 MINUTES

BUTTER
- 1/4 cup [1/2 stick] unsalted butter, softened
- 1/4 cup freshly grated Parmigiano-Reggiano cheese
- 2 tablespoons finely chopped fresh basil
- 1/2 teaspoon kosher salt
- 1/4 teaspoon freshly ground black pepper
- 1/4 teaspoon granulated garlic

- 4 ears corn, husked

1. To make the butter: In a small bowl, mash the butter ingredients together with the back of a fork, and then stir to distribute the seasonings throughout the butter.
2. Brush about 1 tablespoon of the seasoned butter all over each ear of corn. Grill over *Direct Medium* heat until browned in spots and tender, 10 to 15 minutes, turning occasionally. Serve warm with the remaining butter spread on the corn.

MAKES 4 SERVINGS

Leeks
with Romesco Sauce

PREP TIME: 30 MINUTES
GRILLING TIME: 15 TO 25 MINUTES

SAUCE

  2 medium red bell peppers
  1/4 cup whole almonds
  1 medium garlic clove
  1/2 cup loosely packed fresh Italian parsley leaves
       and tender stems
  2 teaspoons sherry wine vinegar
  1/2 teaspoon kosher salt
  1/8 teaspoon ground cayenne pepper
  1/4 cup extra virgin olive oil

  8 to 12 slender leeks, each about 1 inch thick
       Extra virgin olive oil
  1/4 teaspoon kosher salt
  1/8 teaspoon freshly ground black pepper

1. To make the sauce: Grill the bell peppers over *Direct Medium* heat until they are black and blistered all over, 12 to 15 minutes, turning occasionally. Place the peppers in a small bowl and cover with plastic wrap to trap the steam. Set aside for at least 10 minutes, then peel the skins from the peppers and discard the skins, stems, and seeds.
2. In a small skillet over medium heat, toast the almonds until their aroma is apparent, 3 to 5 min-

utes, stirring occasionally. In a food processor, finely chop the garlic. Add the almonds and process until finely chopped. Add the peppers, parsley, vinegar, salt, and cayenne. Process to create a coarse paste. With the motor running, slowly add the oil and process until you have a fairly smooth sauce.
3. Remove the dark green tops off each leek, cutting about 2 inches above the point where the leaves begin to darken. Trim just enough of each root end to remove the stringy parts, but leave enough of each root end to hold the end together. Slit each leek lengthwise, starting about 1 inch from the root end and cutting all the way through the other end. Remove the first layer of tough outer leaves on each leek. Rinse the leeks under water, opening up the layers to remove any dirt. Stack the cleaned leeks in a steamer basket. Steam the leeks over boiling water until a sharp knife inserted in the root end slides out easily, 4 to 5 minutes. [The leeks may be prepared up to this point a few hours ahead.]
4. Pat the leeks dry with paper towels. Lightly brush or spray them with oil and season with salt and pepper. Grill over *Direct Medium* heat until well marked and warm, 3 to 5 minutes, turning once. Serve warm with the sauce.

MAKES 4 SERVINGS

Eggplant
with Spicy Asian Dressing

PREP TIME: 10 MINUTES
GRILLING TIME: 8 TO 10 MINUTES

DRESSING
- 1 to 2 serrano chile peppers, stems and seeds removed, minced
- 3 tablespoons soy sauce
- 2 tablespoons fresh lemon juice
- 2 tablespoons minced yellow onion

- 2 globe eggplants, about ¾ pound each
  Vegetable oil
- 1 teaspoon granulated garlic

1. To make the dressing: In a small bowl, combine the dressing ingredients with 1 tablespoon water.
2. Remove about ½ inch from both ends of each eggplant. Cut the eggplants crosswise into ½-inch slices. Generously brush both sides of the slices with oil and season evenly with the granulated garlic. Grill over *Direct Medium* heat until well marked and tender, 8 to 10 minutes, turning once. Place the slices on a platter in a single layer. Immediately spoon the dressing over the top. Serve warm.

MAKES 4 SERVINGS

Acorn Squash
with Asiago and Sage

PREP TIME: 10 MINUTES
GRILLING TIME: 50 MINUTES TO 1 HOUR

- 3 acorn squashes, 1¼ to 1½ pounds each
- 4 tablespoons unsalted butter
- 1 tablespoon brown sugar
- 2 teaspoons finely chopped fresh sage
- 1 teaspoon granulated onion
- 1 teaspoon maple syrup
- ½ teaspoon kosher salt
- ¼ teaspoon freshly ground black pepper
- ½ cup freshly grated aged Asiago cheese
- 2 tablespoons finely chopped fresh Italian parsley

1. With a large knife, carefully cut each squash in half lengthwise. Scoop out and discard the seeds and strings.
2. In a small saucepan over medium heat, combine the butter, brown sugar, sage, granulated onion, maple syrup, salt, and pepper and cook until melted. Brush the butter mixture all over the exposed flesh of each squash. Grill, cut sides up, over *Indirect Medium* heat for 30 minutes. Sprinkle the cheese and parsley all over the exposed flesh of each squash. Continue to grill until the flesh is very soft when pierced with the tip of a knife and the cheese has browned, 20 to 30 minutes more. Serve warm.

MAKES 6 SERVINGS

Roasted Tomatoes
Stuffed with Grilled Ratatouille

PREP TIME: 15 MINUTES
GRILLING TIME: 16 TO 24 MINUTES

  4 large, ripe tomatoes
     Kosher salt

RATATOUILLE
  1 medium red onion, cut crosswise into
     1/3-inch slices
  1 medium red bell pepper, stem and seeds
     removed, cut into flat pieces
  1 medium zucchini, cut lengthwise in
     1/3-inch slices
     Extra virgin olive oil
     Freshly ground black pepper
2/3 cup grated mozzarella cheese
  1 tablespoon finely chopped fresh basil
  1 teaspoon balsamic vinegar

1. Cut a 1/2-inch slice off the top of each tomato. Discard the tops. With a small knife cut around the inside of the fleshy part of the tomato [do not cut through the bottom of the tomato] to within 1/2 inch of the skin. With a teaspoon, scoop out the tomato flesh, leaving about 1/2 inch of flesh attached to the skin. Discard the juice and seeds to make room for the ratatouille. Lightly salt the inside of the tomatoes and turn them, cut side down, on a plate lined with paper towels while you prepare the ratatouille.

2. To make the ratatouille: Lightly brush or spray the onion, pepper, and zucchini with oil. Season with salt and pepper to taste. Grill over *Direct Medium* heat until tender, turning once. The onions will take 8 to 12 minutes. The peppers and zucchini will take 6 to 8 minutes. Transfer to a cutting board and cut into 1/3-inch pieces. Combine the grilled vegetables in a medium bowl with the cheese, basil, and vinegar.

3. Spoon the ratatouille into the tomatoes. Grill the tomatoes over *Indirect Medium* heat until the cheese is melted and the vegetables are warm, 8 to 12 minutes. Serve immediately.

MAKES 4 SERVINGS

Portabello Mushrooms
Stuffed with Spinach and Dried Tomatoes

PREP TIME: 30 MINUTES
GRILLING TIME: 10 TO 15 MINUTES

FILLING
10 ounces baby spinach leaves, rinsed
    Extra virgin olive oil
¹/₂ cup finely chopped yellow onion
2   teaspoons finely chopped garlic
1   cup finely diced ripe tomato
¹/₄ cup oil-packed, sun-dried tomatoes, thinly
    sliced
¹/₄ cup pitted and coarsely chopped Kalamata
    olives
    Kosher salt
    Freshly ground black pepper

4   large portabello mushrooms, 5 to 6 inches in
    diameter
¹/₄ cup fine, soft bread crumbs

1. To make the filling: In a large saucepan over high heat, cook the spinach just until wilted, 1 to 2 minutes, stirring frequently. Transfer the spinach to a sieve and drain until cooled. Squeeze out the remaining liquid with your hands, and then roughly chop the spinach. You should have about 1 cup.

2. Wipe out the saucepan and warm 2 tablespoons of olive oil over medium heat. Add the onion and cook until golden, about 5 minutes, stirring occasionally. Add the garlic and cook for 30 seconds. Add the diced tomatoes and cook for 1 minute, stirring occasionally. Add the spinach, sun-dried tomatoes, olives, ¹/₂ teaspoon salt, and ¹/₄ teaspoon pepper. Cook until all the moisture has evaporated, 1 to 2 minutes, stirring occasionally. Remove the saucepan from the heat.

3. Remove and discard the mushroom stems. With a teaspoon, carefully scrape out the black gills from the mushroom caps and discard. Generously brush or spray the mushroom caps with oil and season them with ¹/₄ teaspoon salt. Grill, smooth sides up, over *Direct Medium* heat until well marked, about 5 minutes. Transfer to a work surface, smooth sides down. Spoon a thin layer of the filling onto the mushrooms, spreading it evenly to the edges.

4. In a small bowl toss the bread crumbs with 1 tablespoon of oil, and salt and pepper to taste. Sprinkle each stuffed mushroom evenly with a thin layer of crumbs. Grill the mushrooms, smooth sides down, over *Direct Medium* heat until the crumbs are browned and the mushrooms are tender, 5 to 10 minutes more. Serve warm.

MAKES 4 SERVINGS

German Potato Salad

PREP TIME: 40 MINUTES
GRILLING TIME: ABOUT 30 MINUTES

- 1 large red onion, cut crosswise into ½-inch slices
- 3 tablespoons extra virgin olive oil, divided
- 2 pounds red-skin potatoes, each about 2 to 3 inches in diameter, scrubbed
- ½ teaspoon kosher salt
- ½ teaspoon freshly ground black pepper

DRESSING
- ½ pound sliced bacon, cut into 1-inch pieces
- ⅔ cup medium diced celery [about 2 stalks]
- ½ teaspoon granulated sugar
- ⅓ cup apple cider vinegar
- 2 tablespoons stone ground mustard
- ½ teaspoon freshly ground black pepper
- ¼ teaspoon kosher salt
- ⅓ cup diced dill pickle
- ¼ cup finely chopped fresh Italian parsley

1. Brush or spray both sides of the onion slices with 1 tablespoon of the oil. Grill over *Direct Medium* heat until tender, 8 to 12 minutes, turning once. Cut into ¼-inch pieces. Cut the potatoes in quarters and put them in a large bowl with the remaining 2 tablespoons of oil, salt, and pepper. Grill over *Direct Medium* heat until tender inside and crispy outside, 15 to 20 minutes, turning every 5 minutes or so.

2. Begin making the dressing while the potatoes are grilling: In a 12-inch skillet over medium heat, cook the bacon until crispy, 8 to 10 minutes, turning occasionally. Drain the bacon on paper towels. Pour off all but 3 tablespoons of the bacon fat in the skillet. Add the celery to the skillet and cook for 3 minutes. Add the sugar, and continue to cook until the sugar is dissolved and the celery is cooked through, 2 to 3 minutes, stirring occasionally. Add the vinegar and ½ cup water; cook until bubbling and slightly thickened, about 2 minutes, stirring occasionally. Reduce the heat to low. Add the mustard, pepper, and salt, stirring until combined, and cook 2 minutes. Remove the skillet from the heat; add the bacon pieces and the onions, tossing to coat with the dressing.

3. Transfer the potatoes from the grill to a cutting board. Cut each potato quarter in half and place in a large serving bowl. Pour the hot dressing over the potatoes, mixing gently to coat. Add the pickles and parsley. Toss gently and serve warm or at room temperature.

MAKES 4 TO 6 SERVINGS

Franny's Potato Salad

PREP TIME: 40 MINUTES
GRILLING TIME: 40 MINUTES

- 6 chicken drumsticks
  Extra virgin olive oil
  Kosher salt
  Freshly ground black pepper
- 4 large russet potatoes, about 12 ounces each, cut into quarters
- 6 eggs, hard boiled and roughly chopped
- 1 cup mayonnaise
- ½ cup drained, pitted black olives, finely chopped
- ½ cup finely chopped yellow onion
- ⅓ cup drained dill relish
- ⅓ cup drained sweet pickle relish
- ¼ cup drained pimentos, finely chopped
- 3 tablespoons finely chopped fresh chives

1. Lightly brush or spray the drumsticks with oil and season with salt and pepper to taste. Grill over *Indirect Medium* heat until the meat is no longer pink at the bone, 40 to 50 minutes.
2. Meanwhile prepare the potatoes: In a large saucepan, add the potatoes, cover with water by 1 inch, and add 1 tablespoon of salt. Cover the saucepan with a lid. Bring to a boil over high heat, and then reduce the heat and simmer, with the lid off, until the potatoes are very tender, about 25 minutes. Drain in a colander and let cool.
3. When cool enough to handle, pull the skin off the chicken drumsticks and discard. Pull the meat apart into shreds or roughly chop it. Add the chicken to a large mixing bowl. Peel the skin off the potatoes and discard. Roughly chop the potatoes and add them to the mixing bowl. Add the remaining ingredients, including salt and pepper to taste. If not serving right away, cover the salad with plastic wrap and keep cool in the refrigerator.

MAKES ABOUT 10 CUPS

Grill-Roasted New Potatoes

PREP TIME: 10 MINUTES
GRILLING TIME: 15 TO 20

- 2 pounds new potatoes, each 1½ to 2 inches in diameter, scrubbed and quartered
- 2 tablespoons extra virgin olive oil
- 2 teaspoons minced fresh rosemary
- ½ teaspoon kosher salt
- ½ teaspoon freshly ground black pepper

1. In a medium bowl, combine all the ingredients and stir to coat the potatoes. Grill over *Direct Medium* heat until tender and browned on all sides, 15 to 20 minutes, scooping and turning with a wide spatula every 5 minutes or so. Serve warm.

MAKE 6 TO 8 SERVINGS

Grilled Bread Salad
with Fresh Tomatoes and Garlic

PREP TIME: 15 MINUTES
GRILLING TIME: 1 TO 3 MINUTES

- ½ cup unsalted butter
- 1 tablespoon minced garlic
- ½ loaf day-old Italian bread, about ½ pound, cut crosswise into ¾-inch slices
- 2 pounds ripe, fresh tomatoes [about 6 medium], cored, seeded, and cut into ¾-inch pieces
- ¼ cup minced red onion
- ¼ cup extra virgin olive oil
- 2 tablespoons balsamic vinegar
- 2 tablespoons finely chopped fresh basil
- 1 tablespoon finely chopped fresh tarragon
- ½ teaspoon kosher salt
- ¼ teaspoon freshly ground black pepper

1. In a small saucepan over medium heat, combine the butter and garlic. Cook until the garlic is just turning light brown, 2 to 3 minutes. Evenly brush the garlic-butter mixture on both sides of each slice of bread. Grill the bread slices over *Direct Medium* heat until well marked, 1 to 3 minutes, turning once [but check the bread often as it can burn quickly]. Transfer the bread to a cutting board and cut into ¾-inch cubes. Place the cubes in a large bowl.
2. Add the remaining ingredients to the bowl. Mix thoroughly. Adjust the seasonings if necessary. Serve at room temperature.

MAKES 6 TO 8 SERVINGS

Red Cabbage Coleslaw
with Creamy Caesar Dressing

PREP TIME: 15 MINUTES

DRESSING
- 1 medium clove garlic
- 1/2 teaspoon kosher salt
- 1/2 cup good-quality mayonnaise
- 1/4 cup freshly grated Parmigiano-Reggiano cheese
- 2 tablespoons fresh lemon juice
- 1 tablespoon Dijon mustard
- 1/2 teaspoon Worcestershire sauce
- 1/2 teaspoon Tabasco® sauce
- 1/4 teaspoon freshly ground black pepper

- 3 cups coarsely grated red cabbage
- 1 cup coarsely grated carrot
- 1/2 cup finely chopped scallions, white and green parts only

1. To make the dressing: Roughly chop the garlic, and then sprinkle the salt on top. Using both the sharp edge and the flat side of the knife blade, crush the garlic and salt together to create a paste. Transfer the paste to a small bowl and add the remaining dressing ingredients. Mix well.
2. In a medium bowl, combine the cabbage, carrot, and scallions. Mix well. Add the dressing. Mix well again. Cover the bowl with plastic wrap and refrigerate for 2 hours or until ready to serve.

MAKES 4 TO 6 SERVINGS

Roasted Corn and Black Bean Salad

PREP TIME: 15 MINUTES
GRILLING TIME: 10 TO 15 MINUTES

- 3 ears corn, husked
  Extra virgin olive oil
  Kosher salt
- 2 cans [15 ounces each] black beans, rinsed
- 1 1/2 cups roughly chopped ripe tomatoes
- 1/2 cup finely chopped celery
- 2 tablespoons finely chopped fresh cilantro

DRESSING
- 3 tablespoons extra virgin olive oil
  Grated zest of 1 lime
- 1 tablespoon fresh lime juice
- 1 teaspoon minced garlic
- 1/2 teaspoon ground cumin
- 1/2 teaspoon kosher salt
- 1/4 teaspoon freshly ground black pepper

1. Lightly brush or spray the corn all over with oil and season with salt to taste. Grill the corn over *Direct Medium* heat until browned in spots and tender, 10 to 15 minutes, turning occasionally. In a large bowl, slice the kernels off the cobs. Add the black beans, tomatoes, celery, and cilantro.
2. To make the dressing: In a small bowl, whisk together the dressing ingredients. Pour the dressing over the black bean mixture. Mix to evenly coat the ingredients. Serve at room temperature.

MAKES 6 TO 8 SERVINGS

Grilled Sweet Potato and Red Pepper Salad

PREP TIME: 15 MINUTES
GRILLING TIME: 20 MINUTES

DRESSING
¼ cup extra virgin olive oil
2 tablespoons fresh lime juice
1 teaspoon minced garlic
1 teaspoon minced jalapeño pepper
1 teaspoon kosher salt
½ teaspoon ground cumin
¼ teaspoon freshly ground black pepper

1½ pounds sweet potatoes
4 large red bell peppers
1 cup thinly sliced celery
3 green onions, white and light green parts only, cut diagonally into thin slices
⅓ cup roughly chopped fresh cilantro leaves

1. To make the dressing: In a small bowl, whisk together the dressing ingredients.
2. Trim the ends off the sweet potatoes. Peel and cut them crosswise into slices about ½ inch thick. Lightly brush both sides with some dressing. Grill the sweet potatoes along with the bell peppers over *Direct Medium* heat, turning occasionally. The sweet potatoes are done when they can be easily poked with a knife, about 20 minutes. The bell peppers are done when the skin blackens and blisters all over, 12 to 15 minutes.
3. Cut the sweet potatoes into ½-inch pieces and put them in a large bowl. Add enough dressing to moisten them [you may not need all of it]. Place the peppers in a small bowl and cover with plastic wrap to trap the steam. Set aside for at least 5 minutes, then remove the peppers from the bowl and peel away the charred skins. Cut off the tops and remove the seeds. Cut the peppers into ½-inch pieces. Add the peppers to the bowl along with the celery, onions, and cilantro. Mix well. If desired, add some of the remaining dressing and mix well. Serve at room temperature.

MAKES 6 SERVINGS

Fire-Roasted Pepper and Mushroom Salad

PREP TIME: 20 MINUTES
MARINATING TIME: 30 MINUTES PLUS 1 HOUR
GRILLING TIME: 24 TO 30 MINUTES

MARINADE
1/4 cup extra virgin olive oil
1 tablespoon minced garlic
1 tablespoon balsamic vinegar
1 tablespoon Dijon mustard
1 teaspoon dried thyme
1/2 teaspoon kosher salt
1/2 teaspoon freshly ground black pepper

4 portabello mushrooms, each 4 to 5 inches
  across

4 medium red/yellow bell peppers
1/4 cup finely chopped fresh Italian parsley
1 tablespoon drained capers

1. To make the marinade: In a small bowl, whisk the marinade ingredients.

2. Remove and discard the mushroom stems. Scrape out the dark gills with a teaspoon. Generously brush the mushrooms all over with some of the marinade and reserve the rest. Allow the mushrooms to marinate at room temperature for 30 minutes.

3. Grill the bell peppers over *Direct High* heat until the skins are blackened and blistered all over, 12 to 15 minutes, turning occasionally. Place the peppers in a small bowl and cover with plastic wrap to trap the steam. Set aside for at least 10 minutes, then peel the skin from the peppers, discarding the stems and seeds, and cut them into 1-inch squares. Place the roasted peppers in a medium bowl.

4. Grill the mushrooms over *Direct Medium* heat until tender, 12 to 15 minutes, turning occasionally and, if necessary to prevent drying out, brushing with the reserved marinade. Cut the mushrooms into 1-inch pieces. Add them, along with the parsley and capers, to the bowl of roasted peppers. Add the reserved marinade. Toss to distribute the ingredients. Cover and set aside at room temperature for at least 1 hour. Taste just before serving and, if necessary, season with salt and pepper. Serve at room temperature.

MAKES 4 SERVINGS

Noodle and Green Onion Salad
with Orange-Sesame Dressing

PREP TIME: 20 MINUTES
GRILLING TIME: 2 TO 3 MINUTES

DRESSING
- 3 tablespoons smooth peanut butter
- 2 tablespoons peanut or canola oil
- 2 tablespoons oyster sauce
- 2 tablespoons soy sauce
- 2 tablespoons rice vinegar
- 1 teaspoon freshly grated orange zest
- 2 tablespoons freshly squeezed orange juice
- 2 teaspoons dark sesame oil
- 1 teaspoon freshly grated ginger
- ¼ teaspoon hot chili oil
- ¼ teaspoon freshly ground black pepper

- ½ pound udon noodles or spaghetti
- 12 green onions, white and light green parts only
- 2 tablespoons finely chopped fresh cilantro
- ½ cup dry roasted, unsalted peanuts, finely chopped, divided

1. To make the dressing: In a large bowl, whisk the dressing ingredients until smooth [this may take up to a minute].

2. Cook the noodles in a large pot of boiling water until tender [see package instructions]. Drain in a colander, and then add to the dressing while still warm. Toss lightly.

3. Lightly brush or spray the green onions with oil and grill over *Direct Medium* heat until well marked and tender, 2 to 3 minutes, turning once. Cut them crosswise into 1-inch sections and add them to the noodles. Add the cilantro and about half the peanuts. Mix well. Transfer to a serving bowl and sprinkle the remaining peanuts on top. Serve warm or at room temperature.

MAKES 4 SERVINGS

Honey-Lime Chicken Salad
with Tomato and Avocado

PREP TIME: 30 MINUTES
MARINATING TIME: 1 TO 2 HOURS
GRILLING TIME: 10 TO 12 MINUTES

MARINADE
  - 3 tablespoons fresh lime juice
  - 3 tablespoons vegetable oil
  - 1 tablespoon honey
  - ½ teaspoon kosher salt
  - ½ teaspoon granulated garlic
  - ¼ teaspoon freshly ground black pepper
  - ¼ teaspoon ground cayenne pepper

  - 4 boneless, skinless chicken breast halves, 6 to 8 ounces each

  - 2 ripe Hass avocados
  - 1 tablespoon fresh lime juice
  - 1 pint cherry tomatoes, cut into halves [or quarters if large size]
  - 2 tablespoons minced fresh chives

1. To make the marinade: In a small bowl, whisk the marinade ingredients until the honey is dissolved.

2. Place the chicken in a large, resealable plastic bag and pour in the marinade. Press the air out of the bag and seal tightly. Turn the bag to distribute the marinade. Place the bag in a bowl and refrigerate for 1 to 2 hours, turning occasionally.

3. Remove the chicken from the bag and discard the marinade. Grill over *Direct Medium* heat until the juices run clear and the meat is no longer pink in the center, 10 to 12 minutes, turning once. Remove from the grill and let rest for 2 to 3 minutes before cutting into ½-inch pieces.

4. Scoop the avocado flesh onto a cutting board and cut into ½-inch pieces. Immediately put the avocado in a large mixing bowl and toss with the lime juice. Add the chicken, tomatoes, and chives. Mix well. Adjust the seasoning to your taste. Serve at room temperature or slightly chilled.

MAKES 4 TO 6 SERVINGS

Shrimp and Mango Salad
with Spicy Thai Dressing

PREP TIME: 20 MINUTES
GRILLING TIME: 2 TO 4 MINUTES

DRESSING

- 1 medium garlic clove, coarsely chopped
- 1 serrano chile, stem removed, coarsely chopped
- 2 teaspoons granulated sugar
- 1 small handful fresh cilantro leaves
- 1 small handful fresh mint leaves
- 2 tablespoons fresh lemon juice
- 1 tablespoon peanut oil
- 1 tablespoon fish sauce
- 1 tablespoon soy sauce

- 20 large shrimp, about 1 pound, peeled and deveined
  Peanut oil
- 1 small head butter lettuce, cut into 2-inch pieces
- 1 ripe mango, about 10 ounces, peeled, seeded, and cut into 1/2-inch strips
- 1 cup bean sprouts

1. To make the dressing: Using a mortar and pestle or blender, crush the garlic and chile with the sugar. Add the cilantro and mint, grinding them until they create a paste. Add the remaining dressing ingredients, plus 2 tablespoons water, and mix well.
2. Lightly brush or spray the shrimp with the oil. Grill over *Direct High* heat until the shrimp are firm to the touch and just turning opaque in the center, 2 to 4 minutes, turning once.
3. In a large bowl, combine the lettuce, mango, and bean sprouts. Stir the dressing and add enough of it to lightly coat the lettuce leaves [you may not need all of the dressing]. Spoon the salad onto individual plates and garnish with grilled shrimp. Serve immediately.

MAKES 4 TO 6 SERVINGS

Grilled Calamari and Arugula Salad

PREP TIME: **10 MINUTES**
MARINATING TIME: **1 TO 2 HOURS**
GRILLING TIME: **4 TO 5 MINUTES**

MARINADE
- ¼ cup extra virgin olive oil
- 1 teaspoon freshly grated lemon zest
- ¼ cup fresh lemon juice
- 2 teaspoons minced garlic
- ½ teaspoon kosher salt
- ½ teaspoon freshly ground black pepper
- ¼ teaspoon ground cayenne pepper

- 2 pounds cleaned [about 4 pounds uncleaned] medium squid, tubes and tentacles
- 4 cups loosely packed baby arugula
- 2 tablespoons butter, softened
- 8 slices country-style Italian bread, each about ½ inch thick

1. To make the marinade: In a small bowl, whisk together the marinade ingredients.
2. Place the cleaned calamari in a large, resealable plastic bag and pour in the marinade. Press the air out of the bag and seal tightly. Turn the bag several times to distribute the marinade, place the bag in a bowl, and refrigerate for 1 to 2 hours.
3. Put the arugula in large serving bowl.
4. Drain the calamari in a sieve and discard the marinade. Grill over *Direct High* heat until well marked and tender, 3 to 4 minutes, turning once. Immediately add the calamari to the bowl of arugula and mix well so the heat of the calamari wilts the arugula.
5. Butter the bread slices on both sides and grill over *Direct High* heat until lightly toasted, about 20 seconds per side. Serve the salad warm or at room temperature with the toasted bread slices.

MAKES 4 SERVINGS

Smoky Sweet Baked Beans

Red Chile Rice

PREP TIME: 15 MINUTES
GRILLING TIME: ABOUT 25 MINUTES

- ¼ pound bacon, cut into ½-inch pieces
- ½ cup finely chopped yellow onion
- 2 teaspoons minced garlic
- ¼ teaspoon crushed red pepper flakes
- 1 can [28 ounces] baked beans
- ¼ cup ketchup
- 2 teaspoons Worcestershire sauce
- ½ teaspoon prepared chili powder
  Kosher salt
  Freshly ground black pepper

1. In a large oven-proof saucepan, cook the bacon over *Direct Medium* heat until crispy, 8 to 10 minutes, stirring occasionally. Add the onion and cook until tender, about 5 minutes, stirring occasionally. Add the garlic and red pepper flakes, and cook for 30 seconds, stirring occasionally. Add the baked beans [with their liquid], ketchup, Worcestershire sauce, and chili powder. Bring the mixture to a simmer, stirring occasionally, and then cook over *Direct Low* heat for 15 minutes, stirring all the way to the bottom of the pot occasionally. Taste and adjust seasoning with salt and pepper, if desired. Serve warm.

MAKES 4 TO 6 SERVINGS

PREP TIME: 5 MINUTES
COOKING TIME: 30 TO 35 MINUTES

- 2 tablespoons extra virgin olive oil
- 1 cup finely chopped white onion
- 1 teaspoon pure chile powder
- 2 cups medium-grain rice
- ¾ teaspoon kosher salt
- ½ teaspoon dried oregano
- ½ teaspoon ground cumin
- ¼ teaspoon freshly ground black pepper

1. In a medium saucepan over medium heat, warm the oil. Add the onion and cook for about 5 minutes, stirring occasionally to avoid browning. Add the chile powder. Cook for about 1 minute, stirring occasionally. Add the rice. Stir to evenly coat the grains of rice with oil. Add the remaining ingredients, including 3 cups of cold water. Stir. Bring the mixture to a simmer. Reduce the heat to low, cover the saucepan with a tight-fitting lid, and cook until the rice is tender and has absorbed all the water, 18 to 20 minutes. Remove the saucepan from the heat and leave it alone for 5 minutes. Remove the lid and fluff the rice with a fork. Serve warm.

MAKES 6 TO 8 SERVINGS

Skillet Cornbread
with Bacon and Chives

Prep time: 20 minutes
Grilling time: 20 to 30 minutes

    4 slices bacon
    2 cups yellow cornmeal
1 1/2 cups all-purpose flour
  1/2 cup granulated sugar
    1 teaspoon baking powder
    1 teaspoon baking soda
    1 teaspoon kosher salt
  1/4 teaspoon freshly ground black pepper
  1/4 teaspoon ground cayenne pepper
    2 tablespoons finely chopped fresh chives
    3 large eggs
    1 cup milk
  1/4 cup sour cream

1. In a 10-inch nonstick, oven-proof skillet over medium heat, lay the bacon flat and cook until crispy, 10 to 12 minutes, turning occasionally. Drain the bacon on paper towels. Pour off and discard all but 2 tablespoons of bacon fat in the skillet.
2. In a large bowl combine the cornmeal, flour, sugar, baking powder, baking soda, salt, black pepper, and cayenne pepper. Finely chop the drained bacon and add it to the bowl along with the chives. Mix well. In another large bowl, whisk the eggs, milk, and sour cream. Pour the milk mixture into the cornmeal mixture. Mix well.
3. Pour the cornbread batter in the skillet with the bacon fat and spread it out evenly. Grill over *Indirect Medium* heat until golden brown around the edges and a toothpick inserted in the center comes out clean, 20 to 30 minutes, rotating the pan occasionally for even cooking. Allow to cool completely in the skillet. Invert the cornbread onto a cutting board. Cut into wedges. Serve at room temperature.

Makes 8 servings

Grilled Parmesan Polenta Crostini

Prep time: 40 minutes
Grilling time: 8 to 10 minutes

    1 cup polenta
    2 teaspoons minced garlic
    1 teaspoon dried oregano
    1 teaspoon kosher salt
  1/4 teaspoon freshly ground black pepper
  1/4 cup finely chopped fresh Italian parsley
  2/3 cup freshly grated Parmiggiano-Reggiano cheese, divided
       Extra virgin olive oil

1. In a large, deep-sided saucepan, combine the polenta, garlic, oregano, salt, and pepper along with 3 cups of water. Bring the mixture to a boil over high heat, whisking frequently, then reduce the heat to low. Cook until the polenta is soft, 20 to 30 minutes, stirring occasionally to avoid scorching on the bottom. Add the parsley and 1/3 cup of the cheese. Stir to blend. Line a baking sheet with plastic wrap, letting the ends of plastic wrap hang over the edges by about 10 inches on each side. Scoop the polenta onto the sheet and spread it out into a rectangle about 1/3 inch thick, smoothing the surface with a spatula dipped in water. Allow to cool to room temperature. Cover with plastic wrap and refrigerate for at least 4 hours.
2. Remove the polenta from the pan and evenly trim the edges. Cut the polenta into 2-inch squares. Pat dry with paper towels. Generously brush or spray the polenta on both sides with oil and grill over *Direct High* heat until they are very well marked, crispy, and they release easily from the grate, 8 to 10 minutes, turning once with a spatula. Serve warm with the remaining 1/3 cup of cheese scattered over the top.

Makes 4 to 6 servings

VEG & SIDES

DESSERTS

Dessert Disarray

Years ago, when I was the chef of a winery in Napa Valley, my job was to cook for visiting distributors, retailers, and restaurateurs. I remember one day in particular when a group of important distributors from Los Angeles came for lunch. Grilled food has always been my specialty, so I put together a string of my greatest hits for the starters and main course, though I went a little outside of my usual range for the dessert. I planned to make a lemon mousse roulade, which is a thin, rectangular cake that is layered with lemon mousse and then rolled into a cylinder and cut crosswise so the colorful mousse creates a pinwheel design. Garnished with marinated apricots and a drizzle of raspberry sauce, it would be a terrific match with the dessert wine we sold, as the wine tasted a little like lemon and apricots.

The meal started off well. Their table was set outside the winery, under a two-hundred-year-old oak tree. I grilled several appetizers to complement our white wines, and for the main course I served porterhouse steaks with a sun-dried tomato pesto and grill-roasted potatoes, along with our cabernet sauvignon. Back in the kitchen, I went to work on the dessert. I cut into the rolled cylinder of cake and immediately noticed a problem. The mousse that was meant to hold a perfect pinwheel design poured out of the cake as if it was lemonade. I had not used enough gelatin to "set" the mousse. The cake was nothing more than a sweet, wet mess. I couldn't possibly serve it to the distributors, yet I had to come up with something...fast.

I looked around the kitchen and spotted some pineapples set aside for a breakfast meeting the next day. I peeled two of them and cut them into chunks. Then I melted some butter and sugar with orange juice, lemon juice, and a bit of ground cloves. I poured the syrupy mixture over the pineapple chunks to glaze them and went outside to check the temperature on my grill. Trying to appear perfectly in control, I waved to my guests who were happily sipping wine, with no clue that their dessert was in disarray.

Sometimes simple can be most sensational.

I returned to the pineapples and slid the chunks onto wooden skewers. Then I grilled the skewers outside until the fruit was warm and tender, brushing them with a bit more glaze as they caramelized. I arranged the golden skewers on a platter and presented them "family-style" in the center of the table. I thought maybe, just maybe, I had survived this embarrassing afternoon, but no, it turned out that this dessert was a food-and-wine epiphany. I hadn't even reached the kitchen when the distributors were calling me back to the table. "Jamie, this pineapple is amazing," they said. "How did you do this? Please can we have the recipe?"

Later that day, as I was writing the recipe for them [see page 288], I thought to myself, this is a good lesson. It just goes to show you that sometimes simple can be most sensational.

Cutting Pineapple into Chunks

1. Set the pineapple on its side and cut off and discard about 1 inch from the top and bottom.

2. Stand the pineapple upright and cut lengthwise to remove and discard the tough, outer peel in strips.

3. Go back around the pineapple and cut off any remaining hard bits of peel called "eyes."

4. Cut the pineapple in quarters lengthwise through the core.

5. Lay each quarter flat on the cutting board. With your knife at an angle, remove and discard each section of core.

6. Cut each quarter in half lengthwise. Then cut them into chunks.

Grilling Guide for Fruit

Type	Thickness/Size	Approximate Grilling Time
Apple	whole	**35 to 40 minutes** Indirect Medium
Apple	½-inch-thick slices	**4 to 6 minutes** Direct Medium
Apricot	halved, pit removed	**6 to 8 minutes** Direct Medium
Banana	halved lengthwise	**6 to 8 minutes** Direct Medium
Nectarine	halved lengthwise, pit removed	**8 to 10 minutes** Direct Medium
Peach	halved lengthwise, pit removed	**8 to 10 minutes** Direct Medium
Pear	halved lengthwise	**10 to 12 minutes** Direct Medium
Pineapple	peeled and cored, ½-inch slices or 1-inch wedges	**5 to 10 minutes** Direct Medium
Strawberry		**4 to 5 minutes** Direct Medium

Note: Grilling times for fruit will depend on ripeness.

DESSERTS

Spiced Banana Chocolate Sundaes

PREP TIME: 10 MINUTES
GRILLING TIME: 2 TO 3 MINUTES

CHOCOLATE SAUCE
 ½ cup heavy cream
 3 ounces semisweet chocolate, finely chopped

 4 tablespoons unsalted butter
 ½ teaspoon ground cinnamon
 ¼ teaspoon ground ginger
 ⅛ teaspoon ground cloves
 4 bananas, ripe but firm, peeled

 1 pint vanilla ice cream

1. To make the chocolate sauce: In a small saucepan over medium-high heat, bring the cream to a simmer. Remove the pan from the heat and immediately add the chocolate. Stir until the sauce is dark and smooth.

2. In a large skillet over medium heat, melt the butter. Add the cinnamon, ginger, and cloves and stir to evenly combine the ingredients. Remove the skillet from the heat. Place the bananas in the skillet and brush them on all sides with the butter mixture. Gently pick the bananas out of the skillet and grill over *Direct Medium* heat until warm and well marked but not too soft, 2 to 3 minutes, gently turning once. Transfer the bananas to a work surface and cut them on the bias into ½-inch slices.

3. Reheat the chocolate sauce over medium heat. Scoop the ice cream into bowls. Top with the warm bananas and chocolate sauce. Serve immediately.

MAKES 4 TO 6 SERVINGS

▲▲

The key to grilling fruit is picking ones that are ripe but not mushy. You don't want them to collapse and slip through the grate. To be absolutely sure a banana will hold together, cut it in half lengthwise [with the skin still on]. Brush the cut sides with melted butter and spices and grill the banana cut side down. Once it is warm and soft, slip off the peel.

▼▼

Grilled Bananas
with Raspberries and Rum

PREP TIME: 5 MINUTES
GRILLING TIME: 5 TO 7 MINUTES

- 2 tablespoons caramel sauce
- 1 tablespoon dark rum
- 4 bananas, ripe but not soft, unpeeled
- 16 fresh raspberries
- 4 scoops vanilla ice cream [optional]

1. In a small bowl, mix the caramel sauce and rum until smooth. Cut each banana in half lengthwise but do not cut through the skin on the bottom. Open each banana slightly, like a book. Drizzle the caramel mixture evenly over the cut sides of each banana. Evenly space 4 raspberries inside each banana. Grill over *Direct Medium* heat until the bananas are warm and the skins are dark, 5 to 7 minutes, turning once. Peel the bananas and serve warm with ice cream, if desired.

MAKES 4 SERVINGS

Grilled Apricots
and Brie Drizzled with Honey

PREP TIME: 5 MINUTES
GRILLING TIME: 5 TO 7 MINUTES

- 3 tablespoons unsalted butter
- 2 tablespoons granulated sugar
- 6 ripe apricots, halved lengthwise and pits removed
- 4 ounces brie cheese, cut into 4 wedges
- 2 tablespoons honey
- 4 lemon wedges

1. In a large skillet over medium heat, melt the butter and sugar. Coat the apricots evenly with the butter mixture. Grill over *Direct Medium* heat until soft and warm, 5 to 7 minutes, turning occasionally.
2. Arrange 3 apricot halves on each plate with the brie. Drizzle honey all over. Garnish with a lemon wedge for guests to squeeze all over. Serve while the apricots are warm.

MAKES 4 SERVINGS

Grilled Figs

with Cherry Sauce and Toasted Coconut

Prep time: 20 minutes
Grilling time: 2 to 4 minutes

2/3 cup heavy cream
1/3 cup cherry jam
1 tablespoon fresh lemon juice
1/4 cup shredded coconut
2 tablespoons unsalted butter
12 large, ripe black figs, cut in half lengthwise
4 fresh mint sprigs

1. In a medium saucepan over medium-high heat, combine the cream and cherry jam and whisk to break up the jam. Bring to a boil, then lower the heat and simmer until 1/2 cup liquid remains, 5 to 8 minutes, whisking often. Add the lemon juice. Pour the sauce through a sieve into a small saucepan.
2. In a large skillet over medium heat, spread the coconut in a single layer and cook until lightly browned, about 5 minutes, stirring occasionally. Pour the coconut into a small bowl to stop the cooking.
3. In a large skillet over medium heat, melt the butter. Add the figs to the skillet and coat them in the butter. Grill the figs, cut side down, over *Direct Medium* heat until well marked and tender, 2 to 4 minutes. Meanwhile reheat the sauce over low heat.
4. Spoon the sauce on the plates. Arrange the figs on top. Sprinkle the coconut over the figs. Garnish with the mint. Serve warm.

Makes 4 servings

Grilled Peaches

with Blackberry Sauce

Prep time: 10 minutes
Grilling time: 8 to 10 minutes

Sauce
6 ounces fresh blackberries, about 1 cup
2 to 3 tablespoons granulated sugar

2 tablespoons unsalted butter
1 tablespoon granulated sugar
4 medium peaches, firm but ripe, halved and pits removed

1 cup vanilla frozen yogurt [optional]

1. To make the sauce: In a food processor, purée the blackberries with 2 tablespoons water. Add the sugar to taste.
2. In a small saucepan over medium heat, melt the butter, then add the sugar and stir to dissolve. Remove the saucepan from the heat. Brush the peach halves all over with the butter mixture.
3. Grill the peach halves over *Direct Medium* heat until they are browned in spots and warm throughout, 8 to 10 minutes, turning them every 3 minutes or so. Serve the peaches warm with the blackberry sauce and frozen yogurt, if desired.

Makes 4 servings

Roasted Pears
with Cinnamon and Brown Sugar Glaze

PREP TIME: 15 MINUTES
GRILLING TIME: 15 TO 30 MINUTES

GLAZE
- 3 tablespoons unsalted butter
- 3 tablespoons dark brown sugar
- 3 tablespoons apple juice
- ½ teaspoon ground cinnamon
- ¼ teaspoon ground ginger
- ⅛ teaspoon ground cloves

- 6 firm, ripe pears, such as Comice

1. To make the glaze: In a 10-inch ovenproof skillet over medium heat, stir the glaze ingredients until the butter and sugar have melted.
2. With a vegetable peeler or small knife, peel the pears, leaving the stems intact. Remove a small slice off the bottom of each pear so they can stand up easily. Working from the bottom of each pear with a melon baller, remove the core and seeds from each pear. Stand the pears upright in the skillet. Spoon some of the sauce over each pear.
3. Place the skillet over *Direct Medium* heat and cook until the pears are warm and tender, 10 to 20 minutes, carefully basting with the hot liquid about every 5 minutes [be careful to hold the hot handle of the skillet with a barbecue mitt]. Using a large slotted spoon, transfer the pears to serving plates. If needed, continue to cook the liquid over *Direct Medium* heat until it reduces to a syrupy glaze, 5 to 10 minutes. Carefully pour the hot glaze over the pears. Serve warm.

MAKES 6 SERVINGS

Pineapple Skewers
with Brown Butter and Orange Juice Glaze

PREP TIME: 25 MINUTES
GRILLING TIME: 6 TO 10 MINUTES

- 4 tablespoons unsalted butter
- ⅓ cup light brown sugar, firmly packed
- ½ cup fresh orange juice
- ¼ teaspoon kosher salt
- ¼ teaspoon freshly ground black pepper
- ⅛ teaspoon ground cloves
- 1 tablespoon fresh lemon juice
- ½ ripe pineapple

1. In a medium skillet over high heat, melt the butter and cook until it begins to turn brown. Add the brown sugar and stir until it dissolves. Add the orange juice carefully, as it will bubble up when it hits the hot syrup. Stir until the mixture is smooth. Season with the salt, pepper, and cloves. Cook until the mixture turns syrupy [there should be about ⅓ cup]. Remove the skillet from the heat, add the lemon juice, stir well, and pour the glaze into a medium bowl to cool.
2. Remove the top, bottom, and all the rough peel from the pineapple [see page 283]. Cut the pineapple lengthwise into quarters and remove the core from each section. Cut each quarter in half and then into 1-inch pieces. Add the pineapple pieces to the bowl of glaze and gently toss to coat them. Thread onto skewers. Grill over *Direct Medium* heat until the pieces are golden brown all over, 6 to 10 minutes, turning occasionally. Serve warm.

MAKES 4 TO 6 SERVINGS

Pineapple Sundae
with Caramel and Toasted Almond Brittle

PREP TIME: 1 HOUR
GRILLING TIME: 8 TO 10 MINUTES

BRITTLE
- 1 teaspoon aniseed
  Vegetable oil
- 1/3 cup slivered almonds, toasted
- 1 3/4 cups granulated sugar
- 1/3 cup whipping cream

- 1 ripe pineapple
- 1 pint vanilla ice cream

1. To make the brittle: In a small saucepan, combine 1 cup water and the aniseed and bring to a rolling boil. Remove from the heat and let steep for at least 30 minutes.
2. Brush a small baking sheet with oil. Place almonds on the sheet in a single, compact layer.
3. Place the sugar in a medium saucepan. Strain the aniseed water over the sugar, pressing down on the seeds; discard the seeds. Cook over medium-low heat until the sugar dissolves, swirling the pan occasionally. Increase the heat and cook until the sugar caramelizes and turns a golden caramel color [160°F or "hard-crack" on a candy thermometer],

washing down any sugar crystals that form on the sides of the pan with a brush dipped in cold water. Carefully pour enough caramel over the almonds to completely coat them. Using potholders tilt the baking sheet to distribute the caramel. Cool until firm, about 10 minutes. Remove from the baking sheet and coarsely chop by hand.
4. Place the remaining caramel back on low heat and carefully add the cream. Cook over low heat until the caramel melts and the cream is mixed in, swirling the pan occasionally. Cool, then refrigerate until serving.
5. Peel the pineapple [see page 283] and cut crosswise into slices, each about 3/4 inch thick. Cut out the core from each slice and discard.
6. Lightly oil the pineapple slices and grill over *Direct Medium* heat until well-browned on both sides, 8 to 10 minutes, turning once.
7. Reheat the caramel sauce in a microwave for a few seconds or over medium-low heat until melted and smooth. Thin with a little more cream if necessary. Place a pineapple slice in the center of each dessert plate and then a scoop of ice cream on top. Ladle warm caramel sauce over the pineapple and ice cream and drizzle more over the plate. Sprinkle with the toasted almond brittle. Serve immediately.

MAKES 6 SERVINGS

Skillet Blueberry Cobbler

PREP TIME: 20 MINUTES PLUS 10 MINUTES TO COOL
GRILLING TIME: 45 TO 50 MINUTES

- 2 tablespoons unsalted butter, softened
- 4 cups fresh or thawed frozen blueberries, divided
- ½ cup granulated sugar, divided
- 1 tablespoon all-purpose flour
- 1 teaspoon lemon zest
- 1 tablespoon lemon juice
- ¼ teaspoon grated nutmeg

- 1¼ cups all-purpose flour
- ½ cup granulated sugar
- 1½ teaspoons baking powder
- ¼ teaspoon kosher salt
- ½ teaspoon cinnamon
- 4 tablespoons unsalted butter, melted
- ½ cup whole milk
- 1 teaspoon vanilla extract
- 1 cup heavy cream, whipped [optional]

1. In a nonstick, ovenproof 10-inch skillet over medium heat, melt the butter. Add 2 cups of the blueberries with ¼ cup of the sugar, stirring frequently until the mixture has the consistency of jam, about 10 minutes. Remove from the heat. Add the remaining 2 cups of blueberries, the remaining ¼ cup sugar, the flour, lemon zest, lemon juice, and nutmeg to the cooked berries and stir to combine. Make sure all of the whole berries are evenly coated.

2. In a large mixing bowl, sift the flour, sugar, baking powder, salt, and cinnamon. Combine the melted butter, milk, and vanilla and add to the dry ingredients. Continue to mix until well combined, scraping down the sides once. There may still be some lumps. Drop the batter over the fruit in large spoonfuls, starting in the middle and working out to the sides, leaving a 1-inch border of exposed fruit around the outside edge. It will seem like there is a shortage of batter, but it will expand while baking.

3. Cook over *Indirect Medium* heat [about 350°F] for 20 minutes. For even cooking, carefully rotate the pan 90 degrees, being careful because the fruit mixture will be bubbling up. Continue to bake until a skewer inserted into the center of the crust comes out clean, 25 to 30 minutes more. Place the skillet on a wire rack and let stand for 10 minutes. Serve while still warm or at room temperature and top with whipped cream, if desired.

MAKES 6 TO 8 SERVINGS

Carrot Cake
with Cream Cheese Frosting

PREP TIME: 20 MINUTES PLUS 15 MINUTES TO COOL
GRILLING TIME: 35 TO 40 MINUTES

    1   tablespoon unsalted butter
 1½   cups all-purpose flour, divided
 1½   teaspoons baking powder
    1   teaspoon ground cinnamon
   ¼   teaspoon ground ginger
   ¼   teaspoon kosher salt
   ½   cup firmly packed light brown sugar
   ⅓   cup honey
    2   large eggs, lightly beaten
   ¾   cup canola oil
    1   teaspoon vanilla extract
   ½   cup raisins
    1   cup firmly packed, grated carrots,
        about 2 medium carrots

    6   ounces cream cheese, softened
    3   tablespoons unsalted butter, softened
    1   cup confectioners' sugar
    1   teaspoon vanilla extract

1. In a nonstick, ovenproof 10-inch skillet, melt the butter.

2. In a medium bowl, sift the flour [reserving 1 tablespoon for the raisins], baking powder, cinnamon, ginger, and salt.

3. In a large mixing bowl, whisk the brown sugar, honey, and eggs until smooth. Mix in the oil and vanilla. Add the dry ingredients to the wet and mix until just combined. Dust the raisins with the reserved 1 tablespoon of flour [so they won't sink to the bottom of the batter]. Fold in the raisins and carrots. Pour the batter into the skillet.

4. Cook over *Indirect Medium* heat [about 350°F] for 20 minutes. Rotate the skillet 90 degrees for even cooking. Continue to bake until a skewer inserted in the center comes out clean and there is almost no jiggle in the center of the cake, 15 to 20 minutes more. Let cool on a wire rack for 15 minutes. Run a knife around the edge of the cake, making sure to run the tip along the bottom of the skillet. Tip the cake out of the skillet and cool completely on the rack.

5. In a medium bowl, mix the cream cheese and butter and sift the sugar on top. With a wooden spoon, beat until thoroughly combined and smooth. Add the vanilla and continue to beat until fluffy, 2 to 3 minutes more. Spread the frosting evenly over the top of the cake. Serve at room temperature. Can be cooled, frosted, and served in the skillet.

MAKES 8 TO 10 SERVINGS

Apple Cake

with Cinnamon Sugar

PREP TIME: 30 MINUTES
GRILLING TIME: 35 TO 40 MINUTES

BATTER
- 5 tablespoons cold unsalted butter, plus more for greasing the pie plate
- 1¼ cups all-purpose flour
- 1¼ teaspoons baking powder
- ½ cup granulated sugar
- ½ teaspoon kosher salt
- ¼ teaspoon ground cinnamon
- ⅛ teaspoon ground cloves
- ½ cup whole milk
- 2 large eggs, at room temperature
- ½ teaspoon pure vanilla extract

- 1 large Granny Smith apple
- 2 tablespoons dark brown sugar
- ¼ teaspoon ground cinnamon
- 1 cup heavy cream, whipped [optional]

1. To make the batter: Generously grease a 10-inch pie plate with butter. Sift the flour and baking powder into a large bowl. Add the sugar, salt, cinnamon, and cloves and mix well. Cut the 5 tablespoons of butter into small pieces and add to the bowl, mixing with your fingertips until you have a coarse meal. Whisk the milk, eggs, and vanilla and add to the bowl. Mix well. The batter should be well combined but still have some lumps. Pour the batter evenly into the pie plate.

2. Core and slice the apple lengthwise into ⅛-inch thick slices. Arrange the slices on top of the batter around the outer edge of the pie plate like petals of a flower, overlapping them slightly. In a small bowl, mix the brown sugar and cinnamon. Sprinkle evenly over the top of the apples and batter.

3. Grill over *Indirect Medium* heat for 20 minutes. Rotate the pan 90 degrees. Continue grilling until a skewer inserted in the center comes out clean, 15 to 20 minutes more. Cool on a wire rack for 15 minutes. Cut into wedges and serve at room temperature with whipped cream, if desired.

MAKES 6 TO 8 SERVINGS

▲▲▲

I use my grill to do all kinds of baking. I have made cakes, cobblers, pies, even soufflés! Think of the grill as an outdoor oven. When you are using indirect heat, with the lid closed, you can bake virtually anything that would cook in an oven.

▼▼▼

Vanilla Cake
with Cherries and Cream

PREP TIME: 20 MINUTES
GRILLING TIME: 35 TO 40 MINUTES

  1 tablespoon unsalted butter
1¾ cups all-purpose flour
  2 teaspoons baking powder
¼ teaspoon kosher salt
  1 cup granulated sugar
  3 large eggs, at room temperature
½ cup whole milk
⅓ cup canola oil
  2 teaspoons pure vanilla extract

  2 pints ripe cherries, pitted and quartered
  4 tablespoons granulated sugar, divided
  1 tablespoon fresh lemon juice
  1 cup heavy cream

1. Grease a 9-inch cake pan [2 inches high] with the butter. In a medium bowl, sift the flour, baking powder, and salt.

2. In the bowl of a stand mixer or using a hand-held mixer, whisk the sugar and eggs until the mixture is pale yellow in color, about 5 minutes. Add the milk, oil, and vanilla and whisk for 2 minutes more. Add the flour mixture and whisk until just combined, scraping down the sides of the bowl. Pour the cake batter into the cake pan. Spread with a spatula to even out, if necessary.

3. Cook over *Indirect Medium* heat [about 350°F] for 20 minutes. Rotate the pan 90 degrees for even cooking. Continue to bake until a skewer inserted in the center comes out clean and there is no jiggle in the center of the cake, 15 to 20 minutes more. Let cool completely on a wire rack. Run a knife around the edge of the cake, making sure to run the tip along the bottom of the pan. Invert out of the pan onto a board. Invert the cake again onto a serving platter.

4. In a medium bowl, mix the cherries, 2 table-spoons of sugar, and the lemon juice. Allow to sit at room temperature for 5 to 10 minutes. Meanwhile whip the cream with the remaining 2 tablespoons of sugar to stiff peaks. Slice the cake and serve with the cherries and whipped cream on top.

MAKES 8 TO 10 SERVINGS

Chocolate Brownie Cake

PREP TIME: 20 MINUTES
GRILLING TIME: 35 TO 45 MINUTES

   1   cup [6 ounces] semisweet chocolate chips
  1/4 pound unsalted butter [1 stick], cut into
       8 pieces, plus more for greasing the pan
1 1/4 cups granulated sugar
   3 large eggs
1 1/4 cups all-purpose flour
  1/4 cup cocoa powder
  1/2 teaspoon ground cinnamon
  1/2 teaspoon baking soda
  1/4 teaspoon salt
   2 tablespoons confectioners' sugar

1. In a medium saucepan over low heat, melt the chocolate chips and butter, stirring often [be careful not to burn the chocolate]. Remove the pan from the heat.
2. In a large bowl, using an electric mixer, beat the sugar and eggs on medium-high speed until pale yellow and thick, 4 to 5 minutes.
3. In a large bowl, sift the flour, cocoa powder, cinnamon, baking soda, and salt.
4. Grease the inside of a round, 9-inch cake pan with butter.
5. With the electric mixer on low, add the flour mixture to the sugar-egg mixture. Then add the chocolate mixture. Mix until just smooth. With a rubber spatula, transfer the batter to the cake pan, spreading it evenly.
6. Cook over *Indirect Medium* heat [about 350°F] until a skewer inserted in the center comes out with moist crumbs attached, 35 to 45 minutes, rotating the pan 90 degrees after about 20 minutes. Let cool in the pan completely, about 1 hour. Invert the cake onto a serving platter. Carefully turn it over. Sift the confectioners' sugar through a sieve on top of the cake. Cut into wedges. Serve at room temperature.

MAKES 8 TO 10 SERVINGS

Chunky Chewy Chocolate Cookies

PREP TIME: 20 MINUTES
GRILLING TIME: 60 MINUTES [3 BATCHES AT 20 MINUTES PER BATCH]

¹⁄₂ cup unsalted butter
 1   package [11¹⁄₂ ounces] semisweet chocolate chunks, divided
 3   large eggs
 1   cup light brown sugar, firmly packed
 1   teaspoon vanilla extract
 2   cups all-purpose flour
¹⁄₂ cup cocoa
¹⁄₂ teaspoon baking powder
¹⁄₂ teaspoon salt
 1   cup coarsely chopped walnuts
 1   cup shredded coconut
 1   cup raisins or dried cherries, or use half of each

1. In a small saucepan over very low heat, melt the butter with ¹⁄₂ package [about 1 cup] of the chocolate chunks, stirring constantly until smooth. Set aside to cool to lukewarm.

2. In a large bowl, using an electric mixer, beat the eggs, brown sugar, and vanilla until light and fluffy. Beat in the cooled butter-chocolate mixture.

3. In a medium bowl, sift the flour, cocoa, baking powder, and salt. Gradually stir into the large bowl of batter. Add the walnuts, coconut, raisins and/or cherries, and the remaining 1 cup of chocolate chunks; stir to blend. The batter will be stiff.

4. Use a tablespoon and wet fingertips to drop 1-inch mounds of the batter onto a cookie sheet lined with parchment paper, keeping the mounds about 2 inches apart [the cookies do not spread when baked]. Grill, in batches, over *Indirect Medium* heat for 20 minutes, keeping the grill's temperature as close to 350°F as possible. Let the cookies cool on the cookie sheet until they are easy to remove with a spatula, 2 to 3 minutes, and then transfer to a cooling rack and allow them to cool completely.

MAKES ABOUT 36 COOKIES

Lemon Italian Ice
with Raspberries

PREP TIME: 30 MINUTES

Grated zest of 2 lemons
1½ cups fresh lemon juice [8 to 10 lemons]
1 cup granulated sugar
¼ teaspoon kosher salt
2 pints fresh raspberries
8 fresh mint sprigs

1. In a medium saucepan over medium heat, combine the lemon zest, lemon juice, sugar, and salt with 2 cups cold water and cook until the sugar is dissolved. Pour into ice cube trays and freeze overnight.
2. Put 6 to 8 cubes in a food processor to make 1 layer. Pulse until the mixture is grainy and fluffy. Remove the fluffy ice to a freezer-safe container and repeat the process with the remaining cubes. Store tightly covered in the freezer until serving. Remove from the freezer 10 to 15 minutes before serving. Spoon into dessert dishes with the raspberries, and garnish with mint sprigs. Serve cold.

MAKES 6 TO 8 SERVINGS

Fresh Strawberry Ice
with Whipped Cream

PREP TIME: 30 MINUTES

1 pound [about 4 cups] ripe strawberries, rinsed, hulled, and quartered
⅔ cup strawberry preserves, divided
4 teaspoons fresh lemon juice, divided
1 cup heavy cream
1 tablespoon granulated sugar
½ teaspoon pure vanilla extract

1. In a food processor, blend the strawberries with ¼ cup of the preserves, 1 tablespoon of the lemon juice, and ¼ cup of water until completely smooth, about 1 minute. Strain the liquid through a sieve into a medium bowl and discard the seeds. Spoon the liquid into an ice cube tray and freeze for at least 6 hours.
2. In a small bowl, whisk the remaining preserves and the remaining lemon juice with 2 tablespoons of water. Pass through a fine sieve into a small bowl and reserve.
3. Whip the cream with the sugar and vanilla to stiff peaks.
4. Put 6 to 8 cubes in a food processor to make 1 layer. Pulse the machine until the mixture is grainy and fluffy. Transfer the mixture to a medium bowl. Repeat with the remaining frozen cubes until all of them are grainy and fluffy. Alternate layers of the frozen strawberry mixture and the whipped cream in cold dessert glasses or champagne flutes. Finish with whipped cream, then top with a drizzle of the reserved sauce. Serve cold.

MAKES 4 TO 6 SERVINGS

INDEX